Ashley Mallett's cricket ambition v————————————————————,
a feat he achieved in his 23rd Test for Australia. Generally
regarded as the best off-spinner and gully fieldsman Australia
has produced, Ashley runs Spin Australia, an international
spin bowling coaching program. As consultant spin bowling
coach to the Sri Lankan Cricket Board, Ashley has established
a Spin Bowling Academy in Colombo, coaching the nation's
coaches on the art of spin and guiding the nation's best
spinners from the Under-13s to the Test squad. The author
of 24 books, Ashley is working on a new biography, the story
of Jeff Thomson, arguably the fastest bowler to draw breath.

One of a Kind

the DOUG WALTERS story

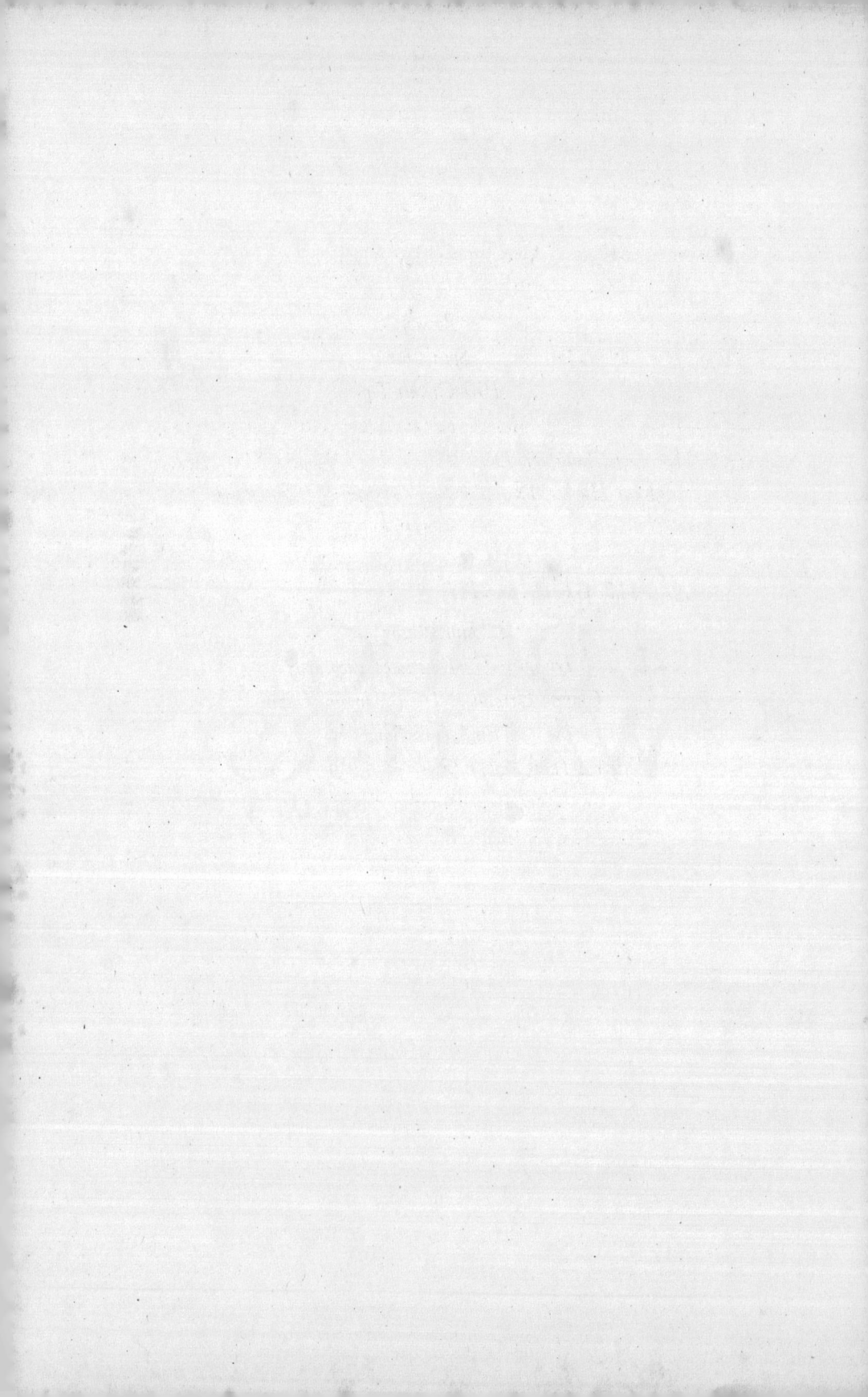

Also by Ashley Mallett

Rowdy
Spin Out
100 Cricket Tips
Master Sportsman Series
Cricket: Don Bradman, Doug Walters, The Chappells, Geoff Lawson,
Kim Hughes, Dennis Lillee, Rod Marsh, Allan Border
Soccer: John Kosmina
Tennis: Evonne Cawley
Australian Rules Football: Mark Williams, Wayne Johnston, Robert Flower,
Tim Watson
Trumper: The Illustrated Biography
Clarrie Grimmett: The Bradman of Spin
Bradman's Band
Eleven: The Greatest Eleven of the 20th Century
The Black Lords of Summer
Chappelli Speaks Out

One of a Kind

the DOUG
WALTERS *story*

ASHLEY MALLETT

ALLEN&UNWIN

First published in 2008

Copyright © Ashley Mallett 2008

Allen & Unwin
83 Alexander Street
Crows Nest NSW 2065
Australia
Phone: (61 2) 8425 0100
Fax: (61 2) 9906 2218
Email: info@allenandunwin.com
Web: www.allenandunwin.com

National Library of Australia
Cataloguing-in-Publication entry:

Mallett, Ashley, 1945-
   One of a kind : the Doug Walters story / author, Ashley Mallett.

   ISBN: 978 1 74175 029 4 (pbk.)

   Subjects: Walters, Doug, 1945--Anecdotes. Cricket--Australia--Anecdotes.
   Cricket--Australia--History. Cricket players--Australia--Anecdotes. Cricket
   players--Australia--Biography. Cricket players--Australia--History.

796.358092294

Set in 13/16 pt Centaur MT by Bookhouse, Sydney
Printed and bound in Australia by Griffin Press

10 9 8 7 6 5 4 3 2 1

Contents

acknowledgements

My thanks to the following: Eddie Barlow*, Dr Donald Beard, Richie Benaud, Fred Bennett*, Big Sid*, Allan Border, Brendan Bracewell, John Bracewell, Sir Donald Bradman*, Sir Ron Brierley, Kevin 'Crazy' Cantwell, Bruce Carter, Greg Chappell, Ian Chappell, Mike Coward, Sir Roden Cutler*, Alan Davidson, Ed Devereaux*, Ross Edwards, Stephen Fry, Lance Gibbs, Trevor Gill, Neil Harvey, David Hookes*, Ray Illingworth, John Inverarity, Terry Jenner, Ray Johnston, Thomas Keneally, Dennis Lillee, Alan McGilvray*, Rod Marsh, Keith Miller*, Clayton Murzello, Norman O'Neill, Kerry Packer*, Len Pascoe, Wayne Prior, Viv Richards, Ray Robinson, Paul Sheahan, Norman Tasker and Jeff Thomson.

A special thank you to Caroline Walters for copying myriad articles from the stacks of cuttings about Doug which May Walters and Caroline had collected for him; to Doug's mum, May, for her words on Doug's early years; and to Freddie (Doug himself) who was ever the fine host during our taping sessions at his home in Sydney, in Colombo and at his favourite watering hole, the Great Northern Hotel, Chatswood.

My thanks, too, to my wife and editing consultant, Christine.

Len Pascoe directed me towards country and western songster Ian Quinn who included his song 'A Legend Like Doug' in his latest album, *River or the Road* (Ringbark Records). Thanks to Ian Quinn and Anita Ree for allowing me to use the lyrics in this book. I even grabbed the title of the song as my heading for Chapter one.

* Deceased

foreword

I have always said I would hate to tour in an Australian side that didn't include Doug Walters. That wasn't just because of his match-winning batting, his almost freakish ability to take a wicket when a dangerous partnership was building or his brilliant all-round fielding. Doug's impish humour and ability to keep a team loose with his dressing-room pranks contributed greatly to team spirit, morale and having an enjoyable time. And if you want someone to write about the off-field side of Walters' character, there's no-one better qualified than his one-time team-mate Ashley 'Rowdy' Mallett, who was often on the receiving end when the 'Dungog Dasher' was devising his antics . . . like the occasion in Durban at the Old Kingsmead ground in 1970.

We were taking a pounding from a strong South African side after an extremely draining three-month tour of India, but that hadn't dulled Walters' ultra-active brain. It was an old dressing-room with wooden floors, wire-fronted lockers and bench seats that lifted up so you could store extra cricket gear. Mallett insisted on walking around in his cricket socks despite the fact that it was easier to score a splinter from the floor than runs against the South African attack. Seizing his opportunity, Walters regularly tossed his cigarette butts in Mallett's path and each time the clumsy off-spinner had to do a military two-step to avoid treading on the fag end of a lighted Rothmans filter.

Eventually Mallett, in taking an elaborate side-step, stumbled backwards, his legs hitting the bench seat and causing him to sit down with a thud. Normally this wouldn't have been a problem, as he was right in front of his own locker, but Rowdy wasn't the tidiest cricketer and he'd left his boots on the bench with the sprigs upturned. His backside no sooner landed on the spikes than Mallett was leaping into the air as though he was trying to catch a lofted Eddie Barlow cut shot. Unfortunately, his second landing was right on one of Walters' strategically placed butts, which caused him to leap backwards again, this time setting him down perfectly on the sprigs of the other upturned boot.

I can't remember what disaster befell his next landing, as I was rolling around on the floor laughing in the company of half a dozen other Australian players. For all I know Walters may have even been rolling about on one of his own lighted butts.

It may sound like a childish schoolboy prank but you must remember people used to crack up watching the *Three Stooges* and this was every bit as funny and it wasn't scripted.

This and many other episodes like it mightn't have been as hilarious if Walters wasn't such a likeable person and, just as importantly, a great player. I use the word 'great' advisedly on the basis that if it describes Sir Donald Bradman then it's difficult to apply the term to any other batsman. Consequently, many people would be surprised I use the word in describing Walters. There was a valid reason.

On three occasions Walters scored a Test century in a session and also repeated the feat in an international match against a Rest of the World team. Other than Bradman, I can't think of another batsman who has surpassed that amazing feat and, as captain of a player with such extraordinary match-winning qualities, you tend to appreciate his contribution.

Typical of Walters he couldn't 'just' score a Test century in a session like Bradman or Sir Garfield Sobers or Victor Trumper; he somehow contrived to add extra drama to the occasion. As this story unfolds you'll better understand Walters' flair for the dramatic.

I can't think of a better subject for a book than Walters, nor anyone more qualified to write about one of cricket's great characters than Ashley Mallett. They broke the mould when Doug Walters came on the scene and thank heavens they had the good sense to wait until after his arrival.

Ian Chappell
Sydney, 2008

meet DOUG WALTERS

Over the years Doug has been showered with adulation, but it's all water off a duck's back. Whether he got a hundred or a duck, Doug remained the same. In Australia Doug Walters is a constant: a national treasure like the Opera House or the Sydney Harbour Bridge. Cricket fans embraced him as one of their own, for here was a national batting hero who did the sort of stuff they did: he drank and he smoked, he had a bet and a laugh. They loved it when, in 1977, news broke that before his 250 for Australia against New Zealand at Christchurch, he spent the previous night in the hotel bar with a team-mate. The little right-hander with the gap-toothed smile drank all night and batted all next day, hitting his highest Test score. Youngsters loved Doug's cricket for his red-blooded strokes and his obvious enjoyment: ever on the attack and win; lose or draw he always sported that famous grin.

Doug hails from Dungog, dairy farm country in the middle of the Hunter Valley some 200-odd kilometres north of Sydney. There he learnt to bat on his homemade ant-bed pitch, defending a kerosene tin which stood in front of the old wood-walled, corrugated tin-roofed dunny. He milked cows and he could spin a milk can. But just like Don Bradman, who had an uncannily similar country upbringing, Doug immediately shone with the bat on the Test stage. And it wasn't long before he was labelled the 'new Bradman'.

Doug hit a century in both of his first two Test matches. He batted instinctively and he stuck to his way of doing things. With a fabulous eye and his hand–eye coordination as good as anyone who has ever pulled a boot on for the Australian Test team, it's not hard to see that there was a lot of Bradman in Doug's cricket. Sometimes his bat came at the bowler at a funny angle, but the bowler was rarely smiling as Doug would cane anything remotely short, or full or wide. Four times he hit a century in a session in first-class matches, and three of those occasions were Test matches. And in December 1974 he hit an amazing century in a true 'Bradman-like' innings.

Doug was known for his love of pranks. Throughout his long career he found ways to harass and annoy his team-mates with all manner of mischief. But this only adds to the fact that he is one of the great characters of the game. Who else would hold his 60th birthday party in the front bar of a suburban hotel?

Doug was the most observant cricketer I struck on the field of play. He always casually told anyone within earshot from his spot at third slip that his wife had just arrived and was sitting in number 10 seat, row 14 of the southern stand. It shouldn't surprise anyone that in August 2007 Doug and Caroline Walters celebrated their 40th wedding anniversary.

Country and Western singer Ian Quinn has penned a song about Doug, entitled 'A Legend like Doug', and in this book I wanted to give a close look at the man as well as the legend. Doug talked candidly to me about both life and cricket and throughout the book I've tried to include as much as possible: his thoughts on modern-day players; the need to scrap the Under-19s; his belief in compulsory National Service; our Test selectors 'giving away Test caps'; his thoughts on the 'conspiracy' which saw him, and other high-profile people, press-ganged into the army at the height of the Vietnam War; and the emergence of China as a cricket power.

Some time back, Doug was addressing a group of about thirty youngsters. In his coaching address, Doug stressed the need for everyone involved in the game to dress neatly. He would say, 'Boys, we look like a cricketer.' At the session he noted one youngster to be well attired: immaculate creams, clean shoes and shirt tucked in, and another not so well dressed: a youngster with his shirt hanging out, hair all over the place, shoelaces undone . . .

He asked both boys to stand up and then he addressed the group.

'Now boys,' Doug began, 'can you notice the difference between these two boys?'

A boy was almost beside himself in the group, thrusting his hand skywards and Doug invited him to respond.

'Yes, Mr Walters, I know . . . one of them is black!'

Whether it was on the cricket field, speaking at a show, playing a prank, or shuffling cards, Doug always had an ace up his sleeve. For me, and for millions of Australians, Kevin Douglas Walters is undoubtedly *one of a kind*.

Ashley Mallett

a LEGEND
like DOUG

We just looked at each other... It was a magic moment.
Looking back, I have one regret about the night. I didn't drink
in those days, but I would have liked to have pulled up at a
pub and had a beer with Dad. He loved his beer alright, but
he celebrated with me over a cup of tea instead.

The Doug Walters story is brimming with thrills, spills and endless
laughs. Doug had more than a fleeting brush with sporting genius:
there was a boyish enthusiasm about his batting and that touch of
magic was never far away. Such Doug Walters magic held the
nation in collective awe on December 1974. At tea on the second
day of the match against England, Doug was three not out. At
stumps he was unconquered on 103. Doug had 'done a Bradman',

scoring 100 in a session. It was his second Test century in a session. His first was at Port-of-Spain, Trinidad, in the Third Test of the 1972–73 series in the Caribbean. Ian Chappell regards that innings as the best Test century he had seen against a turning ball on a treacherous spinning wicket. Doug's amazing century in Perth was entirely different. A lightning-fast wicket with extraordinary bounce never deterred Doug as he hooked and pulled and drove his way towards the last ball of the day. He was on 97 when the ungainly, gangly England fast bowler Bob Willis bustled in to bowl that all-important final delivery. The wicket was providing steep, though consistent, bounce and carry to England's interminable Jack-in-the-box—the bending, stretching, annoying, wicketkeeper Alan Knott. Willis' penultimate ball of the day was predictably short. It rose like a striking brown snake, but Doug was ready to pounce.

His bat met the ball bang in the middle—the bittersweet sound of willow on leather like the crack of a stock whip—which sent the ball soaring like a jumbo jet at take-off. All eyes were on that little red sphere which seemed to take on a life of its own, careering like a cannon ball, barely getting above 3 metres but easily clearing the boundary rope just in front of square-leg. The ultra-conservative Ross Edwards stood agape at the other end, marvelling at Doug the legend, the man he had been scolding just seconds before to 'play sensibly...be there for tomorrow...don't do anything silly'.

Walters ignored Rosco's pleas for him to simply hang on in that final over—Doug was always going to trust his own attacking nature. Any red-blooded Australian batsman, who had an eye like a stinking fish, was immensely strong in the forearms, and could hook and pull like a thrashing machine, would never have allowed that Willis delivery to pass unpunished. The ball simply had to GO...

Even before this epic knock, Doug Walters was well on his way to becoming a true legend of the game. In 1968–69 in Australia,

Doug had a Bradman-like average of 116 against the West Indians. In just four Tests he scored 699 runs, including a record 242 and 103 in the Sydney Fifth Test match. As a Test player Doug was hero to thousands of admirers, yet his image of himself never changed—he was an uncomplicated bloke who was one of the mob. What endeared him to his fans was his matter-of-fact, down-to-earth attitude to life, which remains unchanged. With Doug there are no pretensions: he's a bloke's bloke, who lives life to the full, and throughout his cricket career Doug loved a beer, a smoke, a bet and a bat, not necessarily in that order. The only difference is that these days he limits his batting to the odd charity match and shows kids at coaching classes how to cut, pull and drive.

As a teenage teetotaler, Doug scored a century against England at the Gabba in his debut Test match. He followed up that ton with another one in the Melbourne Second Test match, never forgetting advice from the burly Queensland batsman, Peter Burge, who told him to bat instinctively and to always take the attack to the bowler. Peter strode down the track and said to me: 'Bradman once told me the only way to defend properly is to attack sensibly.'[1]

Doug had his first beer at the age of twenty and he started smoking during his two-year stint in the army. Doug doesn't care what people think of his smoking and drinking, but he takes care not to smoke inside, at home or in a restaurant. The only people Doug Walters ever 'offended' were his opponents on the cricket field, especially the bowlers. Doug belted the hell out of some of the greatest bowlers to have drawn breath. But all opponents, including those defeated bowlers, were always welcome to join Doug for a beer and a smoke at day's end.

There is not a hint of pomp or ceremony about Doug, yet fame has thrust him in the limelight: he has chatted with the Queen Mother at Clarence House; collected his MBE from NSW Governor Sir Roden Cutler at Government House in Sydney; dined with

Queen Elizabeth and Princess Anne on the Royal yacht *Britannia* on Sydney Harbour; and in 1982 he took tea one morning with Australian cricket's version of the 'Royal Couple' at the Kensington Park, home of Sir Donald and Lady Jessie Bradman.

Doug toured England four times (1968, 1972, 1975 and 1977); Ceylon (Sri Lanka), India and South Africa (1969–70); the West Indies (1973); and New Zealand (1974 and 1977). Doug's legendary status rose in February, 1977 at Christchurch. There he hit 250 against New Zealand at Lancaster Park after a long night at the hotel bar with Gary Gilmour. Next day both men cleared the cobwebs quickly and settled down to hit a record seventh wicket partnership of 217 in 187 minutes, with Gilmour hitting his maiden Test century, 101. Statistically, Doug Walters played 74 Test matches, hitting 5357 runs, with fifteen centuries at an average of 48.26. He also took 49 wickets at 29.08 runs apiece, plus 43 catches. Doug proved to be one of our most amazing international sporting heroes, yet he never forgot his roots or lost the common touch. His cricketing life was full of thrills and he thrilled those who saw his brilliant batting, partnership-breaking medium pace bowling, and sure hands at slip and brilliant fielding at cover point. But, according to Doug, all of this combined cannot compare to being named in the Test team for the first time. It was his dream, his ambition, even as a child. And he always believed he would make it, no matter how doubtful some of his teachers seemed to be.

> *I used to tell my teachers that I didn't have to do my homework because 'I am going to play Test cricket for Australia'. My English teacher [Ray Johnston] and my Maths teacher [John Gateley] at Dungog High School told me, 'You'll never make it Doug. You'll never play Test cricket. You have to hand your homework in like everyone else.'*

So I guess those two guys were my greatest inspirations because they told me that I couldn't do what I had dreamed of doing and I went all out to prove them wrong.

Ray Johnston retired from teaching a few years back and lives in Dungog. He well remembers the young Doug Walters. 'Doug and I began at Dungog Central School together in the same year, 1958. He did his Intermediate Certificate in 1960 and he was a pretty good student.'

Ray then corrected himself. 'Well, you could say Doug did as much as he needed to do to get through. As his English teacher I noted that he had a good command of the language. His written expression was good and I reckon he used the dictionary to a great extent to write a story. He had neat handwriting.'[2]

What was Doug like at school?

'Quiet,' Ray mused. 'But really he was as he is now, almost exactly the same. Only thing is in those days he didn't drink and smoke. Otherwise little has changed with him. Quietly spoken, laid-back...'

And what does Ray say of Doug's claim that he, along with fellow teacher John Gateley, told the young Doug Walters that he wouldn't make it in Test cricket?

Ray replied, 'Frankly, I cannot remember saying anything of the sort. I think it's something Doug made up.'[3]

Who indeed would want the world at large to learn that he had once told the schoolboy Doug Walters, who grew up to be one of Australia's greatest batsmen and a true legend of the game, that he wouldn't make Test cricket?

Time can fade our memories. But anyone who knows Doug Walters will tell you that he has the memory of an elephant. He doesn't forget. I'll give you an example of his incredibly accurate memory. In 1968 I was with Doug at London's Waldorf Hotel when he ordered a ham and tomato toasted sandwich. But there was a problem, said the hotel staff. The toaster was on the blink. So Doug had to do without his toasted sandwiches for the duration of his stay. In 1972 I was in a room of the same hotel in London when he ordered toasted ham and tomato sandwiches. The staffer told Doug they couldn't do toasted sandwiches. 'Jeez,' said Doug, 'haven't you fixed that bloody toaster yet?'

Whenever Doug returns for a visit to Dungog, he invariably looks up Ray Johnston (sadly John Gateley passed away six years ago) and his first words as they order their first beers are along these lines: 'Thanks, Ray, I would never have made it if you two guys hadn't told me I'd never make it.'

But Doug was never arrogant in his ambitions. Leading up to the then quaintly called Marylebone Cricket Club (MCC) match and during it, he was being hailed as the newest batting star in the land; the newspapers were full of his being 'certain' of Test selection. Having hammered the cream of the England attack against MCC at the Sydney Cricket Ground in the lead game to the first Test in Brisbane, Doug had this nation of sports lovers hoping that his name would be among the players chosen for the First Test. He had had a good double, 129 and 39, but he had his own doubts and fears, and he tried not to think too much about all the talk.

On the last night of the MCC match, I packed my bag and walked out of the SCG with Dad, who had come down from the country to watch the game. And the Test team was being named that night. Dad was expecting me to get picked in the twelve, but I was certain I wouldn't be selected and was concerned about how disappointed Dad was going to be. We were driving home in the Mini when the team was announced. Dad stopped the car and we listened to the announcement.

It was 30 November 1965 and Doug's life was about to be changed forever. As he listened with his father, the Australian team was announced, with the captain and vice-captain named first, followed by the other ten players in alphabetical order: B. Booth (NSW—captain); W. Lawry (Victoria—vice-captain); P. Allan (Queensland); P. Burge (Queensland); W. Grout (Queensland); N. Hawke (South Australia); G. McKenzie (Western Australia); P. Philpott (NSW); I. Redpath (Victoria); T. Vievers (Queensland); D. Walters (NSW)...

They stopped the car by the side of the road, trying to comprehend the enormity of it all. Ted Walters was overwhelmed, ecstatic and rightly proud, but for Doug, it was all a bit too much to absorb—getting picked in the Test team was every Aussie kid's sporting dream:

'D. Walters'... I couldn't believe it. I honestly thought they'd name the twelve players and I would miss out. It's a bit hard on a young bloke, I can tell you, when they read names out in alphabetical order and your name starts with a W. I could take you to the exact spot in town where I heard the news. It was right outside the Darlinghurst Post Office, just down from Taylor Square. Dad and I were both overcome and we hardly exchanged a word between us. We just looked at each other, both choked with emotion. It was a magic moment. Looking back, I have one regret about the night. I didn't drink in those days, but I would have liked to have pulled up at a pub and had a beer with Dad. He loved his beer alright, but he celebrated with me over a cup of tea instead.

Sadly, poor health prevented Ted Walters getting to Brisbane to watch his son play in his First Test match, but he was able to listen to the radio broadcast and watch snatches of play on television.

During that match Doug expected to carry the drinks, but the Victorian pace-man Alan Connolly was named twelfth man and Doug got his chance. With Australia four wickets down for just over 100, Doug joined the stoic Bill Lawry. Wily England off-spinner Fred Titmus was bowling with good rhythm and gaining considerable turn. Doug met the first good length in the middle of his bat. Although he had only pushed the ball back to the bowler, Doug's face lit up. And his smile got bigger and bigger as he watched the rocking motion of the bowler. Titmus cradled the ball in both hands as he moved in. He had a classical sideways action, spending lots of time on his front foot. He rocked back and forth, spun the ball appreciably at times and was unerringly accurate.

But Doug had 'seen' it all before. He had watched Titmus' action for years: the family would gather around a roaring fire in their lounge room, and they would all listen intently to the wireless as the Test series in England was being fought out.

You could say I was taught the game of cricket by Alan McGilvray . . . The commentators, Alan McGilvray, John Arlott and Brian Johnston, were terrific. Their commentary gave you every minute detail about a player. They described my heroes—Len Hutton, John Edrich, Peter May, Colin Cowdrey, Ted Dexter, Fred Trueman, Tony Lock, Jim Laker, Alec Bedser, Richie Benaud, Alan Davidson, Neil Harvey, Garfield Sobers, Wes Hall, Lance Gibbs and Rohan Kanhai.

Alan McGilvray was indeed the voice of cricket in Australia. He covered Don Bradman's 1948 'Invincibles' tour of England for the Australian Broadcasting Commission. And he was fiercely Australian. McGilvrary was clever. He could paint a word picture so clearly you were transported to the very arena where the action he described was being played out. In those days, McGilvray was the ball-by-ball caller and he had an off-sider: the expert commentator. Once it was Vic Richardson, then Lindsay Hassett, then Norman O'Neill.

In backyard Test matches with his brothers Warren and Terry, and sister Colleen, Doug would emulate the actions of all the

English bowlers. When Doug played these backyard Test matches, he says he simply had to do as his heroes did:

> *If Alan Davidson came on to bowl, you bowled as Davo bowled, left-handed. John Edrich was a left-hand batsman, so you had to bat the way John batted as an England opener. Ray Lindwall was a fast bowler, so you raced in and bowled as fast as you could. When Richie Benaud was bowling, you bowled leg-breaks. I could 'see' through the radio the blokes who hitched their pads or fiddled with their box.*

Doug's fertile mind was able to conjure up a picture so vivid, he had all the England bowlers in his head. He felt he knew all their mannerisms, all their little tricks of the trade. In his mind's eye he had 'watched' them closely. Just as Don Bradman was his own sports psychologist, Doug was living the visualisations that many elite athletes today think to be a modern form of sporting mental awareness. So there he was at the Gabba in his First Test, reading Titmus like an old favourite book; tracking every aspect of his craft, every Titmus verb and adjective; every consonant, every twist and turn of the bowler's rhythm. Titmus' exclusive, rocking action was so familiar to Doug it made him smile and, as he says, it provided him with an instinctive competitive edge that made him very confident:

> *My second ball from Titmus was flighted a bit higher than the first. I latched on to the length early and jumped down the track to hit it wide of mid-on for four. I guess when you're playing your first Test match at the age of nineteen, nerves don't really come into it. And if I had any nerves at all, they disappeared with that boundary to get off the mark. Nerves usually do disappear when you get off the mark.*

Ray Johnston would have smiled at this. At high school during the winter months, Doug used to travel with Ray to Newcastle to play baseball for the Wallsend Robin Club. Fielding at short-stop never worried Doug, but he sometimes had trouble with the bat. Ray says:

> He had the habit of jumping down the ground towards the pitcher, just as he would advance to the pitch of the ball against a spin bowler. In baseball it caused him a bit of strife, for he was invariably given out for batting out of the box.[4]

Given Doug's fabulous eye and his penchant for the horizontal-bat shots, the pull and the cut, one would think that he would have been a sensational batter in baseball.

> *Baseball wasn't my game. I used to terrorise pitchers. I could never hit 'em in the middle. I could always get wood on the ball, but it would be either too high or too low on the bat; never in the middle. I think I only ever hit one home run in my life. Anyone who could pitch properly had me struggling. I couldn't lay a bat on an outcurve.*

And there was also the problem of jumping out of the batter's box to get to the pitcher. Fatal footwork in baseball. But that same swift footwork in Test cricket was to serve Doug well. His first scoring shot was something of a signature stroke for he would bring his front and back feet together in a snapping-at-the-heels drive through mid-on; his come-to-attention shot. The great bowler Bill 'Tiger' O'Reilly, the man Bradman named as the best bowler of any type he had ever played with or against or seen, praised Doug's debut Test knock in his regular *Sydney Morning Herald* column:

> Australia had lost, in quick succession, the wickets of Cowper, Burge and Booth and four wickets were down for 125 runs— a situation expressly designed to try the temperament of a

much more mature man. And to emphasise the problem he [Walters] was facing, England's captain Mike Smith crowded two short legs and a silly point in to the close positions for Fred Titmus to give Walters a searching personality test. The youngster came through it like a veteran. In fact, he shaped up aggressively. Throughout his long innings it was quite obvious that Walters was holding many of his aggressive shots in check. The lofted on-drive, for instance, seldom came into play but I am sure that the English bowlers will have not been hoodwinked about that now the young man has made his mark and secured his position. I can only remember one false step on Walters' part. That was the wind-and-water shot outside the off stump when David Brown was using the new ball.[5]

Doug's temperament shone through in that innings. He says the experience of listening to the Tests on the radio had left an indelible impression on him:

When I finally played against some of these blokes I had never seen, I found myself thinking that I know so much about their approach and mannerisms that I felt like I had been batting against them for a couple of years. When Titmus was almost into his delivery I found myself thinking: 'Gee, how good is this? I have this bloke's run-up to a tee.' I didn't have a clue what these blokes looked like. I certainly wouldn't have been able to recognise them if I'd walked past them in the street, although I do recall Colin Cowdrey being described as 'rotund'.

Doug knew what to expect from all the players except for one: Len Hutton. For some strange reason Doug always envisaged Hutton as being a left-handed batsman. How he came to make such an error, Doug cannot explain. However, years later, he discovered that liquor salesman Arthur Battie spent many days at the Sydney Cricket Ground during Sheffield Shield matches and Tests throughout the Bradman era and it was not until Don Bradman had been retired for fifteen years that Battie learnt that the champion batsman of all time was a right-hander. As Doug explains, Battie had always thought Bradman was a 'Molly-Dooker':

Arthur used to always have his back to the play at the SCG and he would spend hours at the Members' Bar looking at the cricket in the reflection of the huge mirror which was affixed to the wall at the back of the bar. Not once did Arthur turn around to watch the game through the window, so he had spent all that time looking at Bradman in the reflection in the mirror, batting 'left-handed'.

Doug's debut Test brought him 155. He had two days to get a hit, given that only 111 minutes of play was possible on the first day of the game and the second day was washed out without a ball being bowled. When he was on 89, a little dog rushed onto the ground and play was stopped. Again, with Doug on 93, the little dog returned, but the youngster remained calm. He reckoned the incident helped him relax and to forget about the nervous nineties:

I think the little dog was a kelpie. He had to be caught twice, but those delays helped. Rather than upset my concentration, the stoppages gave me a breather, although I did tighten up in the nineties because it took me some time to move from ninety to a hundred.

An elated Doug Walters walked from the ground with an unconquered century to his name. Doug and Bill Lawry (166) put on 187 for the fifth wicket. First to extend a congratulatory handshake was Ken Barrington, followed closely by the bespectacled Yorkshire opening batsman Geoffrey Boycott.

It [his debut Test century] was a great feeling, but it was nothing like the thrill I got when I first learnt I was in the Test team. That feeling could never be beaten.

Doug Walters played 74 Tests, scoring 5357 runs in 111 completed innings at an average of 48.26, with a highest score of 250. He is now a true Australian sporting legend, and many regard him as one of Australia's national sporting treasures. Songwriter Ian Quinn, who has written for such singers as Slim Dusty, was so taken with his first meeting with Doug Walters that he was moved to pen a song about him. Entitled 'A Legend Like Doug', the song is part of an album, *River or the Road*, which Ian released in January 2007. These are the lyrics:

A LEGEND LIKE DOUG
You swung the mighty willow on the wickets around the world
Broke many partnerships with that in-swinging ball
And no matter how tough the game
You've always seen it through
And it never took the bush or Dungog out of you
You couldn't care a dollar if you never made a cent
But you held a nation's spirit when it nearly up and went
The changing of the guard underneath the lights
Wearing coloured clothing as the red ball turned to white
So let's go back to Melbourne
In the shadow of Don Bradman
To those battles with the Windies, let's take 'em on again
To the SCG in Sydney
Where you were king and always will be

Doug you'll always be a legend
Like you were back then
So Doug I'll shake your hand and shout you one before you go
We miss you from the game
Just thought we'd let you know
We miss that bit of larrikin
We miss that real true blue
No-one could fill the shoes of a legend Doug like you
So let's go back to Melbourne
In the shadow of Don Bradman
To those battles with the Windies, let's take 'em on again
To the SCG in Sydney
Where you were king and always will be
Doug you'll always be a legend
Like you were back then
So let's go back to Melbourne
In the shadow of Don Bradman
To those battles with the Windies, let's take 'em on again
To the SCG in Sydney
Where you were king and always will be
Doug you'll always be a legend
Like you were back then[6]

But legends don't just happen.

Kevin Douglas Walters was born in Oomabah Hospital, Dungog in country New South Wales on 21 December 1945. Ted and May Walters had four children and Kevin Douglas was their third. Doug's mum, May Walters, said:

I wanted to christen him Kevin James. His father was Edward James. However, Ted said he liked Doug. I think one of his favourite cricketers at the time was Doug Ring [the Victorian leg-spinner, who toured England with Bradman's 1948 'Invincibles']. And so we settled on Kevin Douglas, but he's always been known as Doug.

May describes Doug as 'a very casual baby'. 'Nothing worried him in the slightest,' she says. 'When Ted and I were playing tennis, Doug would sit in the pram all afternoon.'

It was, May recalls, 'just after he took his first steps' that Ted put a cricket bat in Doug's hand. 'We always knew Doug would make it as a sportsman for he always had the ability to do what was wanted. He would find a way.'

His team-mates know too well about that trait. As Bob Willis came in to bowl the last ball of the day in Perth back in 1974, Doug had to hit it for six to complete the century in the session. Ian Chappell said of Doug: 'Somehow the little bastard will find a way.'

chapter two

the BIG SMOKE

The natural thing for a calf is to drink with his head up, because that's where the 'taps' are on his mum, so it is the devil's own job to make the calf put his head down into a bucket of milk. This particular day Pat Malone had the acknowledged world-champion calf at baulking the bucket. After the umpteenth try, Pat calmly picked up the bucket of milk and poured the lot over the calf. 'Maybe that will soak in,' he said.

Doug was only six or seven years of age when he would go out into the bush with his dad and the other timber workers to help drag out or 'snig'—as he called it—the fallen logs.

Dad was a timber cutter. He worked for a local timber mill and I loved going out into the bush with him to collect the wood. We sometimes had a bullock team, but usually two old draught horses did the trick. We'd throw a chain around a log that had been cut down and snig it out of the bush. The use of the horses was before the tractor and bulldozer days and from very early on I learnt to harness horses or a bullock team.

The Walters family lived in a little town called Dusdodie, which was about 15 kilometres out of Dungog, where Doug was born. He was the third child: first was Warren and Colleen, then Doug, then youngest brother, Terry. It was at Dusdodie that Doug first busied himself catching rabbits and began to make money. In Doug's childhood days Australia was still a nation which literally rode on the sheep's back. A quid was a quid, and the beer had to be cold and downed mighty fast with the pubs' six o'clock closing time. Homes in the cities were full of chrome, vinyl and laminated bench-tops. We drove FJ Holdens and raved over Elvis. The celebrated 'cow's lick', which years later the Fonz made famous in *Happy Days*, was a revolutionary hair-do, a thumbs-down to the short-back-and-sides which so conditioned the older brigade. The prime minister, Bob Menzies, seemed immovable at the political crease, the nation was entranced by the ABC radio epic *Blue Hills*, and the Snowy River Hydro-Electric Scheme was completed. Momentous years for Australia.

Meanwhile Doug Walters was milking the cows, playing cricket and tennis, and hunting rabbits:

In those days trapping rabbits brought good money. We'd collect two shillings and sixpence a pair, selling them to the local butcher. On a good weekend I made more money than my Dad was earning at the mill and I eventually convinced him to come rabbiting with me so that he might earn himself some extra pocket money.

Doug's first school was at Wangat, a one-teacher school with less than twenty students. The trip home to Dusdodie was some five miles but, according to Doug, the journey could be cut by at least a mile by walking the pipeline. This was the main water pipe which was linked to the huge Chichester Dam which, at that time, fed most of the Hunter Valley, including Newcastle and the surrounding areas. In those early school days Doug was like any other fearless kid, blissfully unaware of the hazards of walking along the pipe, which wasn't much wider than a dining table:

My mate and I would race each other along the pipe and pass one another. There we were, running full pelt, our school bags bouncing about on our shoulders. At its highest point the pipeline was about 300 feet above the ground and cold shivers run down my spine these days when I look back at the danger we ignored. It is amazing that neither of us fell from a height. We did, of course, push one another off the pipe, but only when it was a few feet off the ground. Common sense must have prevailed when we were very high up on that pipe.

Cricket was in the Walters family's blood. Ted Walters was a keen club cricketer, who played regularly for Telligra Bs and May Walters kept wicket for a local ladies team. Doug, Warren, Colleen and Terry spent many afternoons racing about the backyard engaged in fierce combat, and sometimes Ted and May joined the children for a three-a-side contest.

At Wangat Primary School the children played a form of French cricket, and whenever a shot beat the field, the ball scuttled down a steep slope, sending Doug and the other kids into a helter-skelter race to retrieve it:

Tossing the ball back up the slope was probably how I developed my throwing arm. I went to that school for about three years, then it folded for lack of numbers, which had dropped to seventeen before the authorities decided to close it.

Doug reckons the school was destined to close down, given that it didn't even have sufficient numbers to field two cricket elevens.

The family moved to Alison, about five miles east of Dungog, where eight-year-old Doug attended the Alison Primary School. His mate, John Hooke, lived next door and the Hooke family had a grass tennis court so the boys played both tennis and cricket on the court's surface:

> *It was only about one and half miles from our home in Alison to the school. We used to ride to school and were there by 7.15 a.m. John Hooke and I got there early so we had the school tennis court to ourselves. We used to knock the ball about until the start of classes.*

Alison was another one-teacher school and that teacher was sports-mad Jim Fuller. He would join in with the boys in those pre-class hit-ups and often brought along his brother, Earl, to practise after school:

> *Usually the teacher had to tell us to get on our bikes and go home as we batted on until darkness fell. But often John Hooke and I were pitted against Jim and Earl Fuller. On many an occasion when we were prac-tising for the school sports carnival, we would be outdoors training for the whole day, never seeing a classroom during that intense build-up. During my three years at Alison Primary School, I think we won every sports carnival in our grouping. Jim Fuller was very sports-minded. Practising the high jump, running, a few sets of tennis, instead of being in class was great. I won most of the blue ribbons for events in those days. I was pretty good in the running.*

Before Doug began any sort of competition cricket, he watched his dad play for Telligra. Doug was among a number of kids who'd sit on the boundary line, all proud of their dads playing in the middle and all of them hoping that there would be a massive power strike so that half the players would be delayed, hand-milking cows: on the occasion when a player was late, one of the kids on the boundary would be allowed to field with the grown-ups. When one of the kids got the chance as a stand-in fieldsman, they were given the run-around, third man up one end then sent to fine leg at the end of the over. Doug reckons they would cover more ground than the Leyland brothers, but they loved the experience and no-one complained. Years later in the Caribbean in 1973, Test captain Ian Chappell ran Doug from third man to fine leg for all of one morning session. It was a disciplinary measure, but all of that was to come much later.

Doug began competition cricket when he was ten, turning out for the Under-15s, with his older brother, Warren. Soon after, Doug moved on to a team called Colts, whose home ground at the quaintly named town of Dingadee, just out of Dungog, was part of a large, privately owned property. There were half a dozen trees on the playing area, including a large gum tree which stood only about 20 metres from the bat. Every time a batsman hit a ball into the tree, four runs were awarded, and even a ball touching a leaf on the tree resulted in four.

The tree was at square leg, about 45 degrees behind square and everyone— the kids and the grown-ups—hit across the line of the ball to try and hit the tree.

Over the years cricket lovers came to love Doug's horizontal bat shots. Anything remotely short of a length and Doug sprang into action: he went back and across, his judgement of length was swift and sure, hitting the ball with immense power. How different it might have been if that tree at Dingadee had been stationed at mid-off. In August 1968 the Australian team played Kent at the St Lawrence Ground in Canterbury. At 'cow corner' (deep mid-wicket) stood a famous oak that was long part of the ground's folklore, and well in front of the boundary. Most of the Australians were amazed that a tree stood within the playing area. But not Doug Walters. The famous Canterbury oak passed into history a couple of years back, but local sentiment won and the ground authority has replaced it with a new oak.

In school cricket Doug was something of a hero with the ball. He bowled his medium-pacers, which were deemed 'very fast' by the opposing batsmen. Around the mid-1950s a Dungog farmer, Tom Abbott, was so taken with young Doug's cricket that he had a chat to Ted Walters.

Tom apparently was impressed with some of the figures I was producing in local cricket and he suggested to my father that he wanted to 'buy me the best bat that money could buy'. I had gone to Sydney for some reason. I think one of my mates had moved to Sydney and I spent a week with him on holiday. And part of my duty was to go and get this bat. I think he gave me 40 pounds—which was a lot of money in those days. We went into Mick Simmons Sports Store in Sydney and I bought a Gunn & Moore [Autograph] bat.

Doug spent a long time over his choice of bat and he must have driven the sales staff to despair as he handled every bat on display, then looked through the bats in the storeroom as well. Doug treasured that bat. He even slept with it under his pillow.

That was the first bat where I started writing my scores on the back. I didn't write down the bad ones. When I am coaching these days, I note that the kids write down their scores on the back of their bats too. Sometimes I see their scores. 'Why is this 0, 1 and 8 on the back of the bat?' I tell them, 'Don't put the bad scores down. The bowler and particularly the wicket-keeper will be able to see that and they will say that this bloke can't bat.' I used to only put my good scores on the back of the bat and I believe Don Bradman did the same sort of thing.

Young Don Bradman was probably an exception in that he would have written down ALL of his scores as they were most likely all good.

Sometimes Doug got the chance to field for his dad's team, Telligra, and that was always a thrill. Then he came under the influence of a policeman, Sergeant Vic Moffitt, who was organiser, coach and bus driver for the Maitland Police Boys team. Doug jumped at the chance to play for the team. During the Christmas holidays, Sergeant Moffitt used to drive the team nearly 150 kilometres to play in the Newcastle competition. In one match Doug took an incredible 9/8.

By the time he had reached the age of twelve Doug had developed a great love for bowling; this was his first love in cricket. He loved to see the bails fly when he clean-bowled a batsman. In a match for Maitland Police Boys against Newcastle, Doug took 17 wickets for just 11 runs in the two innings, and he finished the Under-13s season with 61 wickets at an average of 3 runs apiece.

Ted Walters was not a well-to-do man of the land and for the most part of Doug's early life, Ted worked in a saw mill in nearby Clarencetown. Then the company bought a big slice of land— 13 000 acres—in a place called Raglan. They established a dairy farm on part of the property and offered Ted the job to run the dairy. Doug had just begun attending Dungog High School when the family moved to the farm.

The land was heavily wooded and Doug was always keen to go out into the high country with the men and help them drag out or snig the logs. School, schoolyard cricket, snigging the wooden logs, milking the cows, and the hotly contested backyard 'Tests' presented Doug with a variety of interests and a good work ethic.

I used to help Mum and Dad with the chores, especially during the school holidays. My parents would be up at 3.30 a.m. and they'd have a cup of tea and toast for breakfast. I'd skip the tea and toast, asking Mum and Dad to wake me when it was time to go to the milking shed, so I could grab an extra half-hour's sleep. Our first job was to light the kerosene lamps because when we first moved to the farm at Raglan we didn't have electricity.

While Doug had long known how to sit on the stool and use his fingers to milk the cows, the Walters family only resorted to that method when the diesel engine, which powered the milking machine, along with its teat attachments, broke down. The diesel engine failed about once every month. When a breakdown occurred, it was all hands to the wheel; the Walters family frantically working through 150 cows in time for the milk truck.

I hated milking cows by hand. The Walters dairy was first on the line for the milk pick-up. This meant we had to have the milk ready to be collected by 6.30 a.m. It also meant we had to be up and ready to go by 3.30 a.m.

And during those frantic hand-milking mornings they were usually only about half-way through the business when the milk truck arrived, so the driver would lend a hand to get the milking done. On a good day, with all the equipment working, the cows produced about twenty large cans of milk. But when there was a breakdown with machinery, milk production was cut in half.

Doug would do anything to get out of milking, including getting up at the same time as the rest of the family, jumping on a tractor and ploughing all day until nightfall. Turning the wheel of the tractor and heaving about bags of super-phosphate probably helped Doug develop the strong wrists and forearms which later brought such power to his fierce cutting and pulling off the back foot. However, much as he loathed the milking, the daily collection did draw his attention, for it involved the driver grabbing the large milk cans, one by one, heaving the can onto the tray of the truck, then spinning it like an off-break which sent the can wheeling across the tray of the truck at a 'Leaning Tower of Pisa' angle. So expertly did the driver spin the can that it gyrated gently and settled on its base as closely as he could get it to the other neatly stacked milk cans. Spinning a milk can with such precision was a real art. Naturally Doug wanted to give it a go:

I spilt a few cans of milk in the learning, but I eventually got the knack of how to spin the cans into position. It was good fun and saved the drivers a fair bit of back pain. A ten-gallon can of milk was no lightweight.

Life on the dairy farm was tough on the whole family, and although young Doug never shirked his responsibilities, he left it every morning with a sense of relief.

The land was pretty barren, so to make a living we had to milk up to 180 cows a day in summer and about 70 or 80 in winter. It was hard work and I guess I looked forward to getting a lift on the milk truck and getting to school.

At school Doug could have a hit of tennis or a bat and a bowl, soon clearing his mind of the drudgery of milking cows at an 'unearthly' time in the morning. One of the workers on the farm was a bloke named Pat Malone. (Doug insists that was his 'real' name, given the Australian rhyming slang for 'Pat Malone', or 'On your Pat', which means you are alone.) Doug reckons one of the toughest jobs on a dairy is to get a poddy calf to drink milk out of a bucket:

> *The natural thing for a calf is to drink with his head up, because that's where the 'taps' are on his mum, so it is the devil's own job to make the calf put his head down into a bucket of milk. This particular day Pat Malone had the acknowledged world-champion calf at baulking the bucket. After the umpteenth try, Pat calmly picked up the bucket of milk and poured the lot over the calf. 'Maybe that will soak in,' he said.*

One day during the Christmas holidays when Doug and Terry were out together on their way to the woods, they noticed how the car and tractor wheels had squashed the anthills along the track. Where the wheels had passed over the area a few times, the anthills not only flattened out but they formed a base that was rock-hard: perfect, they thought, for the surface of a cricket pitch.

They shovelled the anthill soil onto the trailer which was hooked onto the tractor and they transported the precious cargo to a specially selected area in the backyard of the homestead. Then they got to work with pick and shovel, digging a hole 38 centimetres deep, by about 6 metres long and 2 metres wide.

Doug and Terry filled the cavity with a glutinous mixture of anthill soil and water. They raked the damp soil into place, then spent hours dragging the cement roller over the thick bed. The ants were angry about having their whole neighbourhood relocated, but luckily they were meat-ants and not the larger and more aggressive bull-ants.

It took us a week to complete the job and while the wicket wasn't quite the standard you'd expect at the SCG or Adelaide Oval, it didn't have to last for a mere five days. Our pitch had to last for about three years! So you can imagine that soon enough huge cracks appeared and the ball did some weird and wonderful things. We used to bowl from about 15 metres and bowling on this track may have given me the idea that I was a better bowler than a batsman. Looking back, I reckon I might well have learnt how to defend, for you had to defend soundly to survive the sideways movement on that wicket. Any ball of a full length could be easily played. Very short balls hit the rough grass short of the anthill surface area and lost most of their sting. We used old palings dragged from the wood pile or an old kero tin to double for a set of stumps and bails at the batsman's end.

On this weird and wonderful ground Dougie took off all his heroes: Freddie Trueman, Jim Laker, Tony Lock, Alec Bedser and Len Hutton. He was always the opposition, England or the West Indies, while Colleen and Warren were Australia. There were no quick singles and runs came only in twos, fours and sixes—two for the fence past halfway, four for rolling into the back fence which stood about a metre high and a six for hitting the back fence on the full. Any hit over the side or back fence and the batsman was out—as was a smashed window. When it rained the kids went back to their old pitch under the verandah which surrounded the farm house.

The first time Doug set eyes on the Sydney Cricket Ground the teenager was invited there for coaching along with a bunch of other keen young country cricketers. The coaching classes were run by George Lowe. Camp stretcher beds were set up in the back of the Members' Stand for the two dozen youngsters. That week-long coaching class at the SCG was like heaven on earth for the boys, for apart from nets every day, the NSW Sheffield Shield players and the Test men were extremely encouraging in their talks to them. The experience gave Doug his first taste of Sydney's famous cricket ground, a place that was destined to be something of a Mecca for Kevin Douglas Walters.

Doug was selected in the NSW State Schoolboys Under-14 team for 1959, but he could not take his place in the squad because his birth date fell a few days outside the required date.

It was the first big disappointment of my cricketing life. Because of the registration date I was just ten days too old to take part in the carnival.

However, in 1961, fifteen-year-old Doug was picked for the Emu cricket squad to tour Tasmania. The team comprised outstanding young NSW country cricketers—Doug had cemented his place in the team with a brilliant unconquered 123 for Dungog against Northern Tablelands and a solid 88 against Stroud at Dungog in the preceding months. During the tour of Tasmania, Doug reached double figures in each of his five innings, including 79 against Tasmanian Colts and 72 versus University Seconds.

That same season I was picked to play for the NSW Country Eleven and I played my first match at the SCG. What a thrill to play on the ground which I only knew from 'watching through the radio', thanks to the dulcet tones of Alan McGilvray, and to play against blokes like Warren Saunders. Quite a few blokes from that era remember me most for my baggy caps; my head must have looked far too small for the cap. I still wear size 6 3/4, so I had trouble with the caps at the age of fifteen. Those baggy, baggy caps—that's what people most remember about my early cricket.

A modest double of 22 and 38 in his first hit at the SCG must have impressed some of the good judges in Sydney for the youngster was being spoken about in the highest cricket circles. Doug first came under the notice of the NSW State selectors when he played for a Maitland Eleven against Jack Chegwyn's famous troupe. Chegwyn, who scored more than 10 000 runs for Randwick in Sydney grade cricket, gathered together celebrity players to take their cricket to the country areas of New South Wales. A galaxy of stars such as Alan Davidson, Neil Harvey, Norm O'Neill, Keith Miller, Ernie Toshack, Sid Barnes, Colin McCool, Jim Burke, Ray Flockton, Jim de Courcy, Bill Alkley and Jock Livingstone took part in Cheggy's tours.

At official welcoming receptions, blokes like Ray Flockton, Warren Saunders, Johnny Martin and Sid Carroll entertained the people; Flockton with his race calls, using the surnames of local identities as his 'horses', and Carroll, Martin and Flockton harmonising in song, their most famous being 'I'm Forever Blowing Bubbles'. Legend has it that they could even sing that one backwards. But behind all the fun and laughter there was a serious quest. Chegwyn had his eye out for special talent. In that match against Cheggy's Champions in 1962–63, Doug hit a second innings 51 not out. The innings greatly impressed the visiting team and Chegwyn, especially, was delighted. Then a NSW selector (he was a State selector for more than twenty years) Chegwyn put the name Doug Walters into his little book of future champions.

Jack Chegwyn played five matches for New South Wales during the war before hostilities brought all first-class cricket in Australia to a halt after the 1941–42 season. A right-handed opening batsman, Chegwyn played for Randwick; coincidentally in that same side was Bill West, my uncle and Randwick's wicketkeeper. For New South Wales Chegwyn scored 375 runs at an average of 46.8 with one century, 103. He was built a bit like Danny DeVito and his personality was very similar to the effervescent film star—Chegwyn was a little bloke with a big heart. He made a big impact on Sydney cricket and greatly influenced a generation of country cricketers.

Jack knew his cricket and the cricketers, and he had the knack of picking future stars. He 'discovered' Doug Walters and finger-flick spinner from Tamworth Johnny Gleeson, both of whom toured England together in 1968. Later on, Chegwyn also advised Doug to leave the bush and play in the city, for Cumberland under the leadership of the then Test captain Richie Benaud.

—∞—

Doug's first big break in cricket came just after the Chegwyn match in 1962–63. University exams forced all-rounder Graeme Southwell to withdraw from the NSW Colts team. NSW Cricket Association secretary Alan Barnes made the all-important phone call.

> *Dad answered the call. 'The State selectors have picked your son, Doug, in the NSW Colts team to play Queensland at the SCG number two starting on Thursday. Can you get him down to Sydney in time?'*
>
> *'Of course I can, Mr Barnes.'*
>
> *I was lucky to have been picked. It was only due to a player pulling out, so I treated the match as a bonus game and decided that I would go out and enjoy myself.*

The brilliant Australian novelist and cricket lover, Tom Keneally, is a good friend of Graeme Southwell and he relates Graeme's side of the story about Doug being selected to replace him in the NSW Colts team:

> Graeme was an architecture student and had to make himself unavailable for the team. I believe it was because he had to do a university exam in architecture. Graeme was showering after a game and someone cried out to him.
>
> 'Hey, Southey, they've replaced you with a bloke from the bush named Doug Walters.'

Graeme heard someone else ask, 'Who the hell is Doug Walters?'

The gods are often listening at such a moment, and are inclined to say, if Walters had not himself been inclined by nature to say, 'We'll bloody show you who Doug Walters is!'[1]

And how Doug enjoyed himself...he thrashed the hapless Queensland bowlers unmercifully to the tune of 140 not out, and in the process, he wrote his name into the annals of cricket folklore in Sydney. Every now and again a Sydney newspaper charts those who hit the big sixes. They include Victor Trumper's hit into the box factory over the road from Redfern Oval in 1912; Keith Miller's glorious drive at the SCG; and Doug Walters' hit into the Kippax Lake in 1962, in fact, Doug's mighty six is spoken about with the same reverence as Victor Trumper's.

The ball finished in Kippax Lake alright, but it is a huge carry and couldn't have possibly landed in the lake on the full. But the ball returned wet and I reckon it landed on Driver Avenue and then took a few favorable bounces along a couple of bitumen footpaths leading to the water.

Included with Doug in the NSW Colts team were several players who went on to bigger and better things: fast bowler Graeme Corling and wicketkeeper Brian Taber both of whom represented New South Wales and Australia; opening batsman Gordon Goffet (NSW), left-handed batsman Lyn Marks (NSW and SA), all-rounder Terry Lee (NSW), and opening batsman Peter Kelly (NSW and WA). Country New South Wales has produced some brilliant cricketers, including two of cricket's greatest players—Don Bradman and Bill O'Reilly—who came from the bush. Like Doug they had little formal coaching and played by instinct. They were their own sports psychologists and they played with natural flair, displaying their lack of any fear. Their greatness came from within, and they played with immense passion. Bradman reckoned the best form of defence was attack—sensible, controlled attack—and with not a semblance of a slog he set out to destroy all bowlers.

Richie Benaud was Doug's first club captain. He remembers the time well:

It has always remained one of my greatest disappointments that I had to pull out of the Jack Chegwyn weekend tour to Dungog in the early 1960s. They were always entertaining affairs and the idea of them was to play against country teams and check out if there might be undiscovered talent hidden away from the city.

They found one of the best young cricketers imaginable, Doug Walters, who batted in outstanding fashion against a team containing five Sheffield Shield cricketers and on the Monday morning Jack Chegwyn was on the phone to tell me how impressed he had been.

One thing we knew was that because Jack was a NSW selector, it would have done Doug no harm at all to bat well. When I checked with the other Shield players who had been on the trip, the unanimous verdict was that 'he's pretty good!'.

Doug's success in the annual NSW–Queensland Colts match earmarked him for higher honours. There have been a lot of Sheffield Shield cricketers come from that fixture, Test players too.

When in 1948, the fixture was revived for the first time after World War II, Jim Burke, Alan Walker and I were first of all included in the NSW team and then later in the Australian Test team. Jack Chegwyn arranged for Doug to transfer to Sydney to avoid the travel every weekend and he recommended that he play with Central Cumberland, as it then was and, having made the phone call to Doug, he then called me to say I had a new player about to join the club for the 1962–63 season.

Cheggy wanted him well looked after and we did our best, quite apart from being grateful to have such a fine cricketer and outstanding young man at the club. Quick learner, too!

We played our first match of the season against Gordon at Merrylands Oval and, as is the case with all cricket grounds, it is used for football in the winter. The early-season pitch is completely bare of grass and therefore the ball keeps very low when pitched short. A batsman must, on such pitches, forget the pull shot, which was one of Doug's strengths, and completely ignore the hook.

I was sitting next to Doug and I told him this and explained the reasons.

When he went out to the centre he batted carefully and the bowlers kept the ball up to the bat, until a medium-pacer dropped one short. It hit Doug on the foot right in front and he came back to the pavilion, sat down alongside me and he didn't say a word for ten minutes.

Then: 'I'll remember that, Richie. You won't see it happen again.'

I never did.[2]

Norman Tasker fondly remembers the day he rang young Walters to deliver the good news. The sporting editor had insisted that Tasker get hold of this new batting prodigy on the phone and get some insights into the measured thinking of a seventeen-year-old cricketer on the verge of greatness:

I was a young reporter on the *Sydney Daily Telegraph*, learning the ropes from Phil Tresidder, who was the chief cricket writer in those days. I must have been barely twenty. Doug had already won a certain immortality for hitting a six into Kippax Lake. He did all this when he was sixteen, and there was quite a bit of talk about the kid from Dungog who captured the imagination even before he got a taste of first-class cricket.

It was a Sunday night when the selectors first named him in the NSW side and if Doug was seventeen, he was only just seventeen.

I broke the news to him that he was a first-class cricketer.

I don't know how I got the number, but the Dungog exchange was on an old party line system, where one line serviced several properties and you had to take your turn. I remember it was Marshdale 1U. I asked for young Doug and by the time he was on the phone I think the rest of the valley was on the phone as well. I could hear them in the background.

'It's some reporter from the city... I think Dougie's in the team... Dougie you little beauty!'

I seemed to be in conversation with Maud and Gladys and Beryl and half the bloody town and the interview was as bizarre as any I ever did except perhaps for Chappell in the bath at the Waldorf.

During the 1972 Australian cricket team's tour of England, Norm Tasker interviewed Ian Chappell as the Australian captain lay back in the steaming luxuriousness of a hot bath in his room at the Waldorf Hotel.

Walters himself was sparing with his insights and restrained in his emotion.

'Do you regard this as a great achievement at your age, Doug?' I ventured.

'Dunno.'

'How much work have you put in since you realised selection was a real chance?'

'A bit.'

'What sort of work have you been doing?'

'Few hits.'

'Are you thrilled?'

'Ahhhh, yeah, 'spose.'

And so it went, and not for very long. Meanwhile the rest of the valley, Maud and the girls, seemed to be wetting their pants. Then the line went dead. Marshdale was never a reliable exchange it seems. Doug, of course, excelled in his first game, looking like he was taking a stroll in the park. I always thought his demeanour never changed from the day he started to the day he finished.[3]

Doug's Sheffield Shield debut was against Queensland at the SCG on 31 December 1962. The visitors had won the services of the demon West Indian fast bowler Wes Hall and Doug says that it was with some trepidation that he walked to the crease to face the opposition attack.

I wasn't facing Wes first up. A bloke named Barry Fisher was bowling. I scored a single then let a few out-swingers go harmlessly outside off stump. Then I shouldered arms to a ball which curved back in, a big in-swinger, and lost my off stump.

Queensland's bowler, Barry Fisher, had a smooth, rhythmic approach, similar to his idol, Ray Lindwall. The action was much the same, although Fisher was never, at any stage of his career, as fast as the great Lindwall. But New South Wales were bundled out for 82,

Fisher getting 5/18, including the wicket of Doug Walters, clean-bowled for 1.

That walk back to the NSW dressing-room seemed as far as 10 kilome-tres. As soon as I got back to the rooms, I felt a lot better. The other blokes understood how I felt. They consoled me and were very encouraging. It was New Year's Eve, but neither my dad nor I were in the mood to celebrate.

They had a quiet tea and went to bed early. Doug awoke next day, refreshed physically and mentally:

I woke up to 1963 and thought, 'It's a new year; just think yesterday's failure was a year ago now'.

I hadn't received a ball from Hall in the first innings and was expecting to be peppered with bouncers when I got to the crease in the second innings. I faced about seven overs from Hall and didn't receive a single bouncer from him.

Doug scored a solid 50, before falling to the leg-spin of Westaway. Years later he spoke to Wes Hall about his first match and asked Hall why he didn't bounce him in the second innings. Hall replied: 'Hey, m-a-an. You were just a kid. I wasn't going to bounce a kid.'

In the wake of his first Sheffield Shield match, Doug had approaches from four Sydney clubs: Mosman, Wests, Cumberland and Gordon. Doug decided on Cumberland. Jack Chegwyn's recommendation was sound, given Benaud was the club captain there, and Doug sensed he would be treated well by the team. He had a long chat with his father and they decided that he would move to Sydney from Dungog in time for the start of the 1963–64 season. They travelled to Sydney to talk with Harold Goodwin and other Cumberland officials who arranged for Doug to stay with Goodwin's parents and lined him up with a job.

Accommodation and the promise of a job sealed it for Doug. He was lucky: six members of the Test team—Benaud, Norm O'Neill, Neil Harvey, Brian Booth, Bob Simpson and Alan Davidson—were still on Test duty when New South Wales' next Shield match, against Victoria at the SCG, was played, so Doug got the opportunity to bat for the team. And he didn't disappoint; although he struggled against the pace and fire of Ian Meckiff, he still managed to top-score with 60.

During his first summer of first-class cricket Doug played for North Western NSW against the England team (then called the Marylebone Cricket Club (MCC) for all games other than Tests or ODIs). The match was played in Tamworth.

I batted for thirty minutes and got a duck, getting out to a slow full toss which I tried to hit into the Peel River . . . and missed.

English journalist Ian Wooldridge, a writer with a penchant for a drink or three and a cigarette or two, who easily identified with the Doug Walters of later years—for then Doug was not yet continually wreathed in cigarette smoke and two years away from the pleasures of the amber fluid—first set eyes on him that day in Tamworth:

Young K.D. Walters simply hadn't made an impression. In a curious way that was probably just as well. A dashing century that day and all the Pom writers, not to mention a few Australians, would have been up to their old tricks in unearthing yet another 'next Bradman'. And that is an enormous millstone for any prodigy to carry, as both Ian Craig and Norman O'Neill will confirm. Three years later, of course, the comparison with another country lad who'd taken cricket by storm was quite inevitable. And of all those burdened by it down the years, I believe Walters handled the 'next Bradman' tag better than any. With a laconic outlook, much humour, irreverence and a glorious talent, he remained very much his own man and—to the outsider—the archetypal Australian.[4]

Doug's first trip away with the NSW Sheffield Shield team was to Brisbane. He had been twelfth man a few times and at that stage he didn't drink or smoke and he was surrounded by mischievous characters such as fast bowler Frank Misson, a prankster if ever there was one—Misson once famously nailed Richie Benaud's street shoes to the dressing-room floor during a Test match at the SCG.

In Brisbane Doug roomed with Norm O'Neill, one of his cricket heroes. O'Neill was worried Doug would awaken early, so conditioned was he to getting up and milking the cows, but O'Neill found, to his utter amazement, he had to wake Doug most mornings.

As part of the newcomer's initiation, the rest of the team wanted to discover whether Doug could take a joke. On one trip Misson organised one of the flight hostesses to hand Doug his junior Learn-to-fly wings and colouring-in pencil set. After touchdown in Adelaide, Frank raced ahead of the rest of the team. As the team disembarked and walked to the lounge area in the terminal, a fruit fly inspector sternly approached Doug saying that he had been warned that Doug was in possession of a concealed bag of fruit.

The official was determined to search my bag, pulling out toothpaste, shaving gear and other toiletries. As I stood there, embarrassed while the inspector rummaged through my bag, I saw Frank Misson sporting a huge grin.

Misson's mischief rubbed off on Doug and it probably fired his enthusiasm to frequent trick shops, buying cigarette lighters that gave off a minor explosion, invisible ink, saltpetre and all manner of paraphernalia which Doug used to annoy the hell out of his State and Test team-mates. But in the early years of first-class cricket

Doug was quiet. He listened and learned, and he stored away all his tricks for a later date.

—※—

Australia's 'Voice of Cricket' Alan McGilvray was to the ABC cricket coverage what couch is to the SCG wicket. He painted a word picture so vivid it inspired thousands, especially Doug Walters. And when Doug, who had been 'watching through the radio' for years, came into first-class cricket, McGilvray saw the youngster as the closest player to Bradman in his experience:

> There was a boyish naïvety about him, like Don [Bradman] when he first came into the NSW team. Doug was an engaging character. I came to like him very much and, unlike Bradman, a bit later in his career Doug loved to have a drink. When he came into Test cricket I saw Dougie play some of Test cricket's greatest knocks. He never changed, even during his struggle in England in 1972. Doug was a hero to a generation but, to me he was one of my favourites.[5]

—※—

A cloud descended on the game of cricket in the summer of 1963–64 when, in the First Test in Brisbane, Test opening bowler Ian Medsiff was called for throwing. Doug batted against Medsiff one time and never believed the Victorian fast bowler was a chucker.

Doug's first century in Sheffield Shield cricket came in the second innings against Victoria in 1963. In the first innings, occasional off-spinner Bob Cowper had him caught at first slip by Keith Stackpole for I.

I learned a good lesson that day, for a bowler doesn't have to be using a shiny ball to make a curve in the air. In the second innings I set out to make amends. Peter Philpott and I put on 203 in 195 minutes and I finished with 109 not out. One writer compared me with the great Archie Jackson, but I've never taken much notice of those comparisons. In fact, I've never seen anyone I've been compared with play the game.

Doug loved the camaraderie of playing top-class cricket. Among the ranks of the NSW team at that time, only two players—Doug Ford and Doug Walters—had not played a Test match. Ford never did and Doug's Test days were before him. Doug was soon to discover that a nickname could do wonders for the soul. The two Dougs were relatively short men and the players were finding it hard to differentiate between the pair. At one stage they were calling Ford 'Little Dougal', but when they addressed him in that way both the Dougs would turn around and answer. Doug remembers the confusion:

'No,' they'd say, 'Not you Little Dougal, I meant Tiny Little Dougal over there.' Peter Philpott posed the question: 'What happens if a catch is in the air and you are both under it? We haven't got time to yell, it's not yours Tiny Little Dougal; it's yours Itsy, Bitsy, Tiny Little Dougal.' At the time there was a song on the Hit Parade called 'Itsy Bitsy Teeny Weeny Yellow Polka Dot Bikini'. Someone suggested we take the Bikkie out of Bikini and so I became Bikkie Walters.

When Doug made the Test side a couple of years later, he was given the nickname 'Freddie'. Victorian and Test opener Ian Redpath kept saying that Doug reminded him of Freddie Trueman as he ran in to bowl: Doug's mop of hair bobbing up and down exactly the way Trueman's mane behaved as he tore in to bowl.

After that most blokes called him Freddie, although some of the team were a bit confused as to how his nickname evolved. He wasn't alone of course. In South Africa Brian Taber (he was christened Hedley Brian Taber) somehow got the nickname Herbie; Ian Chappell, sometimes given the tag, Bertie (a team-mate reckoned he attacked the bowling like Bertie the Butcher); and Doug formed a unique club called The Dunce Brothers. There was Freddie Dunce, Bertie Dunce and Herbie Dunce. However, Doug always says he believes his nickname Freddie came from Redpath talking about his bobbing hair a la Freddie Truman as he approached the wicket to bowl.

—៣—

It all happened for Doug in that summer of 1963–64. It was his first season with Cumberland and he became a regular member of the star-studded NSW team. He also got his first job away from the dairy at Raglan and he bought his first car, a grey-coloured Mini Minor, all the rage in those days. He paid £900 for that first car which rewarded him with largely trouble-free motoring for 200 000 kilometres in the ten years he owned it. Doug's first job was as a storeman at David's Wholesale, but he didn't like the work much so he moved to a firm called Grimley's that sold sporting goods and toys.

The South Africans toured Australia that summer and for the first time Doug experienced a day at a Test match. He watched the eighteen-year-old wonder boy of South African cricket, Graeme Pollock, peel off a flawless century. Doug never saw another Test match until he played in one himself in 1965, scoring that brilliant debut 155 against England at the Gabba.

At the end of the summer the Australian team to tour the West Indies would be named. Doug was in the running, but form eluded him at the critical last part of the season and he missed the boat. Despite missing out on the tour, Doug's incredible all-round performance in Adelaide against South Australia had cricket lovers excited throughout the land. Doug hit 253, his highest Sheffield

Shield score, figuring in a record 378-run second-wicket partnership with Lynn Marks.

Herbie [Brian Taber] reckoned he helped my cause a lot because he had 'taken the shine off the ball'.

Taber lasted for eleven minutes and was out for a duck with the score at 9; 136 minutes later Doug had notched his century. After getting 253, Doug then bowled 22.7 overs to take a career-high 7/63. It was becoming clear that this lad Doug Walters was something very special.

Doug finished the season with 536 runs at an average of 53.60; however, along with another promising young player in Ian Chappell, Doug wasn't selected for the West Indies. In hindsight he believes that missing the West Indies tour wasn't such bad luck for he would have been up against the speed and fire of Wes Hall and Charlie Griffith on foreign soil; something he wasn't quite ready to play at the higher level.

While Cumberland skipper Richie Benaud was in the Caribbean covering the tour as a journalist, Doug led the club side to a grand final victory, scoring 138 to help notch the win. It was a first for Cumberland. Never before had a teenager led the club in all of its long history and to win the final without Benaud at the helm was a big plus for Doug. He was also a member of the winning NSW Sheffield Shield team (the first and only time Doug Walters was a member of a NSW team to win the Sheffield Shield) and he sensed there were good things around the corner.

All of his runs that summer were made with the Doug Walters Autograph Grimley bat. There had been some hiccups along the way but in Doug's last few matches he hit form. Too late for a trip to the Caribbean, but enough end-of-season form to give him lots of confidence for the future. Doug was excited about the prospect of playing against the Englishmen when the England team toured from the following October, and 1965–66 promised to be a stellar year for Kevin Douglas Walters.

—⚬⚬⚬—

In top-line sport, one man's misfortune can sometimes be another man's lucky break. And so it was for Doug Walters when Bobby Simpson was hit on the hand by Queensland fast bowler Peter Allen. New South Wales was playing Queensland at the Gabba and was bowled out for 108 in the first dig, with Simpson going for a duck and Walters for 2, caught by Tom Vievers off the clever swing of Ross Duncan. The Queenslanders hit 307 in reply, with a couple of Doug's heroes, Peter Burge (111) and Wally Grout (91) doing the bulk of the scoring. New South Wales was heading for outright defeat, especially after the captain, Bob Simpson, suffered a broken hand early in the second innings. Graeme Thomas rescued the NSW innings with 182 and Doug chimed in with a solid 84. Barry Rothwell was unconquered on 75 and the visitors got out of trouble with a draw.

Simpson's injury meant a vacant spot was there in the Australian team, for he wasn't expected to recover in time for the First Test. Doug was clean-bowled by Graham McKenzie in the match against Western Australia at the SCG, but he hit 76 in the NSW second innings and a week later he was playing against the MCC at his favourite cricket ground. When he read through the names of the England squad, Doug visualised their technique: he had already 'seen' players such as Colin Cowdrey, Mike Smith, Bob Barber, Fred Titmus, David Brown, David Allen and Peter Parfitt by 'watching them through the radio'. Doug scored two centuries in this MCC match—one with the ball. His 15 overs cost exactly 100 runs, then he hit his memorable 129, an innings which brought him into the Test side for the Brisbane Test.

Ian Wooldridge fondly remembered Doug from the day he hardly turned a hair when the youngster tried to hit a full toss into the Peel River and was bowled for a duck against Ted Dexter's England team at Tamworth a few years before Doug's Test debut. Wooldridge had seen enough in the MCC match a week before to believe that Australia had unearthed another teenage international sports star. These are some of the words which appeared in his column in the *London Evening Standard*, for his British audience, under the banner 'Young Bradman all over again':

At half-past five this evening a pale and slender youth gravely removed the billowing cricket cap of Australia and jerked it aloft. Just once. It was one of his few gestures in four and a half hours that lacked the assurance of absolute maturity.

On his first visit to a Test, two years ago, he bought an excursion ticket from Dungog to Sydney and ate his sandwiches on the Hill. On his second, today, he scored 119 not out at the age of 19. Not even Sir Donald Bradman, who stood to lead tonight's ovation, could launch the most ruthless of all Test batting careers on such a resounding note. Walters is the tenth Australian in 100 years to make a century in his first Test against England. He is the first, postwar, to hit 100 on his very first walk to a Test wicket anywhere. Today from the moment he met Titmus' second ball a yard out of his crease and struck it cleanly into the long-off fence, it became impossible to avoid the comparison with Bradman. Walters is straight, correct, deceptively strong, unashamed to loft the ball into the air, unimpressed by any reputation and totally run-hungry.[6]

As Doug walked from the ground in the wake of his debut Test century, Richie Benaud extended his hand and advised Doug to consult him before he 'signed anything'. Doug scored his debut century with the Doug Walters Autograph Grimley bat. He also scored his second Test century, in Melbourne a week later, with the same bat. But Benaud sought a decent bat contract for Doug and after protracted talks he secured for Doug a contract with Slazenger worth £1000 a year for three years. It turned out to be the richest bat contract Doug ever received in his career.

A Test century first try also brought Doug an unexpected reward. A friend, Bruce Burton, presented him with an audio broadcast tape of his first Test innings—Doug's first ever recording of its kind.

Doug scored 410 runs at an average of 68.33 and he took 9 wickets for 283 at an average of 31.44 in his first Ashes series. Only a few days after the Test series ended, Doug was given a civic reception in Dungog. Accompanied by his pretty, dark-eyed girl-friend, Caroline Redman, the girl he was destined to marry, Doug was treated to hero status. More than 2000 people turned out to cheer him as he arrived at the venue in an open-topped sports car, which cruised ahead of the town band and marching girls dressed in smart blue uniforms and big white hats.

Doug sat next to Caroline and near his proud parents. The crowd cheered as Hunter Valley Cricket Association president, Colin Johnston, opened proceedings: 'The whole town of Dungog has turned out to pay Doug Walters tribute and it couldn't have happened to a nicer fellow.'

Doug stood to say a few words. He was nervous, but he sported his famous gap-toothed smile. 'Scoring a century isn't nearly as nerve-racking as speaking here today. As far as I am concerned, Dungog must take full credit for any success I've had in cricket.'[7]

Later at a special lunch given by Dungog and District Cricket Association, Doug's former Alison School headmaster, Jim Fuller, paid his tribute:

... Those were happy days at Alison. Doug was not only good at cricket, but also tennis and the fact is Doug Walters was the greatest schoolboy athlete in this district. He won more ribbons at Bandon Grove, Alison and Dungog than needed to make a large dressing-gown.

When I saw Doug walk to the wicket on Tuesday, I said to myself: 'That's the same Doug Walters who used to sit in the third row at Alison School' and who is just the same today, quiet, unassuming, courteous, as he ever was...[8]

The *Dungog Chronicle* published the playing lists for a number of cricket teams. Doug's brother Warren was in the Telligra B Grade team and his younger brother, Terry, was included in the Dungog John Bull Shield team to play Gloucester, at Dungog, the following Sunday. The 1965–66 summer proved to be Doug's most satisfying season so far.

I enjoyed a terrific season. There was the civic reception in Dungog and to top off my summer I scored 168 against South Australia and 114 against Western Australia in my final two Sheffield Shield games. And I'd won selection in the Australian team to tour South Africa.

But a trip to South Africa with an Australian team had to wait for Doug. All Australian males in their twentieth year were faced with the prospect of being conscripted into the army and a possible tour of active duty in Vietnam. Australia's grossly unfair national service lottery hit our shores and Doug's number came up. He was soon forced to make a decision: would he go to South Africa with the Australian team and then go into the army, or would he forego that Test tour, work through his conscription and then be available for the Australian tour of England in 1968? Richie Benaud advised Doug to go straight into the army, which meant missing the South

African tour, but he would then be available for the 1968 Australian tour of England.

Doug wasn't keen on going into the army, but he won the nation's heart by calmly accepting his fate. Graeme Watson, the Victorian all-rounder who replaced Doug in the Australian side to tour South Africa, was also called up in the same lottery, but Watson had his papers deferred due to university studies. Army service also cost Doug a trip to England by way of an invitation from MCC to play for a World Eleven in a few matches in 1966 against an England Eleven at Scarborough and at Lord's. MCC committeeman Trevor Bailey, an ex-England Test player, penned the invitation to Doug in a letter dated 7 February 1966. He was offered all expenses paid and a fee of £150.

Former Test captain Ian Johnson, for many years secretary of the Melbourne Cricket Club, which manages the Melbourne Cricket Ground, wrote to Doug when he was about to enter his two-year stint in the Australian Army as a conscript. Johnson knew all about the services. He flew Beaufighters for the RAAF during World War II.

Melbourne Cricket Club
26 Jolimont Terrace
Jolimont C2

March 4, 1966

Dear Doug,

First my congratulations upon your selection for South Africa, although this was a foregone conclusion following your wonderful season debut in Test cricket.

However, that is not the main purpose of this letter. I feel compelled to say how very much I admired your statement following receipt of your call-up notice. Your attitude was a credit to all sportsmen and I must say that, because of my long association with cricket, I was proud that a leading cricketer should set such a magnificent example to others in so accepting and facing up to his responsibilities.

As you said, two years is not a long time at your age and you can rest assured that those two years will certainly do you more good than harm. You will come back to cricket the better for it even though the game can ill-afford to lose a player like you for even two years.

As you possibly know a big majority of the 1948 Australian team that toured England had seen five and more years of active service.

Players like Miller, Lindwall, Morris and I all went into the services around your age and because of this did not play Test cricket until our late twenties. Lindsay Hassett is still another. Yet even though we were discharged at a much later age than you will be we still had enough time left to get lots of fun out of Test matches and tours, and I know that not one of us would have missed the five years or so we served.

You will be pleased to know that my views of your attitude are shared by many people in Melbourne, from all walks of life. You would feel so proud of the comments as of your century in Brisbane had you heard some of the things that have been said. My personal admiration has increased tremendously; so too has my pride in cricket. You are a credit to your family and the game.

With all good wishes
Yours sincerely
Ian Johnson[9]

chapter three

I'M *in the* ARMY *now*

I had my draft card in my hand, Kevin Douglas Walters written on it and the old doctor said, 'Sit down. Have you had any complaints? What diseases have you had?'

'I've had hepatitis, and the usual, chicken pox and mumps...and I think I've got rather flat feet.'

And this bloke looked at me through the top of his Coke-bottle glasses and said, 'I've seen every [Sheffield] Shield game at the Sydney Cricket Ground since 1901 and you look fit enough for me!'

Doug Walters was one among 804 286 twenty-year-old Australian citizens who were required to register for national army service between the years 1964 and 1972. Doug went in to the second National Service ballot held on 10 September 1965. It was precisely

48

two months to the day before Doug played his first Test match for Australia, against England at the Gabba. At the time Labor Leader Arthur Calwell declared that 'the Labor Party opposes utterly and absolutely conscription for the youth of this country for service overseas in peace time'.[1]

As the total number of twenty-year-old men was greater than what was needed for the intakes, a ballot was held up to six weeks after the close of each registration. Dougie was always a betting man, but this was one 'lottery' he wasn't keen to win. Marbles with birth dates printed on them were cast into a barrel and the numbered marbles for each of the months in this second national draft—I July 1945 to 31 December 1945—were drawn. If a number on a marble matched your birth date you were well on the way to becoming a conscripted soldier in the Australian Army. For the second intake the dates drawn in the ballot were:

July 3, 6, 7, 8, 16, 22, 25, 26, 31.
August 3, 6, 9, 11, 12, 13, 14, 15, 16, 20, 21, 22, 23, 25, 26
September 2, 4, 5, 6, 14, 17, 21, 25, 26
October 2, 4, 5, 6, 10, 11, 13, 16, 17, 23, 25, 29
November 3, 4, 12, 14, 15, 16, 22, 24, 27
December 6, 10, 12, 14, 17, 18, 19, 21, 24, 25, 26, 28, 31[2]

Doug was born on 21 December 1945, so his number came up. Ironically I was in the same ballot, but 13 July (this time) was lucky; I was among a collective of 567 238 twenty-year-olds whose marble did not fall. In 1965 37.7 per cent of the young men whose birth-date marbles had been picked out of the barrel proved unfit for army service. These 99 010 young men were rejected as they were considered not to have been able to meet the medical, psychological and educational standards required. However, Doug was among the 63 740 men called up and enlisted in the army. Some

19 000 conscripts served in Vietnam and 511 servicemen and one servicewoman were killed in active service in Vietnam.

The servicewoman was Temporary Captain Barbara Frances Black of the First Field Hospital, Australian Nurses Corps, and she died on 3 November 1971 at Vung Tau.

Among the Australian dead in Vietnam were a total of 202 National Servicemen. And there are still six unaccounted for Australian soldiers in Vietnam, officially listed as Missing in Action. In April 2007, the remains of two soldiers were found in Vietnam. They are believed to be two of the six missing in action from the year 1965.[3]

Doug was among numerous high-profile public figures called up for service, along with the likes of Normie Rowe (voted at the time by the nation's teenagers as the 'King' of Australian popular music), future politicians Jeff Kennett, Bill Hayden and Tim Fischer, prominent sailor and wine baron Sir James Hardy and racing driver, the late Peter Brock. Doug has always been skeptical about the conscription 'lottery' system.

I understand it was three birthdays a month they pulled out of the hat. Supposedly it was a ballot system but I doubt very much whoever intro-duced that ballot system got it right. If you went up to the boozer with a thousand guys, which there invariably was, or more, in the bar, of a night, there should have been heaps of guys celebrating a birthday every night in that pub. Now there was never any more than the usual average of two or three guys celebrating a birthday on any given day. As for 21 December, I never struck anyone else in my time in the army who did Nashos with me and shared that birth date with me. I know that there were sets of twins—I met a number of blokes who had a twin brother—whose birth dates matched the selected marbles, but only one of the twins was picked for army service.

Normie Rowe also has grave doubts about the call-up procedure. He, like Doug, believes that he was part of an overall conspiracy. Normie's birth date was 31 January.

'I'd registered in all good faith and was called up. But I found out—ten years after I got back—that there were a whole bunch of people born on my birthday who weren't called up.'[4]

Doug Walters and Normie Rowe were immensely popular youngsters, stars in their respective walks of life. No doubt, the authorities felt that these champions would make fine examples to other young men less willing to conform to the call-up lottery and, if needs be, march headlong into the valley of the shadow of death. We may never discover the truth about how many young men whose birth date matched the drawn marbles were actually called up.

In October 1965, the Department of National Service and Labor (DENS) considered whether National Service for brothers of National Servicemen, for only sons or for twins or triplets constituted hardship. While the government apparently recognised that the call-up of an only son or more than one son in a family could be seen as undue hardship, no man was (officially) exempted from service obligations on the grounds of family circumstances.

So I believe they did have a thing with twins. They'd only take one and not two. How they picked one or the other I don't know.

The army has long been noted for its soldiers having a liking for the demon drink. Doug was no exception, however, it wasn't army life which led him down the path towards having the odd beer. In fact, Doug didn't have an alcoholic drink until after the end of his first Test series against England in 1965–66.

I used to play squash two or three times a week. And because I didn't drink, I was appointed the designated driver. And I used to play my match last; a ploy by the drinkers to have me out on the court while they had a bit more time to spend in the bar having a beer. The squash would finish about 11 p.m. and we would often get home around 4 a.m. I played Wentworthville in D once which was sort of second division at various courts around Sydney. I finished this five-setter one night. It was very hot and they had no soft drink, and I needed a drink. I picked up someone's beer and downed it because I had to drink something.

And I thought 'that tasted better than the sip of beer I had tried three or four years ago'. I sipped on a few more beers that night and gradually got the taste.

Doug Walters was then twenty years old.

However, Doug was a non-smoker when he was called up for National Service. Six weeks before he entered the army, Doug got a job with Rothmans.

When I applied for the job the State manager, Brian Weeks, asked me if I smoked. And I told him I didn't.

'Well, Doug, if we were to give you the job, would you be prepared to carry cigarettes in your pocket and offer them to other people?'

I said, 'That's not a problem for me, of course I would.'

So I got the job with Rothmans and I wasn't a smoker and because I got called up soon after getting the job I spent a lot of time in the office reading sales letters and learning about the tobacco industry.

And they would send me out to the odd shopping centre to promote Rothmans.

And I'd link up with blokes like [Test cricketer] Norm O'Neill and footballers Peter Diamond and Dennis Meaney, both having played rugby league for Australia. I distinctly remember going to the East Lake Shopping Centre in Sydney where they were doing a Consulate menthol promotion.

There we were walking about the shopping centre handing out free Consulates . . . and the very first bloke I offered a cigarette to (and I had a beautiful Dunhill lighter) . . . and he recognised who I was and he said 'Doug, they can't be too bloody good if you are not going to have one yourself.'

'Okay, I'll have one with you.' I put it into my mouth and lit it up and smoke came out of my eyes, my ears, my nose and I started coughing and I can still see this bloke walking away, laughing his head off. After he disappeared round the corner, I put it out, after the one puff. And that was the end of my smoking. It just wasn't for me. In fact, my wife Caroline was smoking at that time and I hadn't even convinced her that it wasn't a very good thing to do and that she should give it away. Soon Caroline had given smoking away . . . and I started.

But Doug had 'resisted the urge to smoke' until the second year of his National Service. Rothmans continued to send Doug a monthly supply of 3000 cigarettes during his years in boot camp.

Doug found himself immensely popular because when he received his monthly cigarette ration he would give them away, tossing a few packets here and there.

They'd be all up the boozer that night smoking my cigarettes. We had smoko breaks every forty minutes on the parade ground and there they'd be sitting on the sidelines smoking my cigarettes. We were up the boozer one night, I'd had a few drinks and I said to this bloke, 'Hey, give me one of my smokes.'

They (Rothmans with genuine Rhodesian tobacco) were the real McCoys in those days. I began with one or two a night and one or two went to a packet overnight. And then it went to two packets. I think my ration worked out at two and a half packets a day—50 cigarettes. By the end of National Service I was smoking more than my allowance and buying a few more at the bar.

Doug used to hear people talk about smoking in excess of a hundred cigarettes a day. He thought that for anyone to smoke that many cigarettes in a day to be extraordinary.

I recall a flight from Sydney bound for Perth to play a Sheffield Shield match against WA. And I thought to myself, 'if there was ever a day I was going to smoke a hundred it was today'.

I decided to keep count, and I kept putting a cross on the back of my cigarette packet every time I had one. I had to score only the ones I smoked, because working for Rothmans I also gave a lot away. As I finished one packet of twenty I transferred the running total to the new packet.

At the end of that day my total stood at 107.

Ah, another Doug Walters century in a session...

Now, I certainly hadn't smoked anywhere near that many in any one day before then or since. That was something like 24 hours and those were days when you could smoke in an aeroplane. In those days the cigarettes had better quality tobacco and lasted longer. What was my average intake of cigarettes in any given day? People ask me that and I guess it depends how long I'm out of bed of a day. And that's true. If I am out of bed for twenty hours in a day I am going to smoke a helluva lot more than if I have eight hours' sleep.

The *London Evening Standard*'s award-winning sportswriter Ian Wooldridge covered Doug's first Test match. In fact, he'd seen him play up-country cricket a couple of years before and he'd studied the young champion.

He is without pomposity, preferring to portray himself not as some sporting idol to millions, but as one of the millions themselves, humanly fallible when it comes to a drink or a bet and the very last champion of the enormous pleasure of smoking cigarettes. I was surprised to discover that he didn't start smoking until he went off, with cynical resigna-tion, for military training during the Vietnam years, which unfortunately coincided with his early days in international cricket. Since his return, many years now, he seems to have been perpetually wreathed in tobacco smoke. 'I can't imagine life—long, short or indifferent—without a cigarette,' he says.'[5]

It doesn't worry me how people perceive me. I was brought up that way. If I was brought up in the modern era then I certainly would have more concerns about it, especially the smoking. I don't blow smoke in people's faces and I always respect their views on the habit. That's fine, but if I am in a smoking area, I like to be able to do want I want and enjoy a smoke. If I am out of order, let them tell me I am out of order. My children have all tried cigarettes and my wife, Caroline, who must be the most anti-smoking person in the world, once did smoke.

Very seldom do I smoke in the house. I go outside, sit in the cold air, get the flu I suppose. I see myself as an average Australian guy who likes a bet, a drink and a smoke and I enjoy speaking with other like people. If I am branded as such a person, that's who I am: that's me. I have always had the philosophy on life that we are here for a good time, not necessarily a long time. I have always had that attitude. And I intend to maintain that philosophy for as long as I can, for as long as I am here.

Wooldridge delighted in talking about Doug's downing a then record 44 cans of beer on an Australia–England flight.

...he simply doesn't care whether you disapprove or not. It's his body, it's his life and just as Jane Fonda clutters up gangways, wakes up small children and arouses evil male thoughts by performing her in-flight aerobics on some insignificant trans-Atlantic hop, Doug Walters drinks. He doesn't disturb anyone, he sleeps like a log on arrival and wakes up fresh as a lark.[6]

—m—

It was a hot afternoon in January 2006. Sixty-year-old Doug Walters was driving me towards his favourite watering hole in Chatswood, the Great Northern Hotel. We flashed past the carved ancient sandstone in the road leading to the Sydney Harbour Bridge. Unsung convict hands fashioned the stone at the birth of a new nation and crafty graffiti vandals thumbed their noses at authority by their blasphemous artwork today. Were we living in the death throes of a once-proud nation, where all respect for property and the old seems to have fallen by the wayside among our young people? We saw enough louts on the streets that day to bring Doug out of his seeming conservative shell.

I think everyone should do three-months' National Service. Everyone has to have discipline and I just think that it is too easy for kids . . . if they don't get discipline at home, it is a lost life . . . somehow. We see too much violence in the streets. Everywhere, right around the world, there is violence and injustice. Yes, I get a bit disturbed about that because I know some of these kids, they are out there robbing banks and doing whatever. They could be good kids . . . they are just misled. They need direction. Three months in the army would certainly help them. The army life would provide the right sort of guidance for them.

During the two-year stint that we had, those guys who lacked discipline were weeded out and shot back out on to the streets. That, to me, defeated the whole purpose for they were the blokes who would have best benefited from National Service.

When Doug speaks about discipline in the army, he's not referring to a more structured life; he maintains that there is a vital need for the Australian youth of today to learn to take orders.

Kids today just don't do as they are told. There are a couple of ways to guide a youngster. You can show a kid and he might follow or you can tell a kid to do it a certain way. In the army you are TOLD what to do and you WILL do what you are told, whether you want to do it or not. The blokes who rebelled in my time in the army got kicked out. That was a soft way to deal with them. There was an alternative: getting locked in the slammer for a few days until they eventually decided to conform and do as they were told.

Doug believes that Australia needs to reintroduce a scaled-down model of National Service for the sake of the nation's youngsters, to bring our youth to understand the importance of respect and discipline.

However, two years' army service in Australia is far too long. Two years is a long time out of someone's life. Today, apart from our numbers in Iraq and Afghanistan, there is no need for Australia to have trained soldiers over a long period. I think three-months' army life is ideal for young men. You get discipline in the first three months. After that they eased off you a bit.

Doug Walters underwent National Service from April 1966 until March 1968. His recruitment training was at Wagga (called Kapooka), then he was transferred to Singleton for Core Training.

Next stop was Holdsworthy (near Liverpool, NSW) when he was assigned to the 1st Battalion, which had just returned from a tour of combat duty in Vietnam. His training at Holdsworthy also included a few weeks' jungle training in Shoalwater Bay, Rockhampton, where he was among a group masquerading as the 'enemy' for another group destined for the killing fields of Vietnam.

Doug never made public complaints about his treatment while undergoing National Service, and believes he was drummed into the army as part of a government 'plan' of targeting certain people to serve.

> *... They picked out a marble for a cricketer (Doug Walters), they picked out a marble for an Aussie Rules player (Karl Ditterich); they picked out a marble for rugby player (Bob Fulton). They picked out Normie Rowe. I'm sure it was a deliberate ploy by the government to prove there weren't any exemptions, because here they were willing to select high-profile people in the community. As a result of that I was made a scapegoat for my military training. We were supposed to undergo a series of X-rays in Kent Street or somewhere in Sydney and everyone was to see a number of doctors, ensuring they hadn't flat feet and all that sort of stuff.*
>
> *We were queued up in alphabetical order and 'W' (for Walters) was near the end of the line and there were TV cameras, radio and press gathering to talk to me. I had begun my Test career well and news of my call-up had the media out in force. Everyone was taking a long while getting through all this. They went through six different doctors. I saw an old doctor. He was well into his eighties.*
>
> *I had my draft card, Kevin Douglas Walters written on it and the old doctor said, 'Sit down. Have you had any complaints? What diseases have you had?'*
>
> *'I've had hepatitis, and the usual, chicken pox and mumps ... and I think I have rather flat feet.'*
>
> *This bloke looked through the top of his Coke-bottle glasses and said, 'I've seen every [Sheffield] Shield game at the Sydney Cricket Ground since 1901 and you look fit enough for me!'*

Unlike all the other conscripts he got to know in the army, Doug says this was the only doctor he was 'examined' by.

> *Everyone else had umpteen X-rays and saw five or six doctors. My card was obviously already stamped 'fit for active service' because this old guy,*

I suspect, wouldn't have recognised Kevin Douglas Walters anyway on my card. My card was obviously a special one.

Doug's 'special card' clearly did not mean he would get special treatment of the preferential kind. In fact, Doug was soon to learn that some people within the army were hell-bent upon making his two-year stint a relative nightmare.

I went down to Wagga by bus. We got to the camp at about 3.30 a.m. We had to go to the store to collect our sheets and blankets and gear and by the time we got to bed we wouldn't have had much sleep at all, then all hell broke loose with Reveille at 6 a.m.

It was the middle of winter. Everyone had to race out to the middle of the parade ground, carrying your two bed sheets, for roll-call. The idea of taking the sheets was to ensure that you had to make your bed again.

At the end of that this little smart lieutenant who had only just been through Nashos the intake before me and was taking over his first platoon said, 'Recruit Walters, I want to see you in my office.' So I went to his office and he roared, 'Don't think you are going to get any fuckin' preferential treatment in this outfit.'

I said, 'I don't.'

And he replied, 'Well, I'm gonna make sure that you don't. You'll be picking up every garbage bin, cleaning every latrine after roll-call, every day. Understood?'

'That's okay,' I said.

As a result of that conversation at 6.15 a.m., after roll-call every morning this bloke would say, 'I want three volunteers to do the garbage and latrines this morning . . . it will be Recruit Walters, you and you . . . every day it was me and two others, never the same two. And this happened every day for the three months I was at Wagga. I then got transferred to their corps training at Singleton and we had a little sergeant looking after us and he was only about four foot high and he was our platoon leader.

Then he started. The three required men were now privates. 'We want three volunteers to do the garbage and the latrines ... it will be Private Walters, you and you ...'

Jesus, nothing's changed from Wagga to Singleton and here we go again.

Three weeks this has gone on in Singleton and I was resigned to the fact that it was going to happen for the next three months.

I'm starting to wonder how much longer this could possibly keep up for because I never once complained about doing it. Finally, our lieutenant, a great guy, the man in overall charge of the camp, turned up at roll-call. He rarely came to the roll-call, but he had obviously got wind of what had been going on for almost four months. He put his head around the corner of the hut after parade call, after Sergeant McEvoy had picked out Private Walters, you and you, and said, 'Excuse me Sergeant McEvoy, I'll be doing the volunteers this morning. You three hop back in line. We will have you, you and you.'

And I never got another garbage-latrine duty from that day on.

Sadly, the bloke who rescued Doug from the clutches of the unrelenting Sergeant McEvoy, later volunteered to go to Vietnam and was killed within a week of getting there after stepping on a landmine.

Doug's army service caused him to miss the 1966–67 Australian tour of South Africa. In that series, Brian Taber, Doug's friend and NSW Colts' team-mate, made his Test debut in the First Test against South Africa at the New Wanderers ground in Johannesburg. During his two years' National Service, Doug accumulated leave by not taking due days and holidays and so he returned to civilian life in time to make the 1968 tour of England.

Doug didn't set eyes on the officious platoon leader from Wagga again during his National Service days, but their paths did cross a few years later. The platoon leader had found himself a job as the aide-de-camp to former war hero, VC winner and then governor of New South Wales, Sir Roden Cutler.

We were playing a cricket match at the cricket ground (SCG) and I had just got a hundred against somebody. Sir Roden used to walk down the stairs at the end of the day's play and if someone had done well he made a point of being down the bottom of the stairs and shaking the hand of the player concerned just before they went into the dressing-room.

He was there with his hand out and he said, 'Congratulations.' And I looked behind Sir Roden and I saw this fella, the smart-arse from Wagga, Martin was his name, and he had his hand out as well and I said, 'You can go and get stuffed.'

And I veered straight into the dressing-room. I saw Sir Roden a few days later and he said, 'Doug, you didn't go very well on my aide-de-camp the other day, you didn't have any nice things to say to him,' and I said, 'No, he was the prick who fucking gave me a hard time in National Service.'

Sir Roden laughed, 'I gave him the arse myself, today!'

chapter four
JUST
the TICKET

'Good for your image, Doug,' the company commander said, in trying to convince me that a tour of duty of Vietnam would do me the world of good.

'Can you, Sir, guarantee me a return ticket?'

Of course, he couldn't have done that, so I added: 'Sir, I have been picked to go to England with the Australian cricket team. And they CAN guarantee me a return ticket to Australia, so that's what I'll be doing... playing Test cricket in England.'

Doug's life in the army had hardly been a bed of roses. During his two-year stint as a National Serviceman, Doug did not get much leave for playing representative cricket. In February 1966, Doug hit 114 for New South Wales in Perth and he didn't play another first-class match until April 1967 when he got a week's special leave from the army to turn out for The Australian Team to Tour South Africa versus The Australian Team to Tour New Zealand at the MCG. Starved of top-class competition, Doug says he managed to play a lot of army cricket.

The inter-services matches were pretty good, although the wickets were often dubious.

Once, a bloke was killed after being struck under the heart with a rising ball on the Victoria Barracks wicket. There was a clock on the stand at the little ground at Victoria Barracks and myth had it that if someone hit the clock from the centre pitch, there was a keg of beer on the line. I tried every time, but never hit the clock. Sometimes the ball sailed over the clock, but never actually hit it. All the guys tried, but no-one hit it, so we'll never know whether the keg of beer story was myth or fact.

During an inter-service series at Albatross in early 1968, Doug's farewell appearance for the army, he hit a quick 23 against the navy and 66, including ten fours and a six, against the RAAF. With the ball, Doug excelled, taking 7/26 from 11.7 overs against the navy and in just four overs of medium-paced out-swing, he took 3/8 against the RAAF, including a hat-trick. On the front page of the 15 March 1968 *Navy News*, there is a photo of Doug kneeling to help adjust a navy all-rounder's batting stance: there is a packet of Rothmans Filters protruding from Doug's shirt pocket. He always promoted Rothmans, the company for which he would continue to work after he left the army.

While Doug says he didn't get 'a lot of high-standard cricket' in the army, he did learn the not-so-genteel art of throwing a hand grenade. He could fire a gun, but his regimental sergeant major was none too pleased with Private Walters and how he handled his rifle. Doug has this enduring memory of his time in uniform:

> *They weren't impressed with my ability with the rifle. I can still see the RSM yelling from the dais on the parade ground at Holsworthy. 'Get that rifle up, Private Walters. Get it up. Get it up. It's not a cricket bat you've got in your hands you know.' I didn't win any awards with my work on the rifle range, but I am proud of the pewter mug I have on my bar that I won for hand-grenade throwing. I was in the winning team for grenade throwing at Holsworthy.*

Three important events occurred during Doug's army days: he turned 21 on 21 December 1966; his father died on 13 February 1967; and he got married on 26 August 1967. Doug's 21st birthday party was held among 50 family and friends at a hall in Clarencetown. He got a day off army duty to be there and he reckoned he would never again have to buy another pair of winter pyjamas, so many pairs was he given that night. Only a few weeks later his dad died:

> *Dad's death didn't come as a shock because he'd been very ill for more than a year, having suffered a number of heart attacks. I got home for his funeral and it took me a long time to get over Dad's death. I was very close to him. It is so difficult to come to terms with the loss of someone you love.*

His thoughts went back, way back to the times Ted Walters used to drive him to matches and how he had quietly said to himself the instant he brought up his debut century in Brisbane in December 1965 ... *That's for you, Dad.*

On 26 August 1967 Doug married Caroline Joy Redman, youngest daughter of Mr and Mrs Ray Redmond of Moore Street,

Dungog, at the Dungog Methodist Church. Doug still had more than six months to serve in the army. He says:

We both attended Dungog High School together, but we didn't start going out together until I had moved to Sydney and Caroline was going to Teachers' College in Newcastle. In winter we'd both go back to stay with our families in Dungog and I'd take Caroline out to dances and the movies at weekends. I guess our getting married was something everyone sort of took for granted.

Caroline looked stunning in her nylon-lace princess-line gown and circular tulle veil that was held by a flowered pillbox head-dress. The Reverend John Killingly performed the ceremony. He gave the groom some sage advice: 'Doug Walters, you are embarking on a career that will take responsibility, team-work and team spirit.'

Among the 117 guests at Doug and Caroline's wedding were NSW selector Jack 'Cheggy' Chegwyn, Test players Brian Taber, Grahame Thomas and Dave Renneberg, and NSW Sheffield Shield team-mates Lynn Marks and Barry Rothwell.

My young brother, Terry, was best man. There was quite a crowd at the wedding and one TV station filmed the ceremony. Caroline, for once in her life, arrived on time, but she had to cool her heels outside the church waiting for the TV crew to make some minor adjustments to their gear. Caroline wasn't too impressed when we found out later that something had gone wrong and the film didn't come out.

Doug and Caroline had a nine-day honeymoon in Adelaide, travelling there via the Snowy Mountains. On 26 August 2007, they celebrated their 40th wedding anniversary.

What a partnership Caroline and Doug have formed. They have four children—Brynley, 30, Lynton, 24, Hannah, 22 and Mitchell, 20. Brynley holds a science degree, majoring in resource management, from Macquarie University. He now works for the Hawkesbury–Nepean Catchment Management Authority. Lynton has a degree in electrical engineering and telecommunications from the University of NSW and currently works in programming for SBS television. Hannah is studying accountancy at Hornsby TAFE and works for an accountancy firm at Epping. Mitchell is in his second year at university and works in a bottle shop. Understandably Doug and Caroline are very proud of their children.

'All the boys have grown up with a love for and keen interest in cricket,' Caroline says. 'They couldn't understand their father's fame, because Doug retired when Lynton was born [1981] and Brynley was only five. But they did understand that other friends like Dennis Lillee and Rod Marsh were famous and our boys got so excited whenever Dennis or Rod rang Doug.'[1]

Brynley, Lynton and Mitchell all played cricket during school, and Brynley also played tennis. Hannah played softball and continues to dance in jazz ballet and tap.

—⚋⚋—

In December 1967, Doug played for New South Wales against South Australia at the SCG. It was my first match on the famous ground and Doug was the captain of New South Wales. I remember bowling the last over of the day to Doug. It was the NSW second innings; in the first innings, Doug only got 1 and fell after a couple of balls. I'd heard a bit about the legend of Doug Walters and how he had gone into the army for a couple of years, doing what I might have done had my marble been drawn. After play we were having a beer and the instantly likeable Doug Walters said to me:

Now, Mallett. Why did you have a man on the square-leg boundary? I don't sweep. May I suggest that you take your man on the sweep and put him at a wide mid-on. Waste of time having him on the sweep. I might come down the track and hit with the tide past mid-on. That's where you need an extra man.

Next day, South Australian captain Les Favell threw me the ball to start the second over with Doug on strike.

'Righto, Cause [SA opening batsman John Causby], git over there...' Favell said, indicating deep square leg.

'No, need, Les,' I interrupted. 'Doug doesn't sweep. Bring Cause up into the ring.'

Favell dutifully complied and Doug nodded and settled over his bat. He could have 'done' me easily, but that was not then, nor is it now, the Walters' way.

A few overs later, fast bowler Alan Frost got one to move away late when Doug was on 17 and he edged a ball low and hard to my right in the gully. I got both hands under the ball and it went into my palms clean as a whistle. Doug turned to me and said, 'Did you catch that one, Rowdy?'

I nodded in the affirmative and Doug didn't hesitate. He didn't look at either umpire. He simply walked off the SCG.

That evening both NSW umpires tore pieces off me for declaring it was a catch. Both men insisted that the ball bounced, but to me, it was a fair catch. Over the years Doug has never let me forget: 'You know that time in Sydney when you picked me up on the half-volley... Are you still catching them on the bounce?'

When South Australia batted we were bundled out for 95, with Favell unbeaten on 55. Doug bowled 4.7 overs and finished with 5/21. He had me caught on the slog, by a retreating Brian Booth at short forward leg—my attempted hook carried a full three-quarters of a metre.

. Doug came into the Third Test against India later in that year, played at the Gabba. He scored a magnificent 93, followed by an unconquered 62, helping Australia to win a tight match by 39 runs.

Doug Walters was back. In the Fourth Test at the SCG, Doug delighted his Sydney fans with 94 not out, then he was run out for 5 in the second innings, but again Australia won, this time by a convincing 144 runs. Doug's Test runs virtually assured him of a tour berth to England in 1968 and he was duly picked.

A letter from one of his early cricket heroes is something he cherishes to this day:

Sandy Beach Hotel
Worthing, Barbados
West Indies

7.3.68

My dear Doug,

It's not my habit to write to cricketers, but I just felt I had to say how pleased I am to see you going to England. Not that I even thought anything else. But ever since I have watched you start and first met you, I've liked your approach to the game and I have liked you personally. So too did I like the girl you married. So I guess I have an interest in you and what you do. You will love this trip to England. Cricket is different, but there is something that grows on you the more you play there. The grounds are small, crowds very patient, very appreciative. Anyway Doug you shall soon find out and I know you will do well. Writing for the press over there as I do—and the paper I write for like either one of two things—praise or knock—you soon lose friends. Players accept praise, very few accept criticism. It's only natural, I guess. For that reason I rarely mix with them and better all round. Anyway if any time you find things are not going all that well, and you get a bit worried about your game and want advice then don't be frightened to come and ask. I never give advice unless asked as there are far too many advisors around—often bad ones, I'm afraid. Anyway there it is. I don't go to all the matches Australia play there, but if you see me in the press box give me a shout, I'll help if I can. The West Indies have slipped a lot. Hall and Griffiths are half-rat power. A very fine player is Clive Lloyd, tall, strong left-hand bat. England are a pretty useful team now. Anyway Doug, if you have trouble and want advice just yell out. Good trip and best to your charming wife.

Keith Miller[2]

Six weeks before Doug was due to leave the army, his battalion was told it was going to Vietnam. Doug considered himself lucky in that a soldier had to have at least three months to serve before the army would send a National Serviceman to a war zone. The commander of Doug's company tried valiantly to convince Doug that Vietnam would do him the greater good than going to play cricket in England.

In Doug's last week of army life, the commander increased the pressure. Doug was hauled into the commander's office every morning and he asked Doug to seriously consider staying in the army and volunteering to fight with his platoon in Vietnam.

'Good for your image, Doug,' the company commander said, in trying to convince me that a tour of duty of Vietnam would do me the world of good.

'Can you, Sir, guarantee me a return ticket?'

Of course he couldn't have done that, so I added: 'I have been picked to go to England with the Australian team. And they CAN guarantee me a return ticket to Australia, so that's what I will be doing . . . playing Test cricket in England.'

In April 1968, an alert photographer took a shot of Private K.D. Walters of First Battalion at Holsworthy, I RAR, resplendent in his uniform, complete with slouch hat, walking from the barracks for the last time as an Australian soldier. Doug had accumulated enough leave to make the England tour—it was time he discarded his army uniform and swapped his bayonet for a lump of willow. A few days before the team flew out of Sydney bound for England, Private Doug Walters received a letter informing him of his official discharge from the army:

> HEADQUARTERS
> EASTERN COMMAND
> VICTORIA BARRACKS
> PADDINGTON, NSW
> 19 APR 1968

> <u>PERMISSION TO PROCEED OVERSEAS</u>
> Approval has been granted for you to proceed overseas. As you will have completed your 2 year National Service obligations on 19 April 1968 and will be discharged on that date, you will have no further obligation to this Department.

> R.S. Garland
> Lieutenant Colonel
> Assistant Adjutant General
> Eastern Command[3]

—⁓—

On the eve of Anzac Day, 1968, the Australian team bound for the England tour convened at the offices of the Australian Board of Control for International Cricket in George Street, Sydney. The players gathered excitedly, trying on the baggy-green cap (every player was given two baggy-greens for the England trip) and the Australian blazer.

The 1968 Australian cricket team was: Bill Lawry (captain); Barry Jarman (vice-captain); Ian Chappell; Alan Connolly; Bob Cowper; Eric Freeman; John Gleeson; Neil Hawke; Les Joslin; John Inverarity; Graham McKenzie; Ashley Mallett; Ian Redpath; Dave Renneberg; Paul Sheahan; Brian Taber; Doug Walters.

The players were required to sign umpteen autographs—we wondered whether they were for friends and family of the various NSW and Board officials—and final checks over the required vaccinations, passports and luggage were made. Some of the officials accompanying the players on tour were: team manager Bob Parish, of Victoria, an executive in the timber industry and Victorian Cricket Association committee member and Australian Board member; his deputy, the shy and dapper Les Truman, secretary of the Western Australian Cricket Association (Doug would later rid Les of all vestige of shyness); physiotherapist Arthur James, a quiet, gentle and jovial man, who had first gone to England with an Australian team in 1938; and scorer-cum-baggage-man, David Sherwood.

Our team manager Bob Parish, a tall man with a ruddy complexion, revelled in pomp and ceremony. So it was with the air of an outlandish version of a Caesar in ancient Rome that he stood before us at the pre-flight team dinner and addressed his audience. 'No-one here should think they have no right to be on this tour...everyone has been selected on merit,' he said, stating the obvious, or perhaps casting doubts in the minds of some of us who had yet to play a Test match. Doug had a sip of beer and a drag on his cigarette and, like a good card player, he showed no emotion whatsoever. But it was an odd statement from a manager of this team, the 26th Australian cricket team to tour England, and I am sure that the Australian selectors—Sir Donald Bradman,

Jack Ryder and Neil Harvey—would have been relieved to hear that every one of the first-class players they picked in the Australian team was selected 'on merit'.

We left Sydney on a Qantas 707 bound for the United States, with a brief stop-over in Hawaii, while the aircraft was re-fuelled and Doug with Brian Taber, Ian Chappell, Dave Renneberg and myself also 're-fuelled' at the airport bar.

The team spent a couple of days in San Francisco. We attended a short remembrance service at the unknown soldier's grave in the military cemetery, among the thousands of little white crosses covering the manicured sward of green. A cocktail party at the Australian ambassador's home capped off a good, albeit brief, visit.

Then it was on the plane again, this time with an airport stop at New York. Talented young batsman Victorian Paul Sheahan had a few ales en-route from San Francisco and after we disembarked at New York, Paul was found in a locked toilet. Security staff suspected he was a terrorist and next time we saw Paul, he was being dragged through the terminal in a half-nelson wrestling hold. A bit of fast talking by the manager and all was again well with the world. Sheahan was a product of Geelong College and a favourite of Sir Robert Menzies: imagine the former PM's consternation if this little episode had hit the headlines.

We boarded the Trans World Airlines (TWA) flight bound for London and then Bob Parish handed out the autograph sheets. Some 10 000 needed signing. Each sheet had a space alongside the players' names. There were also spots for the team officials. All of the guys dutifully signed the autograph sheets which came in blocks of 100. Bob was most impressed with Doug's effort because he got through the autographs in super-quick fashion. Later the team management realised that Doug, whose name was at the bottom of the sheet, signed only the first two pages and the last two. In between, there were 96 pages Doug had mischievously left unsigned. In 1948 Sid Barnes used a rubber stamp to get through the sheets in quick time. However, his captain, Don Bradman, uncovered Barnes' ploy when he discovered that the bloke who fashioned the stamp misspelt Barnes' first name. It read 'Syd', instead of 'Sid'.

Upon arrival in London, we had a press conference where captain Bill Lawry and manager Bob Parish talked about how the side would endeavour to play attractive cricket; the drone of the conversations threatened to send us all to the land of Nod. In fact there appeared next day in one of the newspapers a lovely photograph of Graham McKenzie fast asleep on the shoulder of spinner John Gleeson. No sooner was the press conference over when Doug, and others, found sanctuary in the front bar of the Waldorf Hotel. The hotel was conveniently situated in the heart of London's West End, close to Australia House and even closer to a German beer hall.

The Waldorf Hotel bar was a splendid place; a quiet refuge from the hustle and bustle of the city of London. But in 1968 London had not yet awakened to the magnificence of ice cold beer; they had lager—Double Diamond, I think they called it—and it tasted a little like luke-warm dishwater. But Doug, being a fully converted drinker by now, figured that after a few it didn't matter anyway.

We soon discovered that our assistant manager, Les Truman, was so stiff and intense that he needed lightening up, lest he fall in a stressful heap. Les would stand outside the team coach and tick off the names of the players, always in alphabetical order. Doug would slip into the bus early and hide behind a seat. The blokes would watch from their seats as Les, ever the master of organisation, scanned his list. Walters? Where was he? Les would then turn on his heel, rush back into the Waldorf reception and ring through to Doug's room.

No answer.

Back to the bus stalked poor, forlorn Les and there would be Doug sitting up the back already immersed in a game of cards.

'Oh, Doug, I thought you were my friend,' Les would lament.

In those days of long Australian cricket tours of England, the first couple of weeks involved practice at Lord's in the morning, then an official lunch-time gathering followed by an even more official evening function. Dinner suits were the go and we had, at all times, to be well groomed. On the night we were to attend the Albert Hall, we had pre-dinner drinks at the bar before we left the Waldorf on the team coach. Then came Doug's clever footwork: he pretended to slip, stumbled forward and crashed into Les, the vintage port in Doug's glass splashing the crisp white shirt of our dapper assistant manager.

Les was dumbfounded. 'How could you, Doug? How could you?' he cried hysterically and rushed from the bar. By the time Les reached his room and looked in the mirror, there wasn't a mark on his shirt. The 'vintage port' had already disappeared. Unbeknown to most in the party, Doug had been frequenting the magic shops in London, stocking up on all manner of tricks, including exploding cigarettes, farting machines and invisible ink.

Les soon discarded his list and he quickly came to watch for Doug's antics. But we all felt Les was still too intense.

The regulars in the front bar—Doug Walters, Brian Taber, Dave Renneberg, Barry Jarman, Bob Cowper and me—reckoned we should treat Les to a night out at the local German beer hall near the Waldorf. There, along with good old traditional fare, including fat German sausages, you could buy litre-sized steins of ice-cold beer. A couple of those and you were well and truly on your ear. Les lost count at three and was soon dancing on the table, much to the joy of his touring companions and the jolly girls waiting the tables.

A few days later Les' humour reached its peak in the confines of the RAF Club where Les found himself signing autographs as 'Bob Parish, Australian Cricket Team Manager'.

It was a warm night and most of us, including Les, had our suit coats hung up in the cloakroom during the function. As the end of the night neared, Freddie moved swiftly about the room, gathering up all manner of silverware, knives, forks, spoons and salvers, and stuffed them into Les' coat pockets in the cloakroom. We duly collected our coats and Les didn't sense anything was wrong as Freddie helped him into his coat. As Les shook hands with our genial host, Doug called out, 'I'd check this man's pockets, if I were you. He can't help himself . . . comes from a long line of kleptomaniacs . . .'

Poor Les. The host discovered a swag of silverware, each piece with the distinctive RAF logo.

There's little doubt Doug's constant antics did much to relieve the boredom, given the Australian team had lost a ridiculous amount of playing time due to rain. Before the First Test in Manchester, which began on 7 June we lost a total of 113 playing hours. The traditional first match at New Road, Worcester, was washed out without a ball being bowled.

'How could Bradman possibly have scored 1000 runs in May?' was an oft-asked question.

Victoria's tall, handsome Paul Sheahan averaged 45 in four Test matches against India and he was, along with Doug Walters, one of the brilliant young batting guns. Sheahan was an upright player with splendid straight and cover drives. He was an outstanding athlete, and admired by Sir Robert Menzies, who, perhaps, in Sheahan, saw a glimpse of his all-time favourite cricketer, Keith Miller. In 1968 that old Sydney–Melbourne rivalry had Doug Walters in one corner and Paul Sheahan in the other. Sheahan, whose nickname was 'Timbers', a take on Prince Charles attending the exclusive Timbertop School in Victoria, recalls the 1968 tour and the rivalry:

I must say I was so wet behind the ears in those days that I wasn't really aware of the issue. But the press saw yet another opportunity to bang the Melbourne versus Sydney drum.

I think Freddie was a really good bloke, one who would have died for the team but you would never have guessed that from his laconic approach to life.

He started his cricket in an era when that sort of approach was not only acceptable but it was almost expected, given that most of the Test team was drawn from New South Wales. He wouldn't be allowed to continue that way today—and the big question is whether players are better off being highly regimented.

I got on quite well with Freddie but we were entirely different people: I was not especially interested in cards and beer and late nights. Funnily enough I was more interested in some of the places we went to visit with 'Truly Wonderful'.

Neither of us was particularly successful in England. In our individual ways, we were both 'feel' players and you need a bit more than 'feel' in England when the ball's moving around a bit. The year 1968 was a wet and green summer when the likes of Ken Higgs, Tom Cartwright, Derek Shackleton and company had a field day, bowling little wobblers that were almost impossible to put a bat on![4]

The 'Truly Wonderful' who Timbers refers to was our erstwhile manager Bob Parish. Some also called him 'Bob the Snob', because he was more inclined to have a gin and tonic with the gentry than buy us a pint in the bar, but everyone on the team referred to him as 'Truly Wonderful'. As we travelled from one venue to the next, Bob would be back in his seat on the coach, speaking into his little voice recorder, making a tape to be sent home to his son: 'Truly wonderful this, son. Truly wonderful. The English countryside is so magnificent...money can't buy it...truly wonderful.'

Doug could never resist. Such as the time when the coach turned down a country lane, past an old cemetery, and Doug said in a tone just loud enough to reach our manager sitting at the front of the bus: 'Hey, Shine [NSW fast bowler Dave Renneberg], truly wonderful that...'

Nine years later, at the outset of the big cricket revolution, when Kerry Packer's Australian squad of World Series Cricketers sat in the team bus about to leave the Old Melbourne Inn for our first practice at Morrabbin, Doug produced another piece of perfect timing: 'Truly wonderful this, boys. Truly wonderful...and Mr Bob Parish...money CAN buy it!'

Bob Parish fitted the time perfectly. He was a bit of a snob, albeit a likeable one. He loved to parade around Lord's Cricket Ground as though he owned it: perhaps a throwback to Lord Frederick Beauclerk, the Vicar of Hertfordshire and a Doctor of Divinity, who was MCC president in 1826 when the administrators ruled the roost, as they most assuredly did in Parish's time on the Australian Board.

Doug scored just 1 in his first innings in England, falling lbw to Barry Knight. He scored an unconquered 5 in another rain-affected match against Lancashire at Old Trafford. Derek Underwood got Doug at slip in his first match at Lord's, scoring only 7, and then came the game at Northampton when he finally got going, hitting a brisk 43 in Australia's 375. Against Somerset at Taunton, Doug scored 61 not out, followed by 34 in the Surrey fixture at The Oval. Doug had produced a string of moderate scores: nothing so far to suggest that he might take the England attack by the scruff of the neck in early June. Doug's most memorable event of those weeks occurred not on the pitch but at the Tavern Bar, the large hotel complex near the WG Grace Gates entrance to Lord's Cricket Ground:

I discovered a good little trick in London and I wanted to test it out. It involved having a one-pound note attached to a very fine piece of fishing line. With the naked eye, you couldn't see the line. I would place the note on the floor and whenever anyone bent over to pick it up, I would pull the fishing line and the note would disappear from their sight. Unbeknown to me, this kid—he couldn't have been more than about ten—was watching me very closely. Then he made his move. I was on one side of a table, and the note was between the other side of the table and a wall. The kid slipped into the aisle and trod on the fishing line, preventing me from pulling the note away. He grabbed the note and fled.

For the First Test in Manchester, the Australian team stayed at a lovely old country house. It had the atmosphere of a nineteenth-century gentleman's residence. I shall never forget having dinner one evening with a few of the blokes, including Doug. A happy, smiling waitress approached our table with a pot of piping hot tea. Doug indicated that he would like tea and the lady poured. She added a bit of milk and asked, 'Do you take sugar, sir?'

'Yes, thanks. I'd like eight spoonfuls, but please don't stir it . . . I don't like my tea sweet.' Doug always loved injecting humour into any situation. It may have links to the old days when as a boy he mixed with the men who 'snigged' like poles. Then stories and jokes were always on show. At that same dinner table, spin bowler Johnny Gleeson said, when asked how he would like his steak, '. . . Rare . . . knock off its horns, wipe its arse and throw it on the plate!'

Bill Lawry won the toss on the first day. It was a pretty good pitch, but it began to take some turn quite early and Lawry, quite rightly, saw a danger man in the Surrey off-spinner Pat Pocock. In one over from Pocock, Lawry hit across the spin sending the ball into orbit for two sixes. He knocked the youngster out of the attack, a grand psychological blow. Both of the young guns batted well, Sheahan (88) and Walters (81), so too Ian Chappell, who got 73.

But it was Doug's second-innings 86 which so delighted the crowd, especially one of the old hands of Australian cricket in the press box, Jack Fingleton, who opened the batting for Australia in 1934. He was one of Australia's best cricket writers and when he wasn't writing about cricket, he was covering Federal Parliament in Canberra. It was Fingleton who helped Harold Larwood, the fearsome England fast bowler of Bodyline fame, to emigrate to Australia in 1950. Fingleton wrote for *The Times* and his piece on the Test paid tribute to Doug's great knock:

Class will tell in adversity and so it was with Walters. I do not think I have ever watched and analysed an innings that gave me as much enjoyment as this one. At no time was this an easy batting pitch.

True it was only the occasional ball that did not behave itself but that was sufficient to bring a furrowed brow on every batting head that came to the middle and it is significant that 13 wickets fell in the day.

It was not an easy pitch on which to play strokes. Every now and then a stroke had to be checked; Cowper and Sheahan showed against Pocock what happened when it was not. Each lobbed a gentle catch back. Walters had not had any great experience. This is his first trip outside Australia. He might have been chosen for our last tour of West Indies but was not, the selectors probably reminding themselves of what happened to Ian Craig when he was sent away at 17. Walters, then in the Army, was not available for South Africa. This then is his first tour, yet on this difficult batting pitch he batted like a true champion. This is a time when class prevails—when the going is difficult. Like all others, Walters suspected the pitch. There were shots which had to be discarded, defence had to be water-tight and Walters's forward defence, the limpness in his fingers sending the ball inertly down, thus frustrating the close fieldsmen, was an object lesson to all. Yet Walters kept his eye peeled for the loose ball and when it came he whirled himself into an exploding bundle of energy, his feet twinkling into position, his bat bristling with aggression. He square cut, he drove, he pulled a magnificent six and he filled me, for one, with warm admiration. It is worth recording Walters's Test score: versus England 155, 22, 115, 23, 35 not out, 0, 60, 81, 86; versus India: 93, 62 not out, 94 not out, 5.[5]

Australia won the First Test at Manchester by a whopping 159 runs, thanks to some adventurous batting by Lawry in the first innings and Doug's great double. Bob Cowper, the occasional Victorian off-spinner, took 4/48 off 26 clever overs, with Graham McKenzie taking 3/33 off 28 overs. England was fired out for only 165 in its first dig, then amassed just 253 batting a second time. McKenzie, Cowper and Alan Connolly each took two wickets and Johnny Gleeson took 3/44 off 30 overs to be the pick of the crop.

Old Trafford was Doug's one happy hunting ground in England where, in six completed innings, he scored 302 runs at an average of 50.33. Australia did not play a Test at Manchester in 1975, the third of Doug's four England tours. Amazingly, Doug's Test average of 50.33 at Old Trafford is far better than Don Bradman's Test record at the same ground. In 1930 Bradman scored 14; in 1934, 30; the Test match was abandoned without a ball being bowled in 1938; and in 1948 Bradman scored 7 and 30 not out: a total of 81 runs at an average of 27.

A day after the Test ended, Australia played Warwickshire at Edgbaston. Doug hit a splendid 55, but the day belonged to Ian Chappell who struck a career-best 202 not out. Brian Taber, second keeper to Barry Jarman, hit a fine double (58 and 81 not out), and I was thrilled having picked up the wicket of one of my cricket heroes, Rohan Kanhai, in both innings.

This was a special game for Doug because Rohan Kanhai was another one of Doug's early heroes. On the backyard pitch or under the verandah back in Dungog, Doug, unbeknown to his team-mates, was often 'Kanhai' with a bat in his hand.

Rohan Kanhai was the great West Indian batsman who had such an impact on the 1960–61 Test series against Australia. He scored at a fast rate, hit a century in each innings in Adelaide, and generally captured the imagination of all budding cricketers. He could hook, cut and drive, and Doug loved to emulate his batting.

Just after Doug's double success in the Manchester Test he received a letter from his old company commander, Major A.W. Hammett, the man who, in Doug's last week of army life, tried to persuade him to stay on in the Australian Army and continue to fight in Vietnam.

From: Major A.W. Hammett   D.Coy

I.RAR

AFV

APPO 4

c/- GPO SYDNEY

14 Jun 68

Mr D. Walters

AUSTRALIAN CRICKET TEAM

c/o AUSTRALIA HOUSE

LONDON UK

Dear Doug,

On behalf of your old Company, I would like to offer you and the team our best wishes for every success on the present tour.

Your progress and performance is followed with a very close personal interest not only by the company but by the whole Battalion—so keep piling up those runs and wickets.

The Company has been involved in a few vicious battles with the North Vietnamese, but we've come out far on top. Unfortunately, we've lost a few fine fellows in the process.

I would also like to commend you for your fine 'innings' as a soldier and for the outstanding example you set to other National Servicemen by your willing acceptance of both National Service and Army life.

Best wishes
A.W. Hammett[6]

Hammett was Doug's old company commander who tried to persuade him that fighting in Vietnam would have been more worthwhile to him than playing cricket for Australia in England. This letter shows that there were no hard feelings towards Doug and that he was proud of him for the path he chose, but the message also conveyed that he would have been as proud had Doug got to the Vietnam War.

Lord's has always been kind to Australia, except perhaps the game which saw Hedley Verity take 15 wickets in a day to destroy Bill Woodfull's team, including getting Bradman cheaply in both innings. For Doug, playing at Lord's was a boyhood dream come true.

Ever since I began watching cricket through the radio, I wanted to play a match at Lord's. One of our first matches in 1968 was at Lord's, against MCC. I remember walking through the famous Long Room and out onto that ground. Ian Redpath was on strike and the very first ball he received after my arrival, he tapped to silly mid-off and said 'C'mon'. I was silly

*enough to go in those days and I was run out by eighteen yards, without
facing a ball. So I didn't get off to a great start. I was running towards
the Nursery End, so I had to wheel around and walk through that mob
again, in the Long Room and up the stairs to the home dressing-room. I
would have loved to have started off getting a few runs at Lord's.*

For the Second Test, England dropped their two big successes of
the Old Trafford match, Basil d'Oliveria who hit 9 and an impressive 87 not out and Pocock who took 0/77, suffering at the hands
of Lawry, Walters and company, before bouncing back in our
Second dig to take 6/79 off 33 overs. The rotund batsman from
Northants, Colin Milburn, came into the side and when England
batted first, Milburn put on a brilliant display of power batting.
Australia was then bowled out for a palpable 78, the lowest score
compiled against England in a Test match since the 65 scored at
The Oval in 1912. Doug Walters battled for a long time to get
to 26 on what had become a treacherous surface. Barry Jarman,
his ring-finger chipped in two places, came to the wicket and
lasted one ball; David Brown raced in, dropped short and the ball
reared, striking Jarman a sickening blow right on the same damaged
finger. It would rule him out of the Third Test match.

That Saturday evening the MCC turned on a gala night to
celebrate the 200th Test match between England and Australia; by
coincidence the 200th Test was the traditional Ashes Second Test
at Lord's. Australia's former prime minister, Sir Robert Menzies,
gave a stirring speech that night, only a few yards away from where
the ten-year-old kid had pinched Freddie's one-pound note. Sir
Robert spoke of the rain and how the 'Lords were in liquidation',
a reference to the rain at cricket headquarters which threatened to
rob England of outright victory or those jolly pollies having the
odd tipple.

There had been the most incredible hail storm at the ground that morning. The entire ground was engulfed in little ice balls and it looked like it had snowed. When they thawed, water flowed across the ground. As we watched from the old pavilion, the water was streaming down the fabled slope and across the uncovered centre of the track (in those days the ends were covered and the wicket area was left open to the elements). We knew there was a 'ridge' at Lord's because when the water hit the ridge, it bobbled, like a flowing brook coming to a pebble in the middle of a stream.

Rain, coupled with some last-day resolute batting by Ian Redpath (53), Lawry (28) and Cowper (32), saw Australia scrape out of the game with a draw. Doug played on to Derek Underwood for a duck and Lawry's men were 4/127 in their second innings when the game ended. A moral victory for Colin Cowdrey's England team, but a draw nonetheless.

The Australian innings began disastrously with Lawry getting a vicious ball from John Snow which reared at his face. The left-hander fended the ball away, but he got the little finger of his right hand jammed up against the handle of the bat. It was a clean break, right through. Lawry would miss the Fourth Test at Leeds. Doug hit a solid 46 in the Third Test at Edgbaston, third top-score to Ian Chappell (71) and Bob Cowper (57). The game was again a draw, the highlight a century (104) for Cowdrey in his 100th Test match.

—⁂—

Around this time, Caroline Walters decided to go to England. She took leave from work and began her journey to the other end of the world.

We had been married for less than a year when the tour started and it was the first time I had lived alone. I hated it, so I planned to take leave from work and travel by ship to Italy and then by train to London to use up some of the time to not feel so lonely. I planned to go with an old friend, about twenty years my senior, and stay in a flat with her in London.

The trip over was okay, but finding a flat we could afford in London was something else. I also missed Doug terribly and the team wasn't scheduled to spend long in London, even though it was towards the end of the tour. I decided to catch trains to all the little places where Doug travelled. The tour only had about six weeks to go at that stage. My companion found she missed her husband and family too much and I wasn't good company, plus I had lost interest in touring with her once I saw Doug, and my friend then decided to go home.

I just stayed anywhere that was within walking distance from the team hotel and Doug would visit most nights. They [the Australian team management] did condescend to give me match tickets and I sometimes had the company of Daphne Benaud [Richie Benaud's wife], but otherwise I was on my own and not welcome most of the time. Doug and I did get to spend our anniversary together, and we dined at some nice places most evenings. The best part of the whole trip was that Doug and I could have a wonderful return trip to Australia together. We chose to travel back via the United States, which was fabulous.[7]

The Australian Board of Control for International Cricket had developed an agreement that each player had to sign and it contained such absurdities as the players forbidden to 'pilot or assist in piloting any aircraft or take any part in the control of any aircraft in which he may be travelling during the tour...'. Wives were also out. A player's wife was forbidden to stay in the same hotel as the Australian team and to travel on any form of transport with him during the tour.

In 1956 NSW pace bowler Pat Crawford wanted his wife to sail to England with him on the same ship as Ian Johnson's Australian team; however, the Board said no and there was the ludicrous situation of Pat waving to his wife as the two separate ships on which each was travelling spent some time cruising parallel to each another a hundred or so yards apart.

Only a couple of weeks before Doug and Caroline's first wedding anniversary, the Australians were playing Hampshire at Southampton. The couple had dinner together then, as 'lights out' approached for the touring team, they went their separate ways. Doug went off to join his fellow cricketers at the modern Skyway Hotel, leaving Caroline to wander back to the Polygon Hotel, a mile away.

> The trouble is that we were not allowed to stay together at all on the tour. It's just one of the things in the contract. I could have dinner with Doug, but I was excluded from all official functions.[8]

Even when the players were relaxing between matches in London, Doug and Caroline had to live apart. In London Doug stayed at the Waldorf Hotel and Caroline had to find accommodation as close as she could to the team hotel.

> I was the only player's wife over there because I wanted to be with Doug and I'd never been to Europe before. I remember thinking that after the tour ends on 7 September, it will be difficult getting used to living together again. We thought we might even have a holiday—in the same hotel.[9]

Doug didn't show his emotions, but the Board's attitude to the players' wives must have annoyed him as much as it did the other married blokes. These days the wives are treated royally.

—⋘—

The 1968 players were each paid $2150 ('or the equivalent thereof and no more'). A sum of $200 was paid in advance to the team leaving Australia and $200 was held by the Board to be paid upon a player's return, subject to his having been on good behaviour on tour. In England the sterling equivalent of $1750 was to be paid to players in four equal instalments. The sterling equivalent was £817. The tour manager deducted a total of £9 from each player to cover the cost of twelve tour ties.

On that tour Doug became good mates with Arthur James, the team physiotherapist. Arthur was one of nature's gentlemen and it was easy to see why Doug and Arthur got on so well. Arthur had been a part of Australian cricket tours to England since the 1930s and had loads of stories about the old days: stories about Don Bradman, Bill Woodfull, Bill O'Reilly, Keith Miller and Ray Lindwall. Players used to go to Arthur for a massage just to hear his wealth of stories. Doug liked playing cards with Arthur. They were almost inseparable in the team dressing-room. One time, Caroline and Doug accompanied Arthur on a day-trip ferry ride to France. It took a few hours to get to France, but neither Doug nor Arthur got off the boat. They played cards non-stop the whole time, until the ship got back to England.

There wasn't a clique among the players in the Australian side, although Doug always seemed to be having a drink with the same bunch of blokes. Simply put, some liked to frequent the bar, others didn't. We had a brief trip to Ireland, which involved a one-day game in Dublin and another in Belfast. The team had just arrived in Dublin the morning of the game: it was a matter of rushing to the ground from the airport, dressing for the match and getting straight into the game.

I remember a few of us having a heart-starter in the bar at the ground. There was Doug Walters, Brian Taber, Dave Renneberg, Ian Chappell and me. Our manager, Bob Parish waltzed into the bar, unusually cheerful and said, 'Well, lads, hope you enjoy your day of rest. What will you have?'

We all ordered pints; the old Imperial pint with a handle.

And we all downed that first pint pretty smartly.

'Another?'

We gulped the second one down in record time.

To our amazement Parish inquired as to whether we could go a third.

Doug enlightened him: 'Sorry, Bob. We can't stand around here drinking all morning. We have a match to play.'

The players loved to take the mickey out of Bob Parish. He was so proper, regimental, seemingly without much of a sense of humour. He had assumed that we all had the game off, otherwise we could not have been getting stuck into a pint. It was worth it to see his jaw drop when we made the announcement about getting ready to take the field.

We took to the field and the players decided to give our skipper, Bill Lawry, a hard time. When the ball passed through to the keeper and Brian Taber flicked it to a slips fieldsman, Walters and Chappell threw the ball in such a way to Lawry at mid-off that he either had to run in to catch the ball on the full or run back and take it overhead. I had my own problems at backward point, falling over and somehow sprigging my left knee in trying to stop an Irish back cut. Despite all our antics we did manage to win the match.

There was precious little time to look about Ireland, but there was time for a beer or two the night after the one-dayer in Dublin. Very early the next morning, Doug turned up at the team hotel and he had trouble finding his room. He banged on the hotel manager's door. 'Hey, mate, what have you done with Room 22? I can't find it, it's disappeared.'

The manager scratched his head as he looked quizzically at the nuggety Australian. 'Toy, toy, not at all, sir. There is no Room 22. Our rooms only go up to the number eighteen!'

Doug was so bleary-eyed he had turned up to the wrong place of accommodation. He'd cop a bit of banter from the blokes, but Doug was well-renowned for having a few beers, often overdoing it. But it was his on-field performance which counted—and his drinking bouts did not appear to affect his run-making ability.

Lawry missed the Fourth Test at Leeds due to his broken finger and Barry Jarman came in to lead the side, but I wasn't the only one who suspected that Lawry was pulling the leadership strings from the boundary line, for Jarman's captaincy was pretty ordinary and very defensive. Doug scored a good double (46 and 56), so too Ian Redpath (92 and 48) and Ian Chappell (65 and 81); however, Jarman bowled Alan Connolly into the ground in the England second innings and hardly bowled the potential match-winner, Johnny Gleeson, at all. In fact. Gleeson bowled only eleven overs for 26 runs as the Poms played out an easy draw. It seemed Lawry was okay with a draw, given Australia was already one-up in the series. Ian Chappell came into the Leeds dressing-room, threw down his baggy-green cap and said something to the effect of: 'If that was Test cricket, you can stick it!'

Doug also felt that the drawn Fourth Test could have been an Australian win:

Lawry said at an after-match press conference: 'We came here to hold the Ashes and we have succeeded.' Both Ian Chappell and I felt we could have succeeded even more in this match had we attacked in England's second innings. On the last day England needed 326 in 295 minutes to win and Ian and I felt we should have attacked them with our spinners.

Although Barry Jarman was the stand-in captain, we had no doubt that Bill Lawry was calling most of the shots from the dressing-room. For most of the day we maintained a medium-pace attack to defensive fields, making sure we weren't beaten, rather than trying to win. Just look at the statistics from that innings: Connolly bowled 31 overs and McKenzie 25, while our main spinner, Gleeson, had only eleven overs and Cowper five. It was a strange situation when you look at Illingworth's 6/87 off 51 overs and Underwood's 2/52 off 45.1 overs in our second innings.

While Doug had a pretty good double in this game, and he eclipses Don Bradman in Old Trafford Test matches, the Bradman record at Leeds would take some beating. In England, especially at Leeds, Bradman turned it on big time. He batted in four Test matches: in 1930, he scored 334; in 1934, he got 304; in 1938, he hit 103 and 16; and in 1948, he scored 33 and 173 not out— 963 runs at an average of 192.6. In 1985 I received a letter from Bradman just after the First Test at Headingly, Leeds:

The TV viewing of the 1st Test was disappointing. Far too many people seem to think that batting becomes impossible when the ball is swinging, or seaming off the pitch. It has always done that at Leeds—I found it playable.[10]

Doug got his highest score—95—of the tour against Derbyshire at Chesterfield, the famous ground where the nearby church spire is as crooked as Freddie's bat (legend has it that the spire will only straighten when a virgin walks the inner stairway). Then just before the last Test, we played the Minor Counties at Torquay.

We'd been in the field for some ninety minutes when we saw John Inverarity wandering along the footpath which ran parallel to the boundary. Invers was in a grey suit and tie and we could see him quite clearly outside

the fence. We had been out there for all that time and no-one noticed that
we had been fielding only ten men! I suspect our twelfth man for the game,
Bob Cowper, knew, but he didn't let on for obvious reasons.

Australia's reluctance to go for a win at Leeds cost us dearly, for
England only had to win at The Oval in the Fifth Test match to
draw the series. And that is what happened. This was my debut
Test and I did okay (3/87 and 2/77) with a wicket (Colin
Cowdrey) in my first over and hitting 43 not out in the Australian
first innings. However, rain gave Derek Underwood use of a treacherous turning and bouncing wicket in the last hour of the match.
A torrential downpour turned The Oval into a patchwork of little
lakes in the outfield and a quagmire in the centre. The ground
announcer called upon the public to help mop up the ground. The
ground authority offered people seven shillings and sixpence for
their efforts and the England captain, Colin Cowdrey, helped
inspire the effort by parading about the ground under a large
umbrella. Underwood swept through the Australian batting to take
7/50 and bring victory with six minutes to go.

In between games Doug played lots of golf with his close
mates Brian Taber and Ian Chappell, and they frequented the
Denham Golf Club whenever the team was in or near London.
Caroline and Doug also got to know Frank and Shiela Russell,
who owned and ran the London Cricketers' Club in Baker Street.
At the club there was always good food, good cheer and cold beer.
Frank and Shiela had been friends with a succession of Australian
cricket teams since the 1953 tourists led by Lindsay Hassett.

While Doug and Caroline flew off to the United States after
the end of the tour, John Inverarity, Greg Chappell (who had been
playing county cricket for Somerset) and I joined Frank Russell's
London Cricketers' Club tour of Germany at Mönchengladbach,
a little town some 20 kilometres from Dusseldorf. We stayed in

the officers' quarters of the British Army Camp at Mönchengladbach where a pint of lager could be bought for a mere four pence. How Freddie would have enjoyed it!

Doug didn't get among the runs in our Fifth and final Test match, scoring just 5 and 1; however, his overall Test figures for that series were pretty good. In the five Test matches, Doug scored 343 runs at an average of 38.11, only five runs behind Ian Chappell, who hit 348 runs in the Tests at 43.50. Doug is typically down to earth about his batting on his first tour of England.

> *I thought I played pretty well in the Tests and the other matches, without setting the world on fire. The wickets took a while to become accustomed to and the England bowlers were accurate and got the ball to move either way... It was tough going, but good experience.*
>
> *The ball seamed a good deal and I saw the ball seam off the wicket. My eyes were pretty good because if the ball deviated off the wicket, I went with it and I found with my method that I hit the ball a lot squarer in England than at home in Australia. The Englishmen set a number of fieldsmen very square in the gully for me.*

I watched Doug bat in England from close quarters in 1968 and on subsequent tours, in 1972 and 1975. Having seen his genius in Australia, India and New Zealand, I, and many other team-mates, were amazed that he didn't consistently dominate the England bowling in Tests there. Long after Doug retired and I reflected upon that extraordinary Walters batting anomaly, I came to the conclusion that his hand–eye coordination was so brilliant he could react incredibly fast to any cut or deviation off the pitch so that he was simply 'good enough' to get a nick to a ball that mere mortals would have played and missed. Dennis Lillee agrees that Doug's hand–eye coordination was so good that on the slower, more responsive English wickets he caught up with the ball with his lightning reflexes. Dennis says: 'Doug played swing well, but it was cut off the wicket, especially in England, which worried him. He was so quick to react to movement off the seam that he managed to get an edge on the ball, where another, less-gifted batsman, would miss the ball completely.' On the hard and fast Australian pitches, Doug found that he either met the ball in the middle of the bat or he missed it.

Sir Donald Bradman was in his late eighties when I put that theory to him about Doug. 'Ah, you'll never convince me with that explanation,' he said.

I sat on my theory until early in 2006, when I asked Doug about his problems in Test matches with the bowling on English wickets.

I'd be trying to hit the ball between mid-off and cover. When I saw the ball 'go', I'd then change my mind and try and hit it between cover and point.

And there they were, the Englishmen, with three or four gullies waiting for the edge. In Australia if the ball deviated it went so quickly you couldn't catch up with the movement. You either hit it or missed the ball completely.

Late in his life Sir Donald Bradman was interviewed by Channel 9's Ray Martin, and Bradman talked about 'turning the blade of his bat' on edge to avoid snicking a ball which deviated off the wicket. Herein lies the essential difference between Bradman's and Doug's method of dealing with the moving ball on English wickets: Bradman was the supreme optimist when it came to batting—where he avoided contact, Walters 'went with it'.

In 1977 at Leeds, England opener Geoff Boycott completed his 100th first-class century in the Fourth Test with a fine 191. Doug's technique couldn't have allowed that, for he would see the ball 'go' and then he'd instinctively react, moving his bat towards the ball and being alert and swift enough in his reaction to 'catch up' with the ball and edge it.

I laughed at Geoff Boycott during this knock. In one over against Dennis Lillee he played and missed something like five balls out of six and he didn't get within five or six inches of the ball. The ball deviated and he kept playing straight down the line. I was at slip laughing. I kept thinking that no top-class player like Boycott could possibly play and miss five balls out of six by that much. I couldn't have done that . . .

Boycott played straight. If the ball moved he missed it, sometimes by a big margin, but the bottom line was that Boycott played and missed—and survived to bat on. The experience of watching Boycott play as he did in that innings got Doug thinking long and hard about his batting technique in England.

—⚬—

Doug has some special memories of that first tour. There was the time when Johnny Gleeson came up with a plan the players thought pretty brilliant to beat the system at the casino. Gleeson announced a roulette system which sounded perfect and looked perfect on paper, so a few of the blokes threw in £5 each and then found the system wasn't so perfect. We were backing red and we decided that we had been desperately unlucky to strike a run of thirteen blacks. So we each put in another £5 and this time we backed black. After we bombed out, we stayed to count the sequence which beat us—would you believe, 27 reds.

At an official function in London, Princess Margaret asked Freddie to sing the 'Wild West Show', a rather bawdy song sometimes belted out on the team bus. Just how the Royals got to hear about this song is beyond me, because as far as I can recall it was something of a hoot with the Nedlands Baseball Club in Perth in the early 1960s. It goes like this:

> [Chorus]
> Oh, we're off to see the Wild West Show ... O ... O
> The Elephant and the kangaroo ... O ... O
> Never mind the weather, as long as we're together
> 'We're off to see the Wild West Show ... O ... O
> [typical verse]
> Next, ladies and gentlemen, is the brown bill duck
> The brown bill duck?
> Yes the brown bill duck can fly as fast as the other ducks,
> but it can't pull up as quick ...
> Oh, we're off to see the ...

This was the first time Freddie discovered that the Royal Family really does have a sense of fun.

Doug's first tour of England was long and testing, but he had done well enough to look forward to West Indian series in the coming Australian summer.

chapter five
a BUMPER HARVEST

I felt really good, but I made the fatal mistake of saying, 'Well, so long as I don't have to open the bowling for Australia, I will be right for the Test match.'

...Next I hear he had phoned the NSW Cricket Association secretary that...'If he is not fit enough to open the bowling, I have no alternative but to rule him as being unfit to play in the First Test.'

After the tour of England, Doug had a few months' rest, then the cricket began in earnest. He had a string of moderate scores early in the summer, with 25 and 16 against Queensland at the Gabba; 43 for a Combined Eleven versus the West Indians in Perth; and he scored 3 in the first innings against WA at the SCG. Batting a second time in the WA game Doug gave a glimpse of the runs avalanche that was to follow with a solid 102.

For New South Wales versus the West Indies Doug hit 24 and 98; the form was beginning to come. A double failure against the Vics at the MCG was a dampener of his early summer, but then came a further blow. Doug strained his hamstring and because it was only a slight strain, he was confident that it would not affect his ability to be fit for the First Test match in Brisbane.

For my fitness test I spent at least three hours out on the track, batting, bowling and fielding. When a doctor sidled up to me after training and asked how things were going, I felt really good, but I made the fatal mistake of saying: 'Well, so long as I don't have to open the bowling for Australia, I'll be right for the Test match.'

The old doctor smiled.

Next I hear he had phoned the NSW Cricket Association and told the secretary that 'Walters said he would not be fit enough to open the bowling for Australia in the First Test, so I cannot pass him fit to play. If he is not fit enough to open the bowling, I have no alternative but to rule him as being unfit to play in the First Test.'

For perhaps one of the few times in Doug's life, his sense of humour back-fired on him. The doctor took him literally and gave him the thumbs down. In those days the doctor's word was final. Often these medicos worked for nothing. It was a way of being feted at the matches, mixing with the present and past great players and having an official standing in the game. Ironically, I also had a fitness worry. I visited the SACA physiotherapist Robin Haskard and through clenched teeth I managed to get my arm just above my shoulder. Doug Walters should have definitely played the First Test and yours truly most assuredly should not have... Doug's replacement, John Inverarity looked out of his depth, falling cheaply to the off-spin of Lance Gibbs in the Australian first innings. Doug's hero, Rohan Kanhai, who had hit 174 not out against the Combined Eleven in Perth, scored 94. Kanhai took his score from 90 to 94 when he 'drop-kicked' me over mid-on, one bounce for four. I asked Lawry to put the man at mid-on (John Gleeson) deeper, but the captain refused, saying, 'No batsman, Rowdy, is going to risk going over the top at 94.'

'Phanto, the batsman's name is Rohan Kanhai, not Bill Lawry!' (Kanhai was like Doug Walters, an attacking batsman of flair; Bill Lawry was dour, slow-scoring and a veritable corpse in pads).

So I secretly persuaded Gleeson to get back deeper and he agreed. Next ball went down Gleeson's throat at mid-on. Kanhai was my only wicket. Second innings I had four overs in three spells, while a tall, strong left-hander, who resembled tennis player Arthur Ashe, tore our attack to pieces.

Keith Miller was right in his letter to Doug: Clive Lloyd was a fine player. Lloyd scored 129 in the West Indies second dig and his century proved to be the difference between the sides.

The off-spinner Gibbs snared Inverarity for a miserable 5 and 9, and Australia lost the match by 125 runs. How much different could it have been had Walters played? He was a brilliant player of off-spin bowling and proved later in the series just how good he was in playing Gibbs. The selectors axed Inverarity and rushed back Walters for the Second Test in Melbourne. While Inverarity was destined to tour England in 1972, he never played another Test match on Australian soil. Lawry (205), Ian Chappell (165) and Walters (76) dominated proceedings as Australia amassed 510. Neither Wes Hall nor Charlie Griffith played in the match and the West Indies lost by an innings and 30 runs. Significantly, the injured Clive Lloyd did not play. While Lawry and Chappell got most of the plaudits, Doug hit grandly for 76. It was the start of an amazing summer's harvest of runs for him.

He played the speed of Garry Sobers and Richard Edwards well, cutting and pulling with great power and he used his feet to counter the flight and guile of Lance Gibbs with ease. The sides were pegged at one-all going into the Third Test in Sydney. Wes Hall came in to bolster the West Indies pace attack, but it didn't stop Australia hitting a first innings 547. This time Doug top-scored with 118. Here was Walters at his finest: he cut and pulled the fast bowlers, making the shots look ridiculously easy because of his swift footwork. And he used his feet to skip down the wicket to get to the pitch of the spin of Gibbs, a number of times thumping the off-spinner wide of mid-on with power-packed on-drives. The crowd rose as one on the Sydney Hill when he played Gibbs with his famous 'come to attention' shot, sending the ball careering to the fence in front of the M.A. Noble Stand.

Doug was like Bradman in that he targeted a bowler. He was ruthless in taking to the spin of Gibbs, who was always there or there-abouts in terms of line and length, but somehow he faltered when Doug got to the striker's end. Doug scored his 118 in 214 minutes. He faced just 185 balls and he hit 12 power-packed boundaries. Gibbs finished with 2/124 off 37.6 overs, figures which would have been substantially better had Walters not been in the Australian Eleven. Eventually Doug fell to Gibbs, playing on to his wicket, via the bottom edge of the bat, to a ball he intended to cut to the point boundary. The scorecard says: 'Walters bowled Gibbs 118', but it might well have been 'Walters tired out'; Doug's arms were surely aching from giving this particular bowler a relentless hammering. Australia won the Third Test by ten wickets and took a 2–1 lead in the series. In two Test innings Doug had scored 194 runs.

As the players headed for Adelaide for the Fourth Test match, Doug's Test batting average stood at 97. In Adelaide Charlie Griffith came into the side, but even his presence failed to stem the Australian tide of runs. Lawry (62), Keith Stackpole (62), Ian Chappell (76),

Ian Redpath (45), Paul Sheahan (51), even Graham McKenzie (59) were among the runs, but Doug Walters' 110 out-shone them all. Doug's innings occupied 194 minutes and he hit 13 fours. He was run out for 50 in the second innings (made in 86 minutes with four fours), but his dismissal was not as dramatic as befell Ian Redpath. The tall, angular Redpath had wandered out of his ground at the non-striker's end as Griffith came in to bowl from the River End. Redpath was looking straight ahead and was probably four or five yards down the track when Charlie smashed a stump out of the ground in the most raucous 'Mankad run-out' imaginable.

A 'Mankad' is considered a thoroughly unsportsmanlike act. Back in 1947–48 during the Second Test in Sydney, Indian left-arm spinner Vinoo Mankad had stopped just before his delivery and pointed to the position of Test opener Bill Brown's feet. He was standing outside his crease as the non-striker and his bat was not grounded behind the crease line. A couple of balls later, Mankad again stopped, noted Brown was again well out of his ground, and he brought the ball down to knock the bails off. Brown was given out, run-out and a 'Mankad' became part of cricket folklore.

Redpath was wandering aimlessly down the track and was yards out of his ground when Griffith stopped and in one foul swoop sent one of the stumps flying and Redpath to the pavilion. No wonder Doug thought Redpath one of the worst runners between the wickets. The Victorian was stunned, as was the entire crowd, but Griffith was totally unrepentant and the umpire, Lou Rowan, had no option but to rule Redpath run out. Sheahan was involved in a number of run-outs during the Test and in the end had to hold out with last man Alan Connolly to salvage a draw.

The West Indians had batted first in the game and on the night before the Test began we attended a rum-punch evening hosted by the West Indian team. At the function Garry Sobers said to a group of players from both sides enjoying a drink together that he would score a century the next day. What confidence! Sure enough though, Sobers scored 110 the next day. He smashed ball from the medium-fast Eric Freeman to the boundary to bring up his hundred, then hit a couple more fours. Freeman was bowling dead straight cannon fodder and Sobers was so casual that he simply hit across a dead straight ball and departed.

The Fifth Test was due to start on 14 February 1969. Doug had already plundered the West Indian attack with scores of 76; 118; 110 and 50: 354 runs at an average of 88.5. Even the man himself could not have imagined that his figures would get a whole lot better.

A few days before the Fifth Test match, Doug had an accident at home, falling down a flight of stairs.

> *Caroline and I were living in a flat and there was a staircase of about thirty steps leading to the door. I was in the process of taking the rubbish out, which meant I had to negotiate all those steps. I was wearing thongs and somehow got one of my feet caught up and I slipped over backwards, my backside thumping down hard on every single one of those steps. I had a pretty badly bruised backside area, reaching up into the small of my back . . .*

After the fiasco regarding his fitness before the First Test when Doug joked about not being able to open the bowling for Australia, this time he was deadly serious.

On the eve of the game the *Sydney Sun* reported on Walters' progress. Under the banner 'Walters Fit to Play in Test Friday', cricket writer Phil Tresidder wrote:

> A specialist has given batsman Doug Walters the all-clear to play for Australia in the crucial Fifth Test against West Indies starting at Sydney Cricket Ground on Friday. Walters is making a quick recovery from a back injury. On Sunday he slipped on a staircase at the back of his Parramatta flat

and jarred his back. The injury was so painful there was some fear of a fracture. X-rays showed no break and Walters is happy with physiotherapy treatment he has received twice a day. He said last night: 'It is a lot better today. I should be right to practise with the team on Thursday. The specialist has given me an all-clear and at this stage it seems certain I will be fit to play.'

Walters' mishap threw a scare into the Australian camp. Skipper Bill Lawry will breathe a sigh of relief at his recovery. Walters missed the First Test because of a leg injury. In the three later Tests he took heavy toll of the West Indian bowlers with scores of 76, 118, 110 and 50. His average of 88.5 runs an innings is only a shade less than Ian Chappell, who tops the averages at 89.5. In those three Tests, Walters played a significant part in the Australian team's mountainous totals of 510, 547 and 533.[1]

And to add insult to injury in the most extraordinary way, the day after Doug fell down the steps at his flat in Parramatta, the NSW Cricket Association sacked him as the State captain. Doug was invited to Cricket House, home of the New South Wales Cricket Association and told to tender his resignation as the State captain. NSWCA secretary Alan Barnes handed Doug the telephone. At the end of the line was State selector Ron James, who said he and his fellow selectors wanted Doug to resign, as 'your batting has deteriorated since your appointment'.

I read some quotes attributed to Dougie Walters in Gideon Haigh's *The Summer Game: Cricket in Australia in the '50s and '60s*, where Doug was quoted as having experienced a 'great surge of anger'; however, when I contacted him by phone in November 2006 (Doug was playing the poker machines at the Great Northern Hotel in Chatswood, and he was in a bright mood, given he'd just

pocketed $150 and had fifteen free shots), he refuted the claim that
he had been angry over being sacked as NSW captain in 1968–69.

*I just accepted their [the NSW selectors] decision and got on with playing
the game. A few years later I was given back the captaincy, I think round
the mid-1970s...*

Richie Benaud was livid. In his *Come in Spinner* newspaper column,
Benaud wrote (in part):

So you thought that red glow over the city on Monday
night was the sun trying to peep through the deluge that
threatened the Fifth Test match. In a bull's foot it was...
The ruddy hue was a reflection of the embarrassment felt
by many cricket followers at Doug Walters' stepping down
from the NSW captaincy... You need a sense of humour
if you're playing cricket in a place where one year they are
grooming you for the Australian captaincy, and the next you're
given the 'sock it to me' treatment.[2]

Although Doug was still suffering from a sore back, he declared
himself fit for the Test match. The NSW State captaincy was one
thing and Doug took the job seriously, but his biggest love was
playing Test cricket and getting lots of runs at the highest level.

Garry Sobers won the toss and invited Lawry's men to bat.
Lawry scored 151 and he figured in a record fourth-wicket partnership with Doug Walters (242) of 336 runs in 480 minutes. He
hit 24 fours. Both Hall and Griffith played that Fifth Test match,
but all the honours went to Doug. He played magnificently, punching
through the covers off either front or back foot; cutting with a ferocity
rarely seen on the famous ground and anything remotely short
Doug pulled it either along the ground between square leg and mid-

wicket, or if the field was in a ring, he simply went over the top. By the end of this Test, Doug had become the second Australian since Jack Ryder to score six 50s in consecutive innings and the first to score four hundreds in a rubber against the West Indies. Doug's innings was a power-laden affair: punctuated frequently with fierce drives, cuts and pulls and he gave the West Indian off-spinner nightmares with his attack of the slow man. Gibbs finally got his man when Walters chopped on, but the West Indian was completely dominated by Walters and his 40-overs stint, for a return of 2/133 was highly flattering to the way he bowled. In scoring 242 Doug beat a long-standing record of 223 against the West Indies, set by Don Bradman at the Brisbane Exhibition Ground in January 1931.

The Australians scored 619 and then sent the Windies packing, dismissing them for a paltry 279, Alan Connolly taking 4/61. Close mate and NSW keeper Brian Taber had not only that week replaced Doug as State captain; he also took over from South Australia's Barry Jarman, who had announced his retirement from Test cricket. Jarman had been the Australian vice-captain to Lawry. Ian Chappell was elevated to become Larwy's vice-captain. Australia held a first innings lead of 340 runs over the West Indians, when Lawry asked Chappell for his thoughts. He indicated that Australia should enforce the follow-on as they had the Windies on the ropes. Lawry replied in the negative: 'No, Chappelli. I'm going to bat on ... give 'em 900 to get.'[3]

Had Chappelli been the captain in this match he would undoubtedly have enforced the follow-on, for the West Indies were trailing by 340 runs. So Doug can thank Lawry for batting again, giving him a chance to add to his impressive run of scores that summer. The first innings' 242 was followed by a brilliant 103, Doug's fourth century of the series. He faced 181 balls in his 196-minute stay at the crease and hit seven fours.

It was late in the Australian second innings that Wes Hall and Charlie Griffith gave their last gasp as truly fast bowlers.

Charlie and Wes had just learnt they had been axed from the West Indian side which was to tour England in 1969. I had hit a double century in the first innings and was seeing them pretty well when I was on about 80 not out in the second when I faced the pair. It was the most frightening half hour's batting of my career. Wes bowled flat out and Charlie reverted to his 'old action'.

One ball from Griffith (he had sent into the pitch short of a length) seemed to rear at me and kept coming straight for me. I almost doubled over backwards to avoid it and actually strained my hamstring in my desperate efforts to avoid being hit. As it was the ball grazed my forehead. It was the closest I had come to being cleaned-up by a fast bowler.

Griffith appeared to be bending the elbow and letting fly. Cricketers did not wear protective helmets in those days and only a batsman of remarkable hand—eye coordination could have evaded that delivery which reared and swung back alarmingly off the pitch at Doug. This was probably what saved Doug from more serious 'damage'.

Doug Walters became the first man in Test history to top-score a double century and a century in the same match. Soon enough in world cricket Doug's Test double was emulated.

Within a few years quite a few blokes achieved the same feat... Greg Chappell in NZ in 1974, Lawrence Rowe, in the West Indies in his First Test and Graham Gooch in England.

There are many big scores in today's cricket asnd the jury is out on whether it is heavier balls which help batsmen to hit harder and further, or a falling away in the general quality of bowling worldwide which has brought bigger scores more consistently.

When Lawry called a halt to the slaughter, Australia was eight wickets down for 394: the West Indies needed 735 runs for victory. Sobers was livid that Lawry had set his team such an impossible task. The West Indian captain smashed 113 in brilliant fashion, and he then threw his wicket away, so too did Seymour Nurse (137), before Nurse swung wildly at John Gleeson and lost his castle. The Windies were all out for 352 and Australia won by 382 runs. But the game belonged to Doug Walters. His season's total of Test runs stood at 699—an average of 116.5 runs per inning.

There was more than a touch of Bradman in Doug's performance. Indeed, Doug's record-breaking effort prompted Sir Donald Bradman to pen him a letter of congratulations:

> SIR DONALD BRADMAN
> 2 HOLDEN STREET,
> KENSINGTON PARK,
> SOUTH AUSTRALIA
> 19.2.69

Dear Doug,

My heartiest congratulations on your record-breaking achievements in the fifth Test. My own performances v West Indies were due to be beaten and I'm glad you did it.

More important still is the pleasing manner in which you have been getting your runs this season.

It is essential in the interests of cricket that batsmen are alive to the necessity to play shots and be aggressive. This does not imply any lack of soundness but in the end, with discretion, the stroke-maker will get more runs. You have had a wonderful season and more than fully recaptured your early form and I hope and expect to see many more fine performances from you to delight everyone. Keep it up.

With best wishes
Yours truly
Don Bradman[4]

The 1968–69 summer was my best, my most memorable in that I scored heavily and consistently.

My best memory of the summer was the 200 and a hundred in the last Test. I didn't realise that I was the first one to get 200 and a hundred in the same Test at the SCG. Bradman never achieved that . . . he might have got 300 and a hundred, but never 200 and a hundred. So I was quite surprised that it hadn't been done before.

I asked Doug if his bumper harvest of Test runs in 1968–69 was all the more pleasing after his moderate tour of England in 1968?

Yeah, look I'd just come out of Nashos. I thought I played okay in England in '68, without doing anything sensational. I didn't even get a hundred in a county match that year. After my season in 1968–69 I couldn't really say that those two years doing National Service in the army interfered too much with my cricket.

At the start of the summer, a youngster penned him a few lines, wishing him good luck for the season. Prophetic words indeed.

I Nyorie Pl
French's Forest 2086

Dear Doug,
I am just writing this letter to wish you luck in cricket this year, and that your captaincy is successful, but doesn't affect your play. If you think you can do it, you will. Good luck.

Yours sincerely,
Stephen Wigney
PS Remember, if you think you can do it, you will.[5]

Doug Walters certainly 'did it' with the bat and he was looking forward to the challenges which lay ahead.

Doug Walters lost the NSW captaincy, but was a certainty to be on the Test tour of Ceylon, India and South Africa. I vividly remember Richie Benaud's words as he left the victorious SA dressing-room after we had beaten New South Wales to secure the Sheffield Shield: 'I hope you enjoy India. It is an interesting place.'

The team for the tour included a few surprises: Victorian wicketkeeper Ray Jordon was one, the other, WA batsman Jock Irvine.

The touring party was Bill Lawry (Victoria, captain); Ian Chappell (South Australia, vice-captain); Laurie Mayne (WA); Eric Freeman (SA); Alan Connolly (Victoria); Ashley Mallett (SA); Paul Sheahan (Victoria); Jock Irvine (WA); John Gleeson (NSW); Doug Walters (NSW); Ian Redpath (Victoria); Graham McKenzie (WA); Keith Stackpole (Victoria); Brian Taber (NSW); Ray Jordon (Victoria). Fred Bennett (NSW) was the manager and Dave McErlane (NSW) was the masseur.

Benaud knew all about the rigours of touring the subcontinent in those days. He led Australia on the 1959–60 tour and the stories which came in the wake of that tour were horrendous. We just hoped they were exaggerated in the extreme.

chapter six

INDIAN
SUMMER

'Hell, fellas, there are 10 000 angry people downstairs. The
bastards are going wild, threatening to tear the place apart.
They all want Bill Lawry's head. It's bloody frightening.'

'Fred. There is only one possible thing this Australian
cricket team can do at such a tense and frightening time...
Hand over Bill Lawry and let's get on with the drinking!'

In 1890 the Tasmanian cricketer Edwin James Kenneth Burn was
picked in the Australian side to tour England. He was selected over
the Victorian John Harry and the New South Welshman Sam
Deane who were vying to become the Test wicketkeeper Jack
Blackham's deputy on the tour. Burn joined his team-mates when
the ship berthed at Melbourne and he announced at the wharf:
'Here I am chaps... but I have never kept wicket in my life.'

Seventy-nine years later, in 1969, Ray Jordon was the deputy keeper to Brian Taber on our tour of Ceylon, India and South Africa, and late into our pre-tour get-together in Sydney, Jordon announced that he didn't realise that each player needed to have a passport. Manager Fred Bennett stood with his mouth open. Fred was stunned and couldn't speak for quite some time, but when he recovered his composure he made hasty arrangements to procure a passport for the somewhat subdued Jordon.

As Bennett and Jordon rushed from the room making for the Immigration Department, they were joined by our team masseur, Dave McErlane—he, too, needed a passport.

Buying a drink in India was more difficult than getting a passport as Doug and his drinking mates soon found out. You had to possess a liquor permit and each time you bought a drink at a bar at the team hotel, the barman would stamp your permit in the same way a customs official stamps your passport. Prohibition existed in many Indian States so only those foreigners armed with liquor permits could legally get an alcoholic drink. To obtain the permit you had to sign a form which branded you as an alcoholic. Doug still has his Indian liquor permit, which he used extensively during the tour.

We began this long, arduous tour in Ceylon (now Sri Lanka), playing three one-dayers and one unofficial 'Test'; one match was played in mountainous Kandy and the rest in the capital, Colombo. In Colombo we stayed right on the beach at the famous Galle Face Hotel. The hotel has since been beautifully restored; however, in 1969, it was in a sad and squalid state. The bar was always a good retreat for Doug and invariably he would be accompanied by Ian Chappell, Brian Taber and me. Skipper Bill Lawry rarely frequented a bar and you usually only saw him at breakfast, at the nets, at the game or, if you happened to be so inclined, at the nearest picture theatre.

Before we left Australia, Dr Brian Corrigan had given us a talk about what to eat and what not to eat on tour and he had issued us with a whole swag of tablets, white ones and brown ones. We didn't really know what they were, although we suspected the brown ones were some sort of anti-malaria medication. Dave McErlane, affectionately known as 'The Doc', brought on tour with him a collection of goodies including Vegemite, cheese spread and Dettol, an antiseptic liquid which guarantees to kill anything remotely resembling a germ. Dave was one smart cookie, a man who would prove to be a loyal and valuable friend to both Australian cricket and every bloke in any Australian Test side during his time.

Lawry put the fear of God in us regarding the quality of the food we would have to endure in the subcontinent. At Kandy he suggested I order lots of boiled eggs, 'just in case', but his advice proved dubious as the second of my eight boiled eggs was rotten. Certainly it was foolhardy to drink water out of a tap. Dairy foods, too, were out because there was some doubt about whether these foods had been pasteurised. Doug found that even the bottles of Lion lager had to be treated with caution:

> It's all in the preservative. If you get a headache next morning, blame it on the preservative . . . and don't shake the bottle because you will then drink most of the stirred-up preservative which usually sits at the bottom of the bottle.

Doug knows his beer and always makes it his duty to test the local brew wherever he might be staying to discover all the beverage's little idiosyncrasies. Anyone who didn't follow his advice about Lion lager invariably suffered the next day.

In the bowels of the Galle Face Hotel there stood a small tailor's shop. Curiosity got the better of Doug and I, so we ventured downstairs and went inside the shop, which was stacked from floor to ceiling with all manner of cloth. It was a dank and humid little place, but the tailor's craftsmanship caught Freddie's imagination. He sidled up to the tailor and said:

'Now then, Mr Tailor, I want a shirt, with four pockets, two at the top and two at the bottom and I'm after a pair of shorts, with two pockets at the front and two at the back.'

Doug then produced a packet of twenty Rothmans Filters and carefully explained:

'Mr Tailor, the pockets need to be of a size to enable me to fit a packet of Rothmans in each. It has to be a snug, yet comfortable fit. Can you do it?'

'Oh, my God, Mr Walters. It would be my pleasure to do this work for you . . . my favourite Australian cricketer. I am velly proud to be of helping.'

'And when today can you have them ready?'

'If you are wanting to come here late this afternoon, I vill have them all ready for the wearing.'

Soon after Doug was seen wandering near the precinct of the Galle Face Hotel, armed to the teeth with eight packets of Rothmans in the various pockets and carrying another packet along with his gold Dunhill lighter which he had bought on the 1968 tour of England.

Doug was ever ready to promote the company and whenever there was a photo opportunity, Doug got in on the act, not for his own publicity but to promote Rothmans. It simply came with the territory. Freddie ensured he had a packet of Rothmans Filters, in either his top pocket or in his hand, whenever there was a camera about. In official team photographs the poor photographer was usually driven to the point of despair because, just as he was about to press the button, Doug would place a packet of Rothmans on the head or the shoulder of the unsuspecting man in front of him. His timing was always good. While Doug never gave up trying, he was stifled to a large extent when, either by accident or by design, he was placed sitting in the front row of team photographs.

We wore black armbands in the West Zone match, mourning the death of former Test captain Vic Richardson, grandfather to our vice-captain, Ian Chappell. It was a sad start to the match but Keith Stackpole (71), Bill Lawry (89) and Doug Walters (68 not out) got some good batting practice on a flint-hard pitch and Ian Chappell, 38 in the first dig, hit an unbeaten 84 in the second. Doug's brilliant first innings knock came with ten sparkling boundaries—all the more amazing considering his previous late night.

The hotel rooms reminded me of the old-fashioned shearer's quarters in the Australian Outback. They were lined up in a quadrangle formation, with concrete floors and concrete verandahs. You could hear a pin drop outside your room. Doug soon realised that sound carried well, for when no-one bothered to join him for a drink the night before the first match around 1 a.m., he gathered up a heap of steel poles and dropped them outside every door. His antics created an unbelievable din, but the players stayed put. Keith Stackpole, or 'Grumpy', as Ian Redpath lovingly called him, was never in good humour whenever his sleep was disturbed, but Doug was determined to find a drinking partner for the night: 'C'mon Stacky. Come and drink with Freddie. Timbers [Paul Sheahan], I know you're there, come drink with Freddie.'

Eventually our manager Fred Bennett reckoned enough was definitely enough and he gingerly ventured outside. But seeing Doug's beligerent stance, poor bleary-eyed Fred was in no mood to stand arguing with Doug, so he gave up and went to bed. Doug drank on alone and was a little worse for wear next day, but it didn't affect his batting.

From Poona we travelled to Bombay and we found we were staying at the Cricket Club of India's ground—Brabourne Stadium. Freddie's top priority was to find a cribbage board. Playing cards was always popular with Freddie, but with all the time on our hands in India and little to do and nowhere to go when we weren't playing cricket, many a player found himself at the card table with Freddie. He recalls:

> *I was given the task of finding or making a cribbage board. Maybe the blokes thought anyone who could work a tractor on a farm would be able to organise something like a cribbage board.*
>
> *I approached one of the carpenters at Brabourne Stadium and explained to him that I needed to drill holes of a certain size, big enough to accommodate the thickness of a match, perhaps slightly bigger. I had selected a miniature cricket bat as my crib board.*

The drill Doug was given looked like a combination of some ancient musical instrument and a cross-bow, but the patient former farmer and Australian Army conscript found a way to make the holes.

> *It was a type of fiddle used for sowing crops. The carpenter was delighted that I was using it to make a cribbage board from a little cricket bat, but it took me the best part of a day to make enough holes in the little bat. When I told him that the bit he had was too big, he took a file from his pocket and filed down an eighth of an inch of the bit until it was the right size. People know how to improvise in India.*

The way Freddie handled that ancient tool, it looked as though he was rubbing sticks to light a fire, so long did it take him to complete one hole in the little cricket bat. But he twirled that Indian drill with a tireless and patient efficiency that perhaps only he among our group could have done.

Initially we thought it was pretty cool staying at the ground upon which we would soon play a Test match, but the rooms weren't too special. Each room had two rather narrow beds. The mattress was about two inches thick and made from horsehair. It was as solid as a rock and felt just as hard to lie on. Under the horsehair mattress was the bed's base, a number of wooden slats set equal distances apart. Overhead was a ceiling fan, a necessity for anyone touring in the subcontinent. When you switched on the fan, it took quite some time to warm up and rotate fast. The gradual process gave Freddie a bright idea. He invited me in to his room one night and said that he had discovered a new way to practise his catching.

Freddie pulled up a chair and stood on it. The fan had four propellers and on the flat end of each propeller he placed an empty can of Fosters. He stepped off the chair, switched on the fan and crouched down as if he was waiting for an edge at second slip. One by one the cans dropped and Freddie caught them all. His 'fielding session' ran a full twenty minutes, and in all that time he didn't miss a chance. Then he slumped into an armchair, and, feigning exhaustion, got down to business: 'After all that catching practice, Rowdy, I think it is time we had a beer.'

Freddie also figured out an ingenious way of getting more comfort from the horsehair-mattress bed. He took the mattress off the bed, removed all of the wooden slats, and tied each end of the mattress to the ends of the bed in such a way that it hung like a hammock.

The monsoon season must have been just on the wane, for our last training day at Brabourne Stadium proved to be the hottest of the summer. It was unbelievably hot, humid and draining. But no-one trained harder than Doug. He ran in like a man possessed, his hair flopping about like Freddie Trueman, with Ian Redpath urging him on, 'C'mon Freddie, get stuck into me.' Redpath's words always took Freddie back to those early days when he 'watched' Fred Trueman through the radio. Having batted and fielded well at training, with runs in the lead-up games, Doug was in good form going in to the First Test in Bombay.

The wicket looked a bit green, which we thought might suit the likes of Graham McKenzie and Alan Connolly. Apparently the grass was grown over a pavement of red bricks, the wicket's base. The ball bounced and McKenzie returned figures of 5/69 off 29 overs, Connolly got 2/55 and Johnny Gleeson 3/52 off 35.4 overs. India was all out for 271, thanks to a fine 95 by the Nawab of Pataudi. He should have been out for 5, but I dropped a sitter off Gleeson. When Pataudi finally skied the ball to me at mid-off, Lawry rushed from mid-on, pushed me to ground and accepted the catch. Freddie didn't miss his chance: 'Well, then Rowdy... You are due to get into a position to catch one!'

That did wonders for my confidence.

Doug scored a bright 48, before he fell to a close catch by Srinivasaraghavan Venkataraghavan off the bowling of Bishen Bedi, the left-arm spinner. Keith Stackpole scored a fine 103. As if battling with Bedi and Erapally Prasanna, the magic off-spinner, wasn't enough to combat, the stifling heat, while not as intense as the previous day, made any time at the crease pretty tough going. Australia hit 345 in reply to India's 271, then the Indians were bundled out for 137, with Connolly (3/20) and Gleeson (4/56) doing all the early damage, and Gleeson bowling Ashok Mankad with a magnificent leg-break, which pitched on the line of leg stump, before turning to hit the top of off stump.

Late on that fourth day there was drama like none of us had ever experienced. Alan Connolly was bowling his usual stuff, nagging length, a little bit of movement either way, when the off-spinner and sometimes dangerous hitter down the order, Venkataraghavan played forward to a leg-cutter and missed the ball by a long way. Brian Taber took the ball and flipped it to Keith Stackpole at second slip, but Stacky was up in appeal. Tabsy didn't appeal and he looked in amazement as the umpire, after a seemingly interminable period, slowly raised his right index finger. Venkataraghavan was temporarily transfixed to the spot before he reluctantly left the scene like the comical character Sad Sack, dragging his bat behind him as he set out for the pavilion.

We gathered around after the dismissal, but there wasn't great elation. Most of us felt that Venkat was 'done'; although Stacky maintained that he had heard a noise, Tabsy reckoned Venkat missed the ball by a foot. The controversial dismissal did not go unnoticed, for the radio announcer kept all those with ears pressed to their transistor radios informed—or misinformed—depending upon your point of view.

There were thousands of people in India armed with transistor radios and to get the full picture I need to take you to page two of the Bombay telephone directory in 1969 where an advertisement with the headline, 'HAVE TWO ... AND THAT WILL DO!' was emblazoned across the page. The Indian government of the time was desperate to cut the birthrate and if a bloke underwent a vasectomy operation after having produced two children, he was presented with a brand-spanking new transistor radio. The ground teemed with people glued to their transistor radios, so there must have been a lot of young men at the ground the next day who had accepted the offer in the Bombay telephone directory, for the crowd went wild when the radio announcer, who was commentating at the game, said that 'Venkat was not out ... Lawry is a cheat ... the Australians cheated.'

Doug was fielding at fine leg to fast bowler Graham McKenzie, and at deepish mid-wicket when I was bowling. On this day Doug wore his white, floppy hat, rather than his usual baggy-green. He found the floppy hat was ideal for catching the small, green limes the crowd was tossing at him. The Doug Walters hat-trick show went on for the best part of the afternoon and the crowd shrieked with delight when he caught a lime in his floppy hat then bowed to the masses. But after the radio announcer made his remarks, the mood of the crowd turned completely. 'Lawry, Lawry, Lawry!' they began to chant and we knew that the mob had turned nasty.

Deck chairs in the outer were stacked high and set alight, and Doug was soon having bottles chucked at him instead of limes. Now he was in need of a crash helmet. I recall fielding in the deep when McKenzie was operating and the members in the stand behind me were cracking the tops off glass Coke bottles and hurling them at me.

I took off and ended up in the gully area. At one point I was bowling and looked over at mid-wicket and saw that Doug had his back to me, so too Paul Sheahan at mid-on and McKenzie at square leg—our men were keeping a close eye on the bottles being hurled over the fence.

A thick pall of smoke curled over the main stand, and apparently the tennis court club house next door and any cars parked near Brabourne Stadium were set on fire. Then a huge mob, at a guess 15 000 people, began to push at a large section of the high cyclone fence which surrounded the playing area. Play was stopped for a few minutes while a 50-strong gang of riot-squad police, armed with batons and wearing face-masks and breast-plates, stormed onto the ground. They quickly gathered up the bottles littering the ground and hurled them back into the crowd. While the police were trying to dissuade the mob from pushing at the fence, a large policeman rushed to the middle of the wicket where we were all huddled. 'May I suggest to you men to grab a stump,' he said, 'for if that mob get through the fence, we are all dead. Grab a stump men and take a few [rioting spectators] with you...'

But Bill Lawry wouldn't have it. He asked the policeman to leave and said, 'Let's get on with the game.'

I was bowling to Erapally Prasanna when there was another disruption. A dapper little man in a grey suit, carrying a leather briefcase, raced to the centre of the ground.

'Who the hell are you?' Lawry enquired. 'Piss off, pal. We're trying to play a Test match here.'

But the little man was undeterred. 'Oh, my God, Mister Lor-ee. I am the official scorer. The smoke is so bad that I cannot see, so Mister Lor-ee, I am going home!'

We later discovered that the official scoring was then taken over by the radio announcer.

So we played on and once again I looked at mid-wicket—there was Doug, floppy hat pulled down hard over his ears, watching the crowd at the fence. I was hoping Prasanna wouldn't hit a catch in that direction lest Doug copped a ball in the back of the head. It didn't happen. Next ball, Prasanna swung and missed and he was bowled. At 9/125 the game was over for the day.

I was dead scared at the time. The crowd was pushing at the fence, the fires and the exploding bottles as they hit the cement stands with people screaming in anger or pain or both was frightening. The last hour of that day's play, up to six o'clock, was sheer hell. I think we were lucky to be staying at the Cricket Club of India in the stadium itself, because I would not have fancied trying to get away from the ground with the mob waiting for the Australian players who had suddenly gone from crowd idols to targets of abuse.

If Doug was scared, you'd never have known it. He always kept his emotions in check, a poker face for the cards and the cricket or anything else you'd care to name. I think I was more concerned about whether I would get my wicket of Prasanna credited than being hit by a missile on our way to the dressing-room. John Gleeson was hit in the back of the head by a bottle thrown at him by a spectator but, despite deck chairs raining down on us from somewhere high in the Members' Stand, no-one else was hit on our way off the field.

We got to the dressing-room and it was a shambles. All the windows were shattered and glass littered the floor. There were numbers of blood-spattered Indian spectators being patched up and we all cleared out to the relative safety of the shower room at the back of the dressing shed. But a few beers there didn't seem ideal on such a traumatic day, so we then decided to barricade ourselves in one of the large rooms in the hotel occupied by Freddie and Tabsy. Freddie had already prepared well. His bathtub was chock-full of cans of Fosters and bottles of Lion lager and there was ample ice, ensuring a cold beer all round.

Outside there was a lot of commotion and there were fears that the fire might spread from the tennis club next door and engulf the Brabourne Stadium itself. And if the stadium caught fire, so too would all of the Australians' rooms. We were sitting, relaxing with a beer when there was a hell of a noise outside the door: the Australian team manager, Fred Bennett, was at his wit's end. 'Hell, fellas there are 10 000 angry people downstairs. The bastards are going wild, threatening to tear the place apart. They all want Bill Lawry's head. It's bloody frightening.'

Doug Walters stood with a can of beer in one hand, a cigarette in the other. He found, as he usually did, perfect timing: 'Fred, there is only one possible thing this Australian cricket team can do at such a tense and frightening time ... Hand over Bill Lawry and let's get on with the drinking!'

Peace reigned on the last day. We had to get one more wicket then after Lawry (2) and Stackpole (11) fell cheaply to the little Indian medium-pacer Rusi Surti; Ian Chappell (31 not out) and Doug Walters (22 not out) carried Australia to an easy eight-wicket victory.

—◦◦◦—

We were keen to leave Bombay behind as we headed to Jaipur, the capital of the State of Rajasthan, a relatively quiet and peaceful place in comparison with the site of the First Test. The match against Central Zone started on 11 November, a day of remembrance alright. Doug took note of the slightly built Indian who rushed over to carry my cricket bag as I got off the bus. Central Zone batted first and managed only 153 and it was the little Indian who carried my bag, Umpire S. Roy, who upheld my appeal against Vijay Pimrikar for lbw. The ball might have missed leg stump, but it was worth an appeal. Next bloke Rajeev Sharma fell first ball. I tried to spin an off-break, the ball pitched on off stump and carried on straight to hit the top of the off stump. Sharma made the fatal mistake of playing for spin. Doug took it all in and at the end of my over he strolled over to Umpire Roy.

The ball was turning from outside off stump and going down leg-side, so anything on the stumps simply had to miss leg by a mile. Rowdy's little umpiring mate gave the most outlandish lbw. I was interested in how the umpire saw proceedings so I said, 'Ah, Mr Umpire, a couple of useful deliveries?'

'Ooh, Mr Walters. That Mallett . . . velly good bowler. The first ball was a top spinner and then the next was a perfectly pitched leg-break!' It is then I thought, 'Now Doug, don't go getting hit on the pad.'

I took 3/42 in the first dig and 7/38 in the second, and despite numerous appeals, I didn't get another lbw. Australia made 321 and we won by an innings and 32 runs. Doug top-scored with a splendid 84, hitting nine fours, and Ian Chappell played a fine cameo of a knock (44) with five fours before he was run out. It was a good lead-up to the Second Test in Kanpur.

For that match we stayed at the Kamala Retreat, which was a magnificent old residence, home of the British governor during the Raj. Each of the rooms had a high ceiling, marble floor and a huge, Roman-style bath, big enough for three or four people. Each room was so spacious you could have fitted a full-sized cricket pitch in the centre. There were acres of parklands about the residence and the whole area was surrounded by an eight-foot-high wall. At the front entrance there was a gate house and within it was a post office. There we were always enthusiastically greeted, but by the end of the Test match we weren't too taken with the postal workers.

Whenever you wrote home from India, it was a bit touch and go whether the mail would get there. From the Kamala Retreat it was doubly hazardous because if you happened to write your name on the back of the envelope as the sender, the postal workers at that little office would cut out the name of the Test cricketer and paste it in their autograph books. They invariably discarded the left-overs. One of the posties once laughingly produced a handful of cut-outs with our players' names on them, and I saw two of Doug's and one of my own.

An official told us of a good fishing spot, so a few adventurous souls, including Doug and Ian Redpath, braved a local swamp which abounded with fish, not to mention leeches and snakes. They caught a few of the local fish and they supervised the cooking of their catch that night. Freddie and Redder were delighted, sporting faces as happy as if they had each scored a century.

Because of the riot in Bombay, each day our team bus had an army escort. Personnel carrier at front and back of the bus completed our odd convoy.

We had heard that our Board had sent the manager Fred Bennett a message to the effect that if there was another riot the team was to return home immediately. Driving to the ground from the Kamala Retreat was full of blokes yelling out, '*Juldi, juldi,* driver follow that bus, there's a riot at the end of it. C'mon driver, *juldi,* let's get to the cricket ground and riot!' *Juldi* in the Hindi language means 'faster'. So we were yelling out 'faster, faster...'

We found out why when we finally got into the ground—it was designed to hold about 30 000 spectators, and was full to brimming.

The wicket at Kanpur was a beauty...if you happened to be a batsman. It was even-paced, flat as a pancake and gave nothing to the bowlers fast or slow. India batted first and openers Farouk Engineer and Ashok Mankad made an opening stand of 111 before I caught and bowled Mankad. Adjit Wadekar, India's brilliant left-hander, was out to Alan Connolly. He hooked a bouncer straight to me at deep fine leg and all I could hear was 'no-ball'. I think that helped me—there were no nerves—and I was content in getting the ball in as quickly as possible to prevent the Indians scoring two. So I caught it and fired it in flat, on the bounce to Taber. Then I heard a collective groan by the crowd and was surprised to see Wadekar walking off. India was all out for 320, with Connolly taking 4/91 off 36 overs and I managed 3/58 off 51.5 overs.

Al Pal (Connolly) and I were rooming together at the Kamala Retreat and that night we decided to relax with a beer and a packet of dry biscuits in our room. We heard a crunching noise and saw the biggest rat imaginable with its head in the biscuits. The packet of biscuits was near the end of a large, mahogany wardrobe, and the rat was behind the wardrobe, poking its head out to dive into the biscuits. So we each took one end of the wardrobe then together we heaved and squashed that big rat up against the wall. We then rang for the bearer to clean it up. Bearer Number 7 arrived—he had the number 7 stitched to the front of his cap—and he was Doug's and Brian Taber's favourite, because Bearer Number 7, for a few rupees, would give you the most sensational head massage, although at the end of the ten minutes your forehead was a mass of red welts. The head massage was just the cure for anyone who had inadvertently shaken a bottle of Lion lager and consumed its preservatives.

We then told Bearer Number 7 that we wanted a bath so he and a gang of thirteen other bearers formed a bucket brigade with hot water to the Roman-style bath. Bearer Number 7 deserved his 25-rupee tip: he organised for the squashed remains of the rat to be taken away and he produced a hot, steaming bath for two very tired bowlers in under fifteen minutes.

Australia didn't ram home the advantage on this perfect pitch. Stackpole got a good start, but was run out for 40; Lawry and Chappell fell cheaply; and Doug was bowled by his spinning nemesis Bishen Bedi for 53. Paul Sheahan, however, batted superbly for 114, playing a grand innings, the type of knock, full of handsome drives, that we had been hoping he would play consistently on the Test stage. In the end, though, we scored just 348, a lead of 28. The Indians replied with 312 and declared their innings closed after they had lost seven wickets. The match ended in a tame draw although we did get a glimpse of the batting skills of Gundappa Viswanath, who debuted with a duck in the first innings and a brilliant 137 in the second.

The Kanpur Test match turned out to be the only one of the series which ran the full five days. It was around that time that Doug Walters and Ian Chappell began their often passionate debates about the relative merits of India's champion spinners, the off-spinner Erapally Prasanna and the rhythmic left-armer Bishen Bedi. Chappelli always maintained Prasanna was 'by far the better' of the two bowlers. Doug would disagree, saying, 'No, way, Chappelli. Bedi is easily the best bowler. Change of pace, great rhythm and he turns away from the bat.'

Prasanna and Bedi were two of the best spinners I've seen, but I rank Bedi ahead of Prasanna. I think most of our players had more regard for Prasanna as a penetrative bowler, but Bedi, calm and phlegmatic, and possessing everything possible in accuracy, flight and change of pace, was the one who seemed to force the Australians into most errors. There is no doubt that Bedi provided the perfect foil for Prasanna at the other end and they worked brilliantly together in tandem. Bedi wasn't a big spinner of the ball, even on the turning Indian pitches, but technically he must rate very highly in anyone's list of spinners of that time.

I felt that without Bedi as his spin partner, Prasanna may not have been as successful as he was, for there were plenty of occasions where Bedi's perseverance and superb accuracy had the Australians at the other end looking to score runs from Prasanna and, as a result, the off-spinner came into his own.

Chappelli and Freddie would continue the debates all night after a curry and chips and more than the odd beer. Ironically, in the Second Test, Chappell was lbw Prasanna for 16 and Walters was clean-bowled by Bedi for 53.

On one of our rest days, the local cricket authorities put on a banquet at the Kamala Retreat. We dined in a large marquee. Soup came first, but when I found a large blowfly flapping about in the bowl I declined to eat it. After the luncheon, we wandered out of the tent looking for a cold beer and saw all the dirty dishes being cleaned: a bloke with a high-powered hose was spraying off the scraps, which ran down the road into a large, open storm drain;

then the cleaned (hosed-down) plates were laid out on the lawn to dry in the sun.

—∞—

We left Kanpur and its armoured personnel carriers, blowflies and postal workers and carried straight on to play North Zone at Jullunder. The match was played in a relatively low-key mode though Ian Chappell hit a stirring 164. Bedi was playing for North Zone, but not Prasanna, and he took 1/43 off his 22 overs. In North Zone's second innings, Paul Sheahan, at fine leg when Ian Redpath was bowling, stunned spectators by reading a spy novel. Redder was unimpressed with his Victorian colleague's show of indifference, and the Indian press weren't taken with the Australians at all, claiming the visitors were not displaying the sort of effort expected of an elite international cricket team. Neither Doug nor I played in that match, but my abiding memories of Jullunder were that we didn't have any electricity at the team hotel for the first two days and how funny Sheahan looked at fine leg, his head in a spy novel.

New Delhi was the venue for the Third Test match, and Doug nearly drove us to distraction with his 'New Delhi, Old Delhi' speak. It all started when a taxi driver explained to him that there was Old Delhi on one side of the ancient Red Fort and New Delhi on the other side. So Freddie began asking, 'Are we in Old Delhi, or New Delhi?' Reasonable enough to ask once, maybe twice, at a pince three times, but a hundred times?

A day prior to the game starting, Bill Lawry announced to the cricket world: 'We'll be fishing in three days.' Lawry's predictions haven't always turned out, but this one was spot on. The Test *was* over in three days—except it was India, not Australia, who won it. The practice wickets were atrocious. They were full of gremlins. The ball turned a foot, bounced outrageously high as if the spinners were bowling with tennis balls, then the odd one would skip off straight, scuttling along the ground like a startled rat. Little did we know that by day two the Test wicket would be no better than the ones we trained on. Freddie decided to just enjoy himself, slogging at everything. Not far from where we trained in the nets there was a huge, crude aqueduct. Akin to a long block of concrete, suspended a hundred feet off the ground, the structure might have put Doug in mind of the water pipe which he and his mate used to run along on the way home from school in Dungog. There was a mob of Indian fans sitting on it, their feet dangling over the side, and Freddie was trying to hit them some catches. Some thought he was trying to knock a few off their perch. When Doug hit a skier near them, they lifted their feet out of harm's way and roared their delight. Sadly Freddie didn't manage to get close enough for one of the fans to make a catch and thankfully not one of the fans fell to their doom.

On the first day of the Test, 28 November 1969, Keith Stackpole played usefully for his 61 and Brian Taber got a tidy 46 in the middle order, but the day belonged to Ian Chappell, who hit a great 138. He used his feet brilliantly, either smothering the spin or launching drives either side of the wicket. Bishen Bedi got 4/71 off 42 overs and his spin-twin Prasanna toiled over 38.4 overs to get 4/111, one of which was Doug for 4. Doug prided himself in being able to play the off-spinners easily and he usually did so; getting out bat-pad for Doug was sacrilege to his way of batting. However, on this day, Doug went back to a short ball from Prasanna and tried to whip it away through mid-wicket. Doug hit it hard, alright, but he succeeded only in smashing it straight into the top of his left pad and the ball ballooned straight up in the air for Eknath Solkar to complete an easy catch at short forward-leg. It was tough luck.

Early on day two India took our last three wickets for just 35 runs and by stumps they had compiled 2/176 with Ashok Mankad unconquered on 89. The wicket was turning a treat, but I hadn't made any inroads and both Doug and Ian Chappell talked to me about my strategy in the middle, especially when operating to Mankad, and Doug said something like: 'Mankad is a terrific off-side player. Look at his stance, very side-on, almost too side-on. I've noted, so too Chappelli, that you need to bowl a straighter line and give him no room at all outside off stump. He simply cannot play on the on-side. You'll get him bat-pad in no time tomorrow.'

Next day of the Test, Mankad struggled to get any sort of flow. Ian Chappell was fielding just around the corner and Doug was in at short-forward leg, about 45 degrees in front of square. Alan Connolly kept things quiet up one end and I bowled a tight line to Mankad. He nicked one and via the pad Doug caught him, but the umpire, Mr Gopalakrishman, who wore a pair of Coke bottle-type glasses, perhaps as thick as the old doctor who passed Freddie fit for National Service without so much as a cursory glance at him, gave it not out. I was so outraged by the decision that, like a truculent schoolboy, I snatched my cap from the umpire and found my way down to third man, where I was, justifiably, pelted with bananas and those small limes Doug loved catching in his floppy hat.

At 97 Mankad once again snicked one from me onto the pad and the ball flew to Doug.

The ball was spinning and bouncing in extraordinary fashion and the Australian bowlers quickly went through the innings, taking 5/17 that morning. India was all out for 223.

Australia was then sensationally bundled out for 107, with Bill Lawry making 49 brave runs on a terrible wicket. Where we sat in our dressing-room you couldn't see the play, but we could hear it: it sounded like ancient Rome as the Christians were being fed to the lions at the Colosseum. With every wicket—and they came at regular intervals—the crowd would roar. Although we made only 107 in our second innings and India had two days in which to score the required 181 runs for victory, Lawry's men believed they were in the box seat given the atrocious nature of the wicket. India was 1/13 at stumps at the end of the second day which realised a total of just 167 runs for the loss of 19 wickets.

Day three was a rest day. We were concerned that the Indian curator, with the help of ground staff, might try to make some alterations to the state of the pitch. Perhaps water and roll it, or whatever. We had an Indian helper, a lovely bloke called Govan, who collected the laundry and was always smiling. He was expected to sleep in the corridor at the team hotel, but Doug and Brian Taber came to the rescue and allowed him to sleep more comfortably on the floor of their room. Manager Fred Bennett gave Govan 500 rupees to go to the ground on the rest day to ensure that there was no hanky-panky with the Test wicket. Govan reported back with a cheery smile and all was well.

On that fateful last day, I started the second over of the morning and really tried to rip one to Mankad. I was mindful of bowling a straighter line to him and I shall never forget it: the ball pitched on the line of off stump. Two days before the ball would have spun a foot and bounced head high to the keeper, but, no, the ball went dead straight and Mankad lost his off stump. Bill Lawry was elated. He rushed up and started chortling something about a brilliant 'arm-ball'.

'Phanto,' I said, 'arm-ball . . . bullshit. That was an off-break and it should have turned a mile. We're playing on a different wicket.'

My statement fell on deaf ears, but I knew something was desperately wrong. This was not the same surface we played on earlier in the match. We duly lost the Test easily, with Ajit Wadekar hitting a great 91 not out and Viswanath playing some delightful cuts and sweeps for an unconquered 44. It was inconceivable that the wicket could have played so well after the events of two days earlier.

—m—

Two years later Ashok Mankad came to Adelaide with a visiting Indian college team and they played some matches against some of our local grade sides. He told me the story of the Delhi pitch.

Ashley, the groundstaff at Feroz Shah moved the wicket a few feet across. We know you paid your man, Govan 500 rupees to keep an eye on the Test track during the rest day. That was easily fixed. We paid Govan double to keep him quiet.

There was no reason for Mankad to have invented such a story, it was also impossible for me to verify the story and no way there would be an investigation.

Today such an event could never happen. Well, I guess we should never say never, but it is less likely to happen, given the way the ICC police the game. In 1969 there were no neutral umpires appointed and there were no match referees. How our blokes would have liked to have batted on that last day wicket. Doug scored just 4 and 0 in the dramatic New Delhi game and he was keen to make amends in the Fourth Test in Calcutta. But first we had a provincial match at a place called Gauhati.

We thought Gauhati was a God-forsaken place. Banners and placards greeted us as we drove in from the airport, most of which had the hammer and sickle sign emblazoned across them. As we found at Brabourne Stadium in Bombay, we 'lived in' at quarters in the Members' Stand. The rooms were reasonably clean when we arrived, but there was no room service, no change of bed linen and every morning at precisely 5 a.m. a little bloke attacked a pile of coal with a pick. Even placid Ian Redpath found that bloke to be a bloody nuisance.

The match began at 10 a.m. and finished each day at 5 p.m. Dinner was not until 8 p.m. and having had a few beers on the first night we decided to go to the kitchen in search of some food. Doug Walters, Brian Taber, Ian Chappell and me decided to duck downstairs, and we ventured into the half-lit dining room. When Tabsy turned on the kitchen light we were greeted with an unbelievable sight: sickly smelling blue-white smoke billowed from a coal-fired stove in the corner. The smoke hung in the air thickly and gave the impression, like Geoff Boycott in his most belligerent mood, of hanging around forever. Water bobbled and gurgled in an obviously clogged drain, and the floor was a live carpet of wall-to-wall cockroaches. As we walked into the kitchen we could feel and hear our shoes squashing umpteen bugs. There were two cats expertly treading their way across the salads in the modern freezer which had its door ajar. Two more cats leapt from their hiding place among the dishes stacked on an open shelf. All manner of dinner, soup and side plates hit the floor with a loud crash.

The cockroaches scattered. We fled. Doug had the presence of mind to grab a few slices of bread. So we decided to set up a barbecue on the floor of Doug's and Brian Taber's room. The rooms were perfect for a barbecue: concrete base, heat resistant. We broke the uprights of a mosquito net and used them to fuel our fire in the middle of the room. Even someone's Australian sweater ended up in the flames.

There was a certain amount of anger directed towards our esteemed Australian Board of Control for International Cricket. Sir Donald Bradman, whose financial meanness was one of the problems the cricketers of our day had to contend with, foresaw problems in the wake of this ill-fated tour of Ceylon, India and South Africa and a few years later, by his insistence, the Board changed its name to the Australian Cricket Board. But the attitude of the Board's administrators had not changed since it was formed in 1906; a thorn-bush by any other name would still constitute a bunch of pricks. Only a few weeks into this tour, most of the players regarded the Board as the 'enemy'—the disregard for our safety and putting us up in hovels rather than decent hotels soured our thinking towards them. Most days we survived on beer and sometimes scotch. We toasted bread to eat with Dave McErlane's cheese spread.

A slug of scotch in the morning before a Test match became a ritual for me. It killed any tummy bugs, or so I thought, and that little tot plus dry toast and at least one banana provided sufficient sustenance to get through a tough day in the field. I was due to have the match off at Gauhati, but was co-opted into the side after someone, I think it was Keith Stackpole, fell sick on the morning of the game. I had had a few beers the night before and was pretty bleary-eyed when I got to the match. Lawry was far from impressed and he gave me a lecture. It went something like this: 'If you give the drinking away, Rowdy, in five years you'll be the best spin bowler in the world.'

It wasn't the sort of thing you really wanted anyone else in the team to hear, especially one Kevin Douglas Walters. Every night after a day's play from then on, Doug would volunteer: 'Ah, now Mallett, let's see ... you have had a few beers tonight, the demon drink has got you again. So you now have to wait five years, one day, two hours, 45 minutes and ten seconds before you qualify to be the best spin bowler in the world.'

In Gauhati Doug scored a handy little double of 32 and 22, batting first drop. Ian Chappell had the game off, so too Keith Stackpole. We won the match by 96 runs. Fast bowler Laurie

Mayne was the surprise packet with the bat, scoring 72. I finished the first day with 5/37 off 20 overs, then I took Lawry's advice and slowed down only to get 1/36 off 20 overs in the second innings. I always reckoned a few beers helped me relax.

The beautiful Eden Gardens was the venue for the Fourth Test match. The police warned that there would be further trouble, perhaps another riot. Shortly after we arrived at our home for the next week or so, the Great Eastern Hotel, right in the heart of the city, a 10 000-strong crowd picketed our hotel. They carried placards, emblazoned across them: 'DOUG WALTERS… GO HOME!' And there were posters plastered all round Calcutta claiming that Doug Walters was a 'Vietnam soldier' who had killed women and children in the Vietnam War. Doug says:

> Calcutta was then very much a communist city and the majority of the protesters were in sympathy with the North Vietnamese [Viet Cong] point of view. They charged that I was among the soldiers who fought against their comrades in Vietnam, but they had not done their homework too well, for the nearest I got to going overseas during my army days was to undergo some training in Shoalwater Bay.

There was a skirmish in the foyer of the hotel when the mob stormed in. Doors were damaged and windows smashed and the Australian players were advised to retire to our rooms and lock the doors. Doug Walters didn't comply. He could be found in the downstairs bar having a cold one. And if any protester wished to join him, he'd buy him one.

One of the English language newspapers had a front page advertisement which stated categorically that the Australians WOULDN'T train at Eden Gardens that day. Security was high and the cricket authorities didn't want both teams' preparation to be disrupted and they certainly didn't want trouble. When our bus arrived at the ground, we found about 20 000 fans. They had turned up on the off-chance that we might train there that day. The practice wickets were on the side of the main playing area and within 50 minutes of the training having started, practice had to be abandoned. The mob converged so close we ran out of room in which to train properly. People started slapping us on our backs and we ran a veritable gauntlet to get through the crowd to the relative safety of the dressing-room.

Next morning we found out that 20 000 people were in a crush outside the Eden Gardens entrance trying to get hold of one of the available 8000 Test tickets for sale. The special police riot squad charged in with their *lathis* (a long stick the police used as a baton) and tear gas, leaving six people dead, crushed in the stampede, and more than a hundred injured. When we arrived at Eden Gardens, I heard a policeman say with a laugh, 'We got six today!'

Australia won the Test easily, with Graham McKenzie taking 6/67 in the first innings. Ian Chappell (99) led the way for Australia, with good contributions from Doug Walters (56) and Keith Stackpole (41). Bishen Bedi was the star for India with 7/98 off 50 overs and Prasanna, who bowled admirably, did not take a wicket in conceding 116 runs. With just 39 runs to knock off for a win, Lawry and Stackpole did it easily, although there was a scare when people on the top deck of the Ranji Stadium started throwing stones at those below and the fans in the lower deck took off straight onto the ground. There was a fifteen-minute delay while those who had transgressed onto the ground were persuaded to sit quietly on the boundary line until the game was over.

We were pretty happy and led the series 2–1, with one to play. Before the final Test we travelled to Bangalore, birthplace of Colin Cowdrey, where Doug learnt the best card trick of his life.

We were somewhere in Bangalore and I was showing a few people a little card trick when this girl approached and said, 'I'll show you a trick.' She produced two new packs of cards and said to me, 'Now you shuffle your cards and I'll shuffle mine, then we'll swap decks.' We duly shuffled the cards, swapped our decks and she asked me to put down the top card. I did and she matched it. This went on for about eight cards. I couldn't believe my eyes. It was amazing. Anyone who knows about card tricks appreciates that it is quite easy to match cards when you CUT the deck. If you cut the deck, the sequence remains the same, even if you cut the deck a million times. But it is very different when you shuffle it because the sequence changes.

It took me months to work it out and I realised that if a person had a genuine photographic memory, he or she could match the whole 52 cards of a pack. I finally worked it out half-way through the South African leg of the tour. Since then I have shown a few magicians the trick and they confirm it's the best they have ever seen. I can't remember that girl's name, but her trick was the best of them all.

On 20 December 1969 we started a match against South Zone which turned out to be a significant event. They batted first and late in the day Erapally Prasanna faced the bowling of Alan Connolly. The big Victorian bowled a ball that, from the side view, seemed to pass outside Prasanna's legs and miss leg stump. But then the leg stump pushed forward. Someone said, 'Prasanna's out, bowled.' Prasanna had scored nine and he was convinced the ball missed the stumps, but Australia's deputy keeper Ray Jordon appealed loudly.

Ian Chappell, who was at close quarters, suspected foul play and he was seething.

The players were taking tea at the afternoon break, when Chappelli decided to vent his anger. He accused Jordon of cheating and the pair had a stand-up slanging match in the centre of the dressing-room. Bill Lawry intervened, saying something along the lines of, 'C'mon fellas, we all know Slug [Jordon] would cheat his own grandmother for sixpence.'

Chappelli later said:

The umpire never gave Pras out—he eventually walked because, Doug Walters told me afterwards, Jordon kept yelling, 'Piss off, you're out mate.' I asked Doug, an honourable person and cricketer, who was fielding square of the wicket at point and had a good view, and he told me the ball bounced off Jordon's pads onto the stumps.

There was plenty more drama in this game. South Zone declared its first innings at 9/239, then bowled Australia out for 195, with Lawry scoring 120, his only century of the Indian leg of the tour. A second declaration by South Zone left Lawry's men with 200 to win in two hours. At the fall of the sixth wicket, Prasanna had 6/9 off nine overs then right on the tea adjournment he had Jordon caught bat-pad. The Victorian was an unhappy camper, swearing and smashing his pad with his bat as he left the field. When Jordon got into the Australian dressing-room, he was still mouthing off. Freddie suggested he take his concern to the umpire so Jordon walked into the umpires' room, where they were sipping black tea, and he said angrily, within earshot of a number of players including me, 'Hey, umpy, there's no way in the world I hit that ball!'

Umpire B.N. Nagaraj Rao rose slowly from his chair. He placed his cup on a table and put his hands together in a gesture of prayer and said: 'Oh, my dear Mister Jordon. If you did not hit the ball . . . you were velly, velly much lbw!'

We were eight down when John 'CHO' Gleeson wandered on to the wicket to join Lawry, who was still not out and didn't look like getting out. CHO stood for 'Cricket Hours Only'. A rather quiet, almost secretive person, during cricket hours was the only time we saw John. Thus it became his nickname, CHO. A win was out of the question, but we did have to survive the last hour or so to draw. Gleeson did not take guard (he had done so weeks before in Bombay) but he did make it very obvious that he wanted a word with each umpire in turn. He went to Umpire N.S. Rishi, at square leg, where we saw Gleeson talking very animatedly to the ump, but strain as we did to hear, we couldn't make out his words. CHO then wandered down to the umpire at the bowler's end, B.N. Nagaraj Rao, and had a bit of a chat. CHO then proceeded to pad every ball away. All the raucous appeals for lbw were knocked back. CHO faced five overs of Prasanna, even scoring two off the brilliant little spinner. In fact, Gleeson (19) outscored Lawry (10).

Play ended prematurely, the fans throwing rocks at our heroes of the hour, Lawry and Gleeson, and we had escaped defeat. Doug wanted to know what CHO said to the umpires before he faced a single ball. CHO explained, 'I went up to the umpire at square leg and said to him, "Mister Umpire, if you give me out lbw, I shall wrap this bat around your head." And I said the same thing to the other umpire.'

That evening most of us went along to a party where there was lots of beer and scotch and just one woman. Her name was Tanya and Tanya had a very loud voice. She told anyone within earshot, and that meant everyone in that gigantic, marble-floored room, that she was Russian and she had walked from the Soviet Union to India. At one stage our physiotherapist, Doc McErlane, was on a couch chatting with Tanya. Suddenly there was a lull in the music and then Tanya let forth, 'Ven I vant sex, I vill ask for it!'

Unbeknown to me, Freddie and Tabsy were very keen that I should have a dance with Tanya, for they knew something about her that I most certainly didn't. In those days I wore contact lenses, but I took them out immediately after play and often didn't wear my glasses at night. The mischievous pair persuaded me to dance with Tanya. She had a very thick collar. Then it moved. And suddenly the head of an eight-foot python was eye-balling me. I instinctively threw Tanya backwards. She hit the wall, the snake flew over her head and I ran for my life. Freddie stored up the snake episode for later.

The Fifth Test was held at Madras. On the first day of the Test, 24 December 1969, the *Sydney Sun* ran a story under the byline of Phil Tresidder, quoting a number of prominent ex-players calling for the tour to be called off. Tresidder had asked the Australian Board of Control for International Cricket secretary Mr Alan Barnes if the tour might be called off, even at this late stage. Bones said: 'The team manager, Mr Fred Bennett, is instructed in the normal course to bring to the Board as a matter of urgency any matters that merit the Board's attention. There has been no special word from Mr Bennett.'

Some former greats of Australian cricket disagreed:

Alan Davidson: 'No sporting side should be subjected to the humiliations our team have encountered in India. This stoning of Lawry and Gleeson is the last straw. Our players are subject to enough risk already in health in a place like India without adding physical dangers. If they can't be guaranteed protection—and that should be a matter for the Indian government—there is no point in going there.'

Jim Burke: 'The stoning of Lawry and Gleeson is just about the end. Stones this time, but is it going to be knives next? The tour should be called off right now and the team sent on to South Africa a week earlier. It is not sport any more.'

Arthur Morris: 'The reports are very alarming. A Test match is coming up this week, but we should clear out if our players are in such danger. They are there to play cricket.'

Brian Booth: 'This is no longer sport. If the players' safety is at stake, then we have to think twice about them playing there again. It is a tragedy when sport comes to this.'

Bobby Simpson: 'Cricket is a game to be encouraged across the globe. But if this is the type of treatment Australian teams are going to get abroad, then we must have second thoughts about sending them away. I don't think we can expose our fellows to this sort of risk.'[1]

Tresidder didn't get it all right, for he wrote: 'Gleeson, of all the Australian players, should be especially happy to see the tour end. In Calcutta he was knocked unconscious for an hour by a bottle.' Gleeson was hit in the back of the head by a bottle thrown from the crowd during the riot in the Bombay First Test, but I never saw him being knocked out by a bottle in Calcutta.

In the Fifth Test match, Doug Walters played a wonderful innings of 102. He hit two sixes and 14 fours in a power-laden display on a wicket that was just right for the spinners. Prasanna took 4/100 off 40 overs and Venkataraghavan took 4/71 off 34 overs. Bedi was strangely quiet, taking 1/45 off 26 overs. Guess who picked up the wicket of Walters? Yes, Bishen Bedi. At one stage Prasanna was operating with just two men on the off-side and Doug was backing away and cutting him through the big gaps. There is a photo which shows Doug cutting a ball and there is no-one else in the picture. The keeper, Farouk Engineer, had gone way down leg-side and Prasanna, operating around the wicket was also out of the picture. Doug's innings was a knock of genius. Only a genius against the spinning ball could have survived let alone hit a century on that treacherous turning wicket.

I got five wickets in each innings (5/91 and 5/53) and despite a few of us having a bout of food poisoning thanks to some imported meat brought especially for Christmas dinner, we won the game by 77 runs with more than two days to spare.

We spent New Year's Eve in Bombay and were accommodated at the Taj Mahal Hotel, one of India's finest. It was like coming out of a military prison for a night at the Officers' Club. But even that move brought anger, for we wondered why we couldn't have stayed at the best accommodation throughout the tour. Despite the conditions on tour, the poor food and accommodation, we managed to perform as a professional outfit on the field.

The tour of India was just so badly organised, the whole thing. When you think about it, we must have played brilliantly to beat India on those spinning wickets. I don't think we had a great side at the time.

Manager Fred Bennett told officials at some official function that, 'Australia was looking forward to playing its First Test match at Gauhati some time in the future.' Fred heard and the officials that heard his patronising words also heard our collective cry of anguish and anger: 'Bullshit, Fred. Bullshit!

In the wake of the tour, one thing I had hoped was that the team manager, Fred Bennett, would lodge a firm report to the Board listing some of the improvements required for future Australian tours of India. I'd have liked to have had some Australian cricket officials with me when we stayed in one place [Gauhati] where conditions were absolutely appalling. Cricket officials might not have laughed off the time when some of the blokes walked into the kitchen at this place to find the floor covered in cockroaches and two cats tucking into the food on the table and in a refrigerator which had its door open.

Subsequent tours of India have seen the Australian team stay in the best hotels, and genuinely embrace the food and the culture.

However, at the time, concern for the players' welfare didn't quite run as far as the Australian cricket officials. The Board had shown, in many ways, that our welfare wasn't a priority. That they had each of the tour member's lives insured for $400 probably said it all.

chapter seven

SPRINGBOK
WHITEWASH

But just as Lawry entered the Australian dressing-room some 40 blokes in blue tracksuits flooded the ground. Each had a lawn mower and they darted to the centre wicket and mowed down every blade of grass. Lawry was aghast. He looked out of the window in anger: 'Shit, they can't do that...we've just tossed.'

Doug Walters was watching too. And he, as usual, had a view on things. 'Phanto, I know they can't do it, but they ARE mowing the pitch!'

New Year's Day, 1970, Bill Lawry's Australian team flew out of India, bound for South Africa.

South Africa was always seen as a great place to tour: good food, good beer and the accommodation and facilities were first class, as good as they are at home. And we were all certainlly looking for better living conditions. A night in Nairobi, Kenya, brought home a sobering reality. Our stomachs had shrunk during our stay in India and we simply could no longer eat a big meal. Most of the blokes were crook that first night in Kenya from trying to eat a full dinner. By the time we got to Johannesburg we were all dead tired, but glad to be out of the dust, grime and the poverty of a country of which, because of our Board's stupidity, we only saw the ugly side.

Missing in India was the presence of any Australian journalists. No-one turned up, not even the ABC's Alan McGilvray. We had no independent witnesses to the dreadful conditions we had to endure. However, they arrived en masse in Johannesburg. The experienced Phil Tresidder of the *Sydney Sun* seemed to be doing most of the reporting for the Australian papers. He liked his NSW players and always had a more sympathetic word or two for the likes of Doug Walters, Johnny Gleeson and Brian Taber. Keith Miller and Alan McGilvray were also there for the Test matches.

Bill Lawry stuck his foot in his mouth from the outset. He was right about 'fishing in three days' in Delhi, but to our disadvantage. Then, at a pre-series press conference he declared that 'Ian Chappell is now the best and most complete batsman in the world'. Chappelli had topped the Test averages in India, scoring 324 runs at 46.28 with one century, 138, in the only lost game of the series in the Delhi Third Test. But in South Africa, Lawry's claim would fall on Chappell like a curse. Originally Bill Lawry's men were to have completed the brief tour to Ceylon, then India, before a Test series in Pakistan.

That made more sense from a cricket point of view but, apparently, it couldn't work financially because of the Pakistani government's strict exchange controls. On 27 October 1968 the Pakistan Cricket Board rescinded its invitation for an Australian team to tour there and the South African Cricket Association immediately offered to fill the void. The Australian Board of Control for International Cricket accepted the invitation, a brave, or stupid (depending on which side of the apartheid fence you sat) political move. South Africa had lost a lot of credibility and sporting friends over its handling of the d'Oliveira Affair, which saw England cancel its proposed tour of South Africa in 1968–69 because the South African government, led by John Vorster, refused an England touring party that included the Cape-coloured-born Worcester all-rounder Basil d'Oliveira. The wickets in South Africa were also a vastly different proposition to the slow, turning tracks in the subcontinent. That alone should have warned off the Australian Board, but no, bugger the players!

Before we left Australia we received all manner of documents, including information from the anti-apartheid lobby. Most of the material emanated from the offices of the teenage anti-apartheid campaigner, Peter Hain. His parents were anti-apartheid activists in the South African Liberal Party and they formed a small band of fighters called the Armed Resistance Movement (ARM). The Hain family fled South Africa and settled in London in 1966. Apart from sending material to members of Bill Lawry's Australian team in 1969, Hain and his followers lobbied against the South African rugby tour of England in 1969 and in 1970 they were instrumental in having the Springbok cricket tour of England stopped. In fact, a private prosecution against Hain had him convicted in the Old Bailey in 1972 of 'criminal conspiracy' in relation to the stoppage of the cricket and rugby tours, and he was fined £200.

In 2004, the volatile Australian leg-spinner Stuart MacGill refused to tour Zimbabwe, taking a political stance against the regime of Robert Mugabe, rather than a dispute with the Zimbabwe Cricket Union over its race-based selection policy. MacGill was playing county cricket for Nottinghamshire, England, when he made his controversial decision.

'I guess in an ideal world, sport and politics would be very, very separate issues,' MacGill said. 'Unfortunately, I don't believe that's the case and, you know, I think history is littered with instances where that can be shown.'[1]

MacGill indicated that he did not want to fuel further speculation by expanding on his private boycott of Australia's tour of Zimbabwe. While his conscience vote won him many fans throughout Australia, the political climate has changed markedly since the 1960s. A cricketer in 1969 who took a stand against apartheid would have probably gained a certain amount of public sympathy, however, the Test selectors would have dumped him like a sack of spuds. We must have been terribly naïve in a political sense and the reality of the horror of apartheid should have hit us, but didn't, in Pretoria on 6 January 1970, where we played North Eastern Transvaal in our pipe-opener match of the tour: it was revealed to us that no coloured-skin people were allowed to attend the match. I think as a collective we had a closed mind to the realities of apartheid. We were there to play cricket and to play the game without outside pressures entering, or really thinking about, the poticial ramifications. Bill Lawry stormed back into form against North Eastern Transvaal with 86 not out, Ian Chappell hit 104, as if to echo Lawry's words about him, and Freddie was unconquered on 20. Alan Connolly and Johnny Gleeson ran through the home side quickly in both innings and left that apartheid stronghold of Pretoria with a first-up 10-wicket victory.

It was in a bar in Pretoria where I thought Freddie was going to be strangled by three huge Afrikaaner rugby players and finally pay for his sense of mischief. The blokes were loud and kept talking about rugby union with a sort of guttural reverence. Freddie was in his element.

'What's all this RUKK-BEE. RUKK-BEE's not a great game. No I think RUKK-BEE's not much of a game at all,' Freddie said to them.

Ian Chappell, Brian Taber and I were trying to stop Freddie from winding up the rugby men. We didn't think it would be a healthy thing for him to persist. But Freddie was at his annoying best.

'Hey, you?' one of these huge Afrikaaners called. 'I am going to fuck you up.'

Suddenly, the biggest of these three enormous men had Freddie in a head-lock. But Freddie continued to take the piss, and said, 'This rukk-bee ... ordinary game you know. What's all this about fucking me up ... ?'

Eventually the big bloke released his hold and announced that he loved the little Aussie and he would buy him a beer. It just isn't possible to stay mad at Doug Walters. Doug had a disarming way about him. The gap-toothed smile and mischievious bent endeared him to all and sundry. The big Afrikaaner sensed the good nature in Doug. Just as well and just in time.

At Kimberley, Lawry hit 157 not out in Australia's 3/324 declared. Freddie was run out for 13 and we easily accounted for Griqualand West by an innings and one run. I bowled some 74 overs for the match and we were operating in 40-degree (Celsius) heat most of the time.

It was a time of growing side-burns. Doug sported a splendid set and mine were just coming to the fore. One night, Doug snuck into my room while I was asleep and cut off ONE of my side-burns. We had been to a diamond mine that day and Freddie had persuaded the mine manager to give him one of the sirens they used for emergencies. After Freddie shaved off my one side-burn, he let me have the siren, full-blast right next to my ear.

Freddie's alarm awoke me to the missing side-burn. So I immediately shaved the right side-burn to even things up. I resolved to even the score with Walters, but I could hardly turn the fire extinguisher loose on him as he refused to leave the confines of the hotel bar.

Our last hit out before the First Test in Cape Town was against Eastern Province at Port Elizabeth. Eastern Province batted first and I got my first close-hand look at Graeme Pollock. He fell for only 11, but the bloke who replaced him at the crease, Laurie Wilmot, was one of the biggest hitters I've seen.

Wilmot was a pineapple farmer and during breaks in work he gave the workers a choice: sit down and have a smoke and a cup of tea, or have a bowl to him. There was a reward for clean bowling Wilmot in these practice sessions. Cigarettes were used instead of bails and if Wilmot was knocked over he gave the jubilant worker–bowler a smoke. When I bowled to Wilmot he struggled to survive, that is, until I tossed one up. Every ball I tossed up he hit into the stand. But he didn't last long, falling to Laurie Mayne's pace for 32. Eastern Province was bowled out for 253 and Australia got 6/297 before we declared. Stackpole got a century (123), Mayne, given a lift in the batting to number four, hit 41, Doug got a duck and Paul Sheahan hit grandly for 93.

Batting a second time, Pollock did get going. He hit me for two successive sixes over mid-off, then holed out to Sheahan on the boundary rope at wide mid-off. Doug also picked up a wicket (at a cost of 45 runs), and Sheahan completed a good double for the game getting 43 not out.

The First Test match was to be played at the beautiful Newlands Ground in Cape Town. Oak trees completely surround this picturesque ground, and it sits in full view of magnificent Table Mountain which literally overshadows the city.

Just before the Test I met the actor Trevor Howard in a Cape Town restaurant. The man who played Captain Bligh on *Mutiny of the Bounty* was, like so many in the theatre and in politics, a cricket tragic, and he was in town to make a film.

'I could have made the film in Sydney, but then Sydney isn't hosting a Test match, right now, is it? I'm in just the mood to see one of my favourite cricketers Doug Walters score a century.'[2]

A couple of days before the Test, South African Prime Minister John Vorster invited our touring group to attend a cocktail party at Government House in Cape Town. Although our host was the man who had refused an England team to tour South Africa if it included the Cape-coloured-born all-rounder Basil d'Oliveira in its squad and, interestingly, was jailed in South Africa during World War II as a Nazi sympathiser, he was surprisingly cordial. His ministers, however, were rude to the black waiting staff.

I can't help but think now how ironic it was that there we were socialising with Vorster while Nelson Mandela sat alone in his cell at Robben Island, no more than 12 kilometres off the mainland.

On 21 January 1970, we trained at Newlands, our last session before the match that was scheduled to start the next day. One of the ground bowlers (players invited to bowl to the Australians at net practice) was a left-arm spinner of Indian extraction, Baboo Ebraheim. He bowled with the sort of guile we associated with the great Indian slow man, Bishen Bedi, but Ebraheim was a non-white cricketer and, therefore, during the strict colour bar executed by the apartheid regime, he was not 'eligible' to play for the country of his birth.

On the day of the match South Africa won the toss and batted on a pitch which appeared to be flat and lifeless. Four new Springbok caps—Barry Richards, Lee Irvine, Derek Gamsy and Graham Chevalier—were brought into Ali Bacher's team for this First Test. We played much the same side that beat India at Madras in the Fifth Test, although the slow bowler Gleeson was brought back to replace Laurie Mayne, who was unlucky to lose his spot given he took 3/60 in 22 overs of sustained pace at Port Elizabeth and then hit 41. In the Springboks first innings, Richards fell for just 29, although at 25 he went to back-cut me, got a glove, and the ball ballooned to Ian Chappell at first slip, who turfed a sitter, his hands closing too soon and the ball hitting his knuckle. I wondered if that little piece of fielding might be a pointer to how we might fare in the series. South Africa played well after we dismissed both openers relatively cheaply (Richards, 29, and Trevor Goddard, 16) and at one stage we had them 4/187. But the tough Eddie Barlow strode to the crease at the fall of the third wicket and Barlow was due to get some runs. He'd had a horror stretch and was only averaging 17 with the bat in Currie Cup cricket. Before he faced his first ball from Alan Connolly, Bill Lawry let forth with a string of expletives. The Phantom (as we called Lawry) was usually the strong, silent type on the field. He was ever on the alert to place pressure on a batsman and he hated any batsman getting an easy ride, but rarely would he sledge an opponent. Maybe it was the aftermath of all the frustration on the subcontinent that finally got to him. Maybe he just wanted to get the pads on and bat on the Newlands pitch, which looked a ripper. Whatever his motive, it was out of character for Lawry, and Barlow stepped away and said to Umpire Billy Wade: 'Billy, can you tell that fucking long-nosed cunt at point to shut up or I won't be facing up at all?'

Thankfully, Umpire Wade had a sense of humour. He had played his first Test against England at Trent Bridge, Nottingham, in June 1935 as captain, and he had led South Africa in all five Tests against Vic Richardson's Australian team which toured South Africa in 1935–36.

'Get on with the game, Mister Lawry, thank you,' he said.

But the vehemence shown by Lawry against Barlow had precisely the opposite effect on the stout South African. Barlow wore rimless glasses and he had forearms like Rodney Marsh's legs. He always rolled his sleeves high on his arms. This day he rolled them even higher. Barlow was fuming.

He hit 127.

Doug got the main man, Graeme Pollock, caught at slip by Chappelli and he also snared Trevor Goddard, to finish with 2/19 off 8 overs. I wondered whether Walters was being used enough at the bowling crease. He always seemed to pick up an early wicket and he was rarely expensive. I had none for 80 at the end of day one.

Some of the umpiring decisions were ordinary to say the least. Barlow should have been out lbw when he shouldered arms to a ball which hit him plumb in front of middle stump. Bill Lawry copped a lot of flak from the crowd as he disputed umpiring decision after umpiring decision. The Johannesburg *Sunday Times* published images of Lawry disagreeing with Umpires Gunter Goldman and Billy Wade. But the facts were, South Africa had scored 382 in its first innings and the pressure was on Australia to hit back.

Australia's reply was disappointing. At stumps on the second day, Australia was in shatters with only Doug Walters (58 not out) standing tall.

Phil Tresidder, writing in the *Sydney Sun*, praised Walters' knock, but was highly critical of his batting team-mates.

Doug Walters' plucky unbeaten 58 stood out like a beacon yesterday as Australia's batting lay in tatters before spirited South African bowling in the First Test at Newlands. Australia 6/107, needs another 76 runs to avoid the follow-on with three days remaining. Ali Bacher's Springboks are magnificently placed to lay the 60-year-old bogy that has haunted South African teams at Newlands. Their speed men, Mike Proctor and Peter Pollock, cut down Australia's ace batsmen like a scythe to the roars of a fanatical Newlands crowd. Only Walters, cool, calm and wonderfully accomplished, rode the storm. But for his 136-minute fight-back, Australia would have been already batting a second time. South Africa have taken up where they left off the last series with all the old trump cards that brought Bobby Simpson's 1966–67 tourists to grief. Indeed, not even Simpson's team pressed the panic button as Lawry and his colleagues did yesterday before the lightning-paced skidding deliveries of 'wrong-footed' Proctor and fiery old trouper Peter Pollock. Admittedly, Australia had spent a wearying nine hours in the field under a hot sun as South Africa surged to a 382 total—their highest against Australia at Newlands. And accustomed to slow Indian wickets, where batsmen took the shine off the new ball before the Indian spinners took over, the Australians were caught unprepared by the Springbok speed blitz. Only the tenacious Walters saved the Australian innings from utter collapse. For a time Walters found a plucky partner in Taber. They pushed Australia's total to 92 before off-spinner Kelly Seymour made a separation. Walters was unconquered at the end of the day. His innings included a superb six over mid-wicket off Chevalier and 15 runs off Barlow's only over.

Denied the 1967 tour of South Africa because of his National Service duties, Walters is making a splendid impact this tour. He drove confidently, used his feet to counter the spinners and punished anything loose. But for Walters, it would have been the bleakest day for Australian cricket in many years.[3]

Doug scored 73 in Australia's first innings 164.

The South Africans also embraced the skill of Walters. A South African writer said of him:

If Doug Walters scores runs he scores them well and when he is dismissed it is usually because he is too eager to attack. Doug, who, at 24, is the same age as Barry Richards, had his career cut short by two years in the Australian Army and it is likely that his best performances in Test cricket are still to come. This is quite a thought when one considers that Walters passed 2000 runs in Test cricket at Newlands in his 35th Test innings, a feat achieved by Graeme Pollock in his 37th innings at the age of almost 26. Unlike Pollock, who is 6'2" and 155lb, he is dark, quietly spoken and has piercing blue eyes. As a batsman he has all the shots in the book and as a bowler he is a lively medium pacer of the Barlow type, capable of dismissing the best batsmen.[4]

The South Africans didn't enforce the follow-on and hit a brisk 232 in their second innings, leaving Australia to score 450 to win. We got 280. Lawry hit 83 and Ian Redpath was 47 not out. Most of the batsmen got mini-starts, but fell in their teens. Doug fell to Mike Proctor for 4. In the first innings Ian Chappell hooked a Peter Pollock bouncer and was caught on the rebound, after the ball bounced off Lee Irvine's right arm and went for a duck, then he lost his wicket in a bizarre manner in the second innings. He had reached 13 when he misjudged a ball from Chevalier. Chappell drove the ball into the back of his left leg and the ball rebounded on to his stumps.

The South Africans eventually won the match by a massive 170 runs. Had Walters had any support in our first innings the match would have gone right to the wire. The spinner Chevalier took a total of five wickets for the game (2/32 and 3/68), but it was patently obvious that the ground bowler of the same spin type, Baboo Ebraheim, was a far better bowler than Chevalier.

After the match Umpires Goldman and Wade wanted to make a presentation to the Australian captain, Bill Lawry, but Lawry refused to accept it.

There was a feeling among the camp that the umpires in this match were either cheats or incompetent, or both. So vice-captain Ian Chappell, on behalf of the Australian team, accepted the gift from the umpires. But from then on the South African press hounded Lawry for his attitude. Truth was, however, bad as those umpires might have been, Ali Bacher's Springbok team was a far superior outfit than our Australian team and they deserved victory.

Alan McGilvray, as proud an Australian as you'd find anywhere, rang my hotel room at 1 a.m. next morning.

'Mallett, come to my room. I want to talk to you.'

Surprised at his call, I staggered down to McGilvray's room, and sitting there were Doug Walters and Brian Taber each holding a glass of scotch. McGilvray had apparently pulled the cork off a bottle of Johnny Walker Red Label and tossed the cork out of the fifth floor window of the hotel.

'Now we drink,' McGilvray said.

It was a drown-your-sorrows little interlude, but it was a good chance to get to know the doyen of ABC radio a little better. He was the man who painted such a great and vivid word picture that he inspired the young Doug Walters to dream of playing in those faraway places that McGilvray had so brilliantly described.

'Never been taken with Lawry as a captain,' McGilvray started, but he never got a bite from any of us.

After an hour or so, McGilvray knocked the top off another bottle and we settled in for a long session. He even woke his South African equivalent Charles Fortune, another splendid broadcaster. I have this vision of Fortune, clad in his brilliant blue-and-red striped pyjamas, sliding slowly down the wall, between Walters and Taber, who were sitting on chairs either side of him. Charles started at the standing position, clutching a full glass of scotch and dry. He was still clutching that glass as his sleeping body gradually slid down the wall towards the carpeted floor.

The loss in Cape Town had Lawry thinking that Australia needed to bolster the lower order batting and to fight fire with fire.

And the latter meant dropping a spinner (me) and bringing in the medium pace of Eric Freeman, who got 4/59 off 21 overs against Transvaal in Johannesburg. I was pissed off given I had taken 28 wickets in five Tests in India and six wickets in the First Test in Cape Town. After all, Freeman wasn't much faster than me and he didn't turn them as much as I could.

The South African fast bowlers Peter Pollock and Mike Proctor were making a huge impact on us. Pollock had slowed down somewhat to his former pace, but Proctor was decidedly quick, about the pace of the great West Indian fast bowler, Malcolm Marshall. Proctor charged in at the batsman like a rampaging bull and because he bowled off the wrong foot he seemed to come on to you a bit quicker than you expected.

Durban, venue for the Second Test, is hot and humid, a lot like Brisbane. The wicket at Kingsmead looked very flat, but it had a crew cut of green on it. The green tinge covered the entire twenty-two yards and we thought that our fast bowlers could do something if we were given first use of the wicket. It was here that the Springbok captain Dr Ali Bacher outwitted Lawry at the toss. He asked Lawry to toss long before play began. Bacher won the toss and decided to bat on a wicket which we all thought might suit Graham McKenzie. But just as Lawry entered the Australian dressing-room some 40 blokes in blue tracksuits flooded the ground. Each had a lawnmower and they darted to the centre wicket and mowed down every blade of grass. Lawry was aghast. He looked out of the window in anger: 'Shit they can't do that...we've just tossed.'

Doug Walters was watching too and he, as usual, had a view on things. 'Phanto, I know they can't do it, but they ARE mowing the pitch!'

Lawry rushed to the centre of the ground and demanded an explanation. To his annoyance he learnt that Bacher had tricked him. Ali Bacher knew the rules backwards and in the small print it stated that the wicket could be mown up to 30 minutes before the start of play. That was why Bacher wanted to toss early, so that if he won it he could do as he had just ordered to be done— mow the pitch bare.

That wasn't a great start for Lawry and the Australian team. On that flat track South Africa amassed 622 runs for the loss of nine wickets before Bacher called a halt to the slaughter. Graeme Pollock hit a superb 274 and Barry Richards 140. They treated our bowlers like truant schoolboys and belted the hell out of them.

Richards should have scored a hundred before lunch but he didn't face a ball for the ten minutes leading to the lunch ajournment. In Durban they talk of the tide affecting the nature of the wicket late in the day. Legend has it that when the tide comes late on an afternoon, the wicket plays all manner of tricks. Ali Bacher failed to give Richards the strike in the last couple of overs before lunch, thus depriving the new champion of a golden chance to hit a century before lunch on the first day of a Test match, a feat achieved by a precious few in cricket history, including Australian greats such as Victor Trumper (versus England at Manchester in 1902) and Don Bradman (versus England at Leeds in 1930).

Eddie Barlow pleaded with Bacher to have a bowl. A medium pacer in the Doug Walters speed range, Eddie had such belief in himself and his ability to get wickets that he was often brought on to bowl to stop him annoying the hell out of his captain and team-mates ... and invariably he took a vital wicket to break a promising partnership. Barlow immediately had Lawry lbw for 15, then he collected the scalps of Ian Chappell (0) and Doug Walters (4). Only Paul Sheahan (62) batted with any sort of authority before Australia fell, all out for 157.

Barlow broke the back of our innings taking 3/24 off 10 overs. He received admirable support from Peter Pollock 2/31, Proctor 2/39 and Trevor Goddard 2/10. Bacher enforced the follow-on and again the wickets tumbled early. Keith Stackpole hit 71 and both Ian Redpath and Doug Walters hit 74 runs apiece. We thought Walters and Redpath were so much in charge that they would amass a huge partnership. But fate took a hand. Doug hit a John Traicos long-hop into the stand for six and then got a similar ball next delivery. Umpire John Draper thrust out his right hand and called 'No ...' There was a definite arm signal and a call from the umpire. Doug tried to hit the ball into the stand, following his previous shot, but he got a top edge and Graeme Pollock ran 30 yards around the boundary to catch the ball right on the fence.

Doug and Ian were astonished to see Umpire Draper with his finger in the air. Walters had been given out. The normally placid Ian Redpath was incensed. He threw his bat onto the ground and cursed. A bemused Doug Walters sauntered off the ground. He never questioned the decision with Umpire Draper, but Redpath did.

'You said, "No", so it is a no-ball.' And the umpire replied, 'No, I thought it was going to be a no-ball and I did not carry on with the call.'

The Springboks won the match easily, by an innings and 129 runs. Barlow got 3/63 off 31 overs in our second innings and again the bowlers shared the spoils, Proctor getting 3/62, Pollock 1/45, and Traicos 2/70.

We then played Border at the Jan Smuts Ground in East London and there Jock Irvine got 56, Brian Taber 46 and Eric Freeman a good batting double of 52 and 67. It was in this game that Freeman and keeper Ray Jordon jostled for a bat-pad catch off my bowling. Freeman was at forward short leg and the ball went from the inside edge to pad and ballooned high in the air. Jordon called 'mine', so too Freeman, who eventually bumped the shorter Jordon out of the way and took the catch. Freeman and Jordon roomed together. They were both ambitious and eager to make a mark even to the extent of trying to outdo one another when a catch presented. Freeman's height advantage won the day, but there was no animosity from Jordon over Freeman having taken the catch away from him. Doug scored a moderate 23 in the first innings and just 2 in the second. He was due for a big hundred. Mind you, he had some mates on that score.

Graham McKenzie was having trouble in a physical sense: he was lethargic and there was a fear that he might have contracted a form of hepatitis. He was given a three-week rest-up on doctor's advice. That put him out of the Third Test match, and Laurie Mayne was earmarked to replace him.

The vital Third Test was being played in Johannesburg. That fair city is situated some 6000 feet above sea level and the rarefied air takes its toll and occasionally one gets a little breathless. At the start of our final training before the big game, Lawry turned up with a bucket of cricket balls and a bat. He gave Freddie the job of going to the centre of the New Wanderers Ground and to hit high catches to the players well-spread at points on the boundary line.

'It is important that we judge the flight of the ball here in Jo-Burg,' Lawry said. 'It is true that in this rarefied atmosphere the ball travels further. Okay, Doug, start hitting them...'

Freddie was at his mischievous best.

He hit the first ball hard and high and it landed thirteen rows back in the grandstand. Each of the next five balls landed in the grandstand and there was Bill Lawry standing on the boundary with his hands on his hips, glaring at Doug.

'You are right, Phanto... the ball does travel a helluva lot further in this rarefied atmosphere.'

That ended our little fielding session and we adjourned to the nets. We were still wearing the widest of grins when the training ended.

The Springboks batted first in the Third Test and were bowled out for a moderate 279. Doug picked up 2/16 off five overs and Alan Connolly 2/49, but again our best bowler was Johnny Gleeson with 3/61 off 21.4 overs. Stackpole, Redpath and Lawry all failed and, finally, Ian Chappell got a decent start. He was looking good until the left-arm medium pace of Trevor Goddard slowed him down. Goddard was bowling very wide of off stump. There was an invitation for Chappelli to drive, but to accept the batsman had to take an enormous risk, for most of Goddard's deliveries were far too wide of off stump. Doug was at the other end, watching events unfold. Eventually Chappelli lashed out at a wide Goddard delivery.

The ball skewed in the air towards Tiger Lance at backward point. Tiger dived forward and from our spot in the dressing-room, square to the wicket, we saw the ball bounce, not once, but twice before Lance clutched the ball.

Chappelli turned to Tiger Lance and asked him, 'Did you catch that Tiger?'

'Ja, Chappelli... I caught the ball.' Chappelli accepted Tiger's reply, he didn't even wait for the umpire to make a decision before he walked off. Later he asked Tiger if he really did catch the ball and Tiger replied, 'Ja Chappelli, I caught it... but you didn't ask me how many times it bounced!'

Chappelli was unimpressed with Bacher. He believed the South African captain should have called Chappell back to the crease for all the players clearly saw that the ball had bounced before Tiger Lance 'caught' it. At the end of the day Eddie Barlow came into the Australian dressing-room and apologised to Chappell.

Doug's 64 was a gem. He cut and drove and pulled with class and power. Again he looked like getting a big hundred, only this time he edged a Peter Pollock to slip where the talented Proctor made no mistake. Paul Sheahan hit 44 and Taber was unconquered on 26. In our second dig, Doug was bowled by Proctor for 15. Redpath scored 66 and Taber was again not out, this time on 18 when the innings folded for 178.

South Africa had thrashed us by 307 runs.

A drawn match against Natal at Kingsmead, Durban, came before the Fourth Test in Port Elizabeth. Ian Chappell (108) and Ian Redpath (118) blazed away as though they had not a care in the world and McKenzie returned from his three-week lay-off, taking 2/53 off 18 overs in the first innings. The match ended in a draw. But McKenzie didn't look right. He was still lethargic in the field and really should not have been considered for the Test match.

At training the English comedian Norman Wisdom turned up at the invitation of Ian Redpath. He bowled off a long, comical run and delighted everyone, except the stern-faced Lawry. Redders allowed the English comedian to bowl him out, but not Lawry. Every Norman Wisdom delivery to Lawry was hit out of the ground. Australia was already three–nil down, going into the fourth and final Test to be played at St George's Park, Port Elizabeth. The Fourth Test went predictably enough. Again it was the batsmen who struggled after another tough time for the bowlers. McKenzie played, but bowled poorly. Clearly he was unfit; probably mentally as well as physically. McKenzie was lethargic and struggled to find rhythm and balance in his bowling. That would not have helped him mentally, for a bowler without rhythm will quickly fall away in a psychological sense, given that cricket is very much a confidence game. The umpiring didn't help his sense of wellbeing. One McKenzie ball to the Springbok keeper Dennis Lindsay had Lindsay snick a ball straight to Ian Chappell at first slip. The ball reached him a good nine inches above the turf, and Chappelli, who fielded poorly this series, caught the ball cleanly, but the umpire, the tall and officious Carl Coetzee, gave Lindsay not out. Next ball from McKenzie saw Lindsay belt it straight over the sightscreen for six. Doug failed with 1 and 23, although Paul Sheahan had a fine double (67 and 46), while Redpath continued his consistent form with 55 and 37. In South Africa's second innings, Ali Bacher (73) struck McKenzie like a rocket to the square leg fence only to tread on his wicket. It was McKenzie's only wicket for the series: 1/333.

We had lost the series four–nil.

Earlier in the tour—with Australia two Test matches down—there were moves by the South African Cricket Union to press for a Fifth Test match, to be played in Johannesburg.

The idea was to play a Fifth Test and scrap the last two (meaningless) matches against Western Province and the Orange Free State. However, to do so the Australian players would have to sign a new contract to enable the tour period to be extended by a few days. Ian Chappell thought this was the opportunity the players should not fail to grasp, a way to air their grievances about the terms and conditions of this long, arduous tour.

Lawry called a team meeting and most of the players voted against playing an extra match, a Fifth Test. Doug was among those who voted against an extra game. Ian Chappell spoke passionately against the extra match, saying that the Board had sold the players 'up the river' and that we should decline the Australian Board's offer to pay us an additional $200 to stay in South Africa to play the game. The Australian players asked for an extra $500, but the Board refused. Then the South African Cricket Board offered to make up the extra $300 to ensure the match got underway. Some voted for playing the game, some against. Doug was among the majority who voted against the Board's offer, the players agreeing that it was our Board that had the responsibility to pay the extra $500 per man in the touring party, something that could not be subsidised by the South Africans.

Bill Lawry then stepped in and said: 'Righto, it's either all in or all out. It's obvious that some of you don't want to play, so it's all over. Forget it.'

Lawry is a man of high principle and he showed a lot of guts on that tour. He took it upon himself to write to the Board outlining the players' concerns. No doubt he was highly critical of the Board's itinerary and their obvious lack of care about the players' welfare. Ian Chappell and Ian Redpath, especially, pleaded with Lawry to have all of the tour party sign any letter of protest he sent to the Board, but Phanto was insistent that he alone voiced the players' concerns. He felt that it was his duty (and responsibility) as the Test captain. Bill Lawry's name would have been placed in the Board's little black book. All they needed now was a loss of form and a few more Test defeats for the axe to fall on him. We played two more matches after that Fourth Test defeat. The first was in Cape Town where we tackled Western Province, a top-rated team with the likes of Eddie Barlow, Mike Proctor and the Test spinners Kelly Seymour and Graham Chevalier.

Doug Walters and Brian Taber were taking turns in providing a 'surprise breakfast'. Tabsy was the twelfth man for the match, but Doug and I were playing. I joined Tabsy and Freddie for their surprise breakfast on the first morning of the game. It comprised a few bits of toast and six bottles of cold Heineken beer. Very refreshing. Taber instigated those early morning lagers for breakfast. The idea caught on!

Australia hit a quick-fire 354 for the loss of only four wickets. Stackpole got 79, Redpath, 84, Irvine, 33, Sheahan 76 not out and Walters scored a highly entertaining 44. Amazingly, Lawry, who we all thought was born with a cricket bat in his hand and who loved batting with a passion, placed himself at the fall of the fifth wicket and he didn't bat in the first innings.

Then came our turn to bowl.

My attitude to the match wasn't great either, and I found myself tossing the ball up higher and shorter to Mike Proctor to see just how far he could hit them. Proctor hit five sixes in a row and Freddie was so taken with the action that he sidled up to me and said deadpan, 'Well then, Rowdy, that's got rid of the reds...now we start on the coloureds.'

Next day we had another surprise breakfast in Freddie and Tabsy's room. This time there were six ice-cold bottles of Castle lager. We got to Newlands and Doug, who'd had a few, was told by Lawry that he would be batting next in. Almost immediately Stackpole, who had been not out overnight, fell to Mike Proctor. Freddie walked to the crease wondering just how well he would sight the ball. As it turned out he hit his only century of the tour, 109, smashing the bowling to all parts of the ground. Perhaps a few beers before play was the key to Freddie's success in this match... A post-match surprise breakfast saw us joined by Alan McGilvray. We had had more than enough beers and missed the early drive to the airport. But all was well because Tabsy had a car and he would drive us to catch the plane. We were desperately late by the time we clambered into Tabsy's car and the drive was helter-skelter. At one stage Tabsy missed a turn and we careered through a bus shelter, people running everywhere.

It was like the Keystone Cops, but we made it. Doug's final innings in South Africa was a century, for he missed the Orange Free State match at Bloemfontein. Lawry also missed the match as did Alan Connolly. In the wash-up of the Test series, the press were scathing in their opinion of the Australian team.

Eric Litchfield in the *Rand Daily Mail* wrote:

'We want Lawry,' thousands shouted at the main grandstand of the St George's Park ground here, where the visitors crashed to a 323-run defeat.

Victorious Springbok captain Ali Bacher and Australian manager Fred Bennett made speeches. But Lawry could not be persuaded to step on to the balcony and say his piece.

This, to say the least, was a remarkable change of attitude because before the start of the series the Australian captain talked quite freely. Indeed before the start of this tour, he made some quite remarkable statements and claims, though, to be fair to him, his prophecies concerning the possible outcome of the series were guarded.[5]

In South Africa's leading Afrikaans language daily, Cape Town's *Die Burger*, an editorial said that the four–nil win was possibly the best contribution South African sportsmen could make to counter the boycott movement against them in the republic.

The Times in London proclaimed: 'If the Australians could catch a ship out of Port Elizabeth this evening, unseen and unsung, that is probably what they would like. In all their history, Australia have never received such a drubbing.' While *The Daily Telegraph* said the South Africans were superior in everything except spin. And there was this from the London *Sun*: 'Out-thought, out-bowled and out-batted is the story of Australia's performance in this series. It was pathetic to see a talented bunch of cricketers reduced to total impotence. But worst of all it was shattering to see how easily they accepted it. For Australia it was shameful, and for Bill Lawry an utterly disastrous end as captain. Lawry showed he is a bad leader when things go wrong. But that's not all. He showed incredible lack of tact in dealing with his own side, the opponents and the umpires.'

Bill Lawry didn't endear himself to the South African umpires at Port Elizabeth when he refused a gift from Carl Coetzee; this echoed a similar refusal for a gift from the Test umpires in Cape Town after the First Test. Bill said later that he would have been a 'hypocrit' to have accepted in view of his thoughts on the standard of the South African umpiring during the series.

The Australian journalist on tour, Phil Tresidder, pulled no punches:

> ... Reputations, hard won against England, West Indies and India in the last two years, have been surrendered with only a token fight. The tour inquisitions will be uncompromising. Even Lawry could face the chopping block as the nation's cricket leader.
>
> Next summer we can expect the Board of Control to issue a 'situations vacant' advertisement for our Test Eleven to combat the MCC. But one wonders if the Board of Control, sitting on a bulging $200 000 tour profit [*sic*], nurses an uneasy conscience. Could the Board members themselves be the chief culprits in this most humiliating chapter in Australian cricket? Reflect back to the originally planned tour in which the Australians were scheduled to visit India and Pakistan. When currency restrictions forced Pakistan to pull out, South Africa was 'substituted'. The Australian team, physically drained from the rigours of three months in India, were asked to tackle the world champion Springboks as a 'substitute' tour. The background for this Four-Test disaster then should be appreciated before the guillotine falls on Lawry's men.[6]

In a few more Test matches, after the Sixth Test of the 1970–71 Ashes series in Adelaide, Lawry was sacked: a fate which also befell Graham McKenzie and Alan Connolly during that series with England. Brian Taber never played Test cricket again, although he did make the 1972 tour as deputy to Rodney Marsh and, soon enough, Ian Chappell would begin a new and exciting era for Australian cricket as Test captain.

Doug batted well at times, but at no stage did he, or any of his batting colleagues, dominate an innings. After batting against all-out spin on turning wickets in India, Doug and company faced a sustained pace attack on the seam-friendly wickets in South Africa.

I can understand why we lost to South Africa because they had a really top side. They were the second best side that ever played against us. It was bad organisation to go from spinning tracks in India to seaming wickets in South Africa. If we had done it in reverse—South Africa, then India—I don't think we would have beaten India.

Graeme Pollock and Barry Richards dominated the series with their brilliant batting. Pollock hit 517 runs at an average of 73.85, with a highest score of 274 in the Durban Second Test match and Richards hit 508 runs at 72.57 with a highest score of 140, also in the Second Test. Doug believed that both Richards and Pollock were great players, but he reserved assessment on Richards because he played so little Test cricket.

I find it hard to rate Barry Richards, particularly because the only four Tests he played were the four against us. Then again, I know if he had played forty-four Tests he would have averaged the same, or even better. Pollock was a magic player. Such a good player, he could count like no-

one else——one to six. Ideally he wouldn't be the bloke you'd like to bat with too often.

Doug also admired the Springbok all-rounder Eddie Barlow.

Barlow was such a fierce competitor. Very good all-round cricketer without being brilliant as a batsman or a bowler. He tried his guts out all day. He had great self-belief.

On the eve of Bill Lawry's team leaving for Australia, manager Fred Bennett promised a 'better showing next time'.

... Our boys were pretty tuckered out after the Indian tour, they've been away from home since October. You can't tell me Graham McKenzie was at his best as a fast bowler. Then there were some of our leading batsmen who never produced the form we know they are capable of.[7]

Ian Chappell, the man Bill Lawry tagged 'the best batsman in the world' at a pre-series press conference, scored only 92 runs at an average of 11.50 in the four Tests. And although he took over from Lawry as the Australian captain, Chappell never got the chance to make amends against the Springboks, for the ills of apartheid had created a huge cloud of uncertainty over the future of sport in South Africa.

chapter eight
CHANGING *of* *the* GUARD

'I place Doug Walters in the same class as Viv Richards in
the context of taking an attack apart. With Viv it was a brutal
assault, but with Freddie it was more touch and placement…
A short time back I caught up with Doug and do you know
the bloke hasn't changed a bit. He's still wearing the same
tight-fitting, light-blue Rothmans Sports Foundation tracksuit
he was wearing in 1971!'

– *Dennis Lillee*

It took members of Bill Lawry's Australian team some time to
recover both physically and mentally from the long tour of Ceylon,
India and South Africa. Doug went back to work at Rothmans
and had a winter 'rest-up' before the challenge of another season's
tough cricket.

Only weeks after Freddie got home, the Walterses received a Royal request for their company over dinner. An invitation card arrived, and under the Royal ER crest came the words:

The Master of the Household is commanded by Her Majesty to Invite Mr and Mrs Douglas Walters to a dinner being given by
The Queen and The Duke of Edinburgh on board H.M.Y 'Britannia' at Circular Quay West on Friday, 1 May, 1970, at 8.15pm for 8.30pm.
A reply is requested to
The Australian Secretary to The Queen
Prime Minister's Department
Dress:
Gentlemen Dinner Jacket
Ladies Long Dress

Doug and Caroline turned up in their little blue Mini Minor which, upon their arrival at Circular Quay West, was politely parked out of sight of the Royal Yacht *Britannia*. The Walterses were among a parade of guests from all walks of Sydney life and, after a short time mingling and having cocktails, the guests were seated in the large dining room. There were starched tablecloths, accompanied by only the best silver and crystal glasses, as befitted the Queen of England and her selected guests.

One Royal—Princess Anne—was late. A renowned horse-woman, Princess Anne had been destined to get a place in the British Equestrian team bound for the Munich Olympics when her mount fell over and broke a leg only a week before the 1972 Games began. Finally she arrived, but before she took her seat, Princess Anne offered an apology.

*'So sorry for being late,' the Princess said, clutching her bottom, 'Ooooooh . . .
my arse is so sore . . . I've been riding horses all day.' And that set the scene
for a memorable night.*

Fortunately, on this occasion, the Princesss did not ask Doug to
sing his rendition of 'The Wild West Show'. It was at a function
in London in 1968 that Princess Margaret asked Freddie to sing
a few bars of 'The Wild West Show' and he obliged . . . briefly.

While the players rested during the off-season, there was much
speculation about the coming summer, for in the wake of Bill
Lawry's men getting a thrashing in South Africa, there were calls
for new faces in the Test team. While Lawry's men were being belted
by the Springboks, Sam Trimble's Australian Second Eleven played
three internationals against New Zealand. That tour saw the
emergence of Greg Chappell, who scored 182 runs at an average
of 60.66 and there was no doubt in the selectors' minds that a
place would be found for him in the Test side for the Ashes series.

A new wicketkeeper was also on the cards. Queenslander John
McLean, a stout fellow behind the stumps, looked as if he would
become yet another of the State's long-serving incumbents in the
Test team, for he stole the march on the likes of WA's Rodney
Marsh for a place on the New Zealand tour. Also Victoria's Alan
'Froggy' Thompson had powered his way to 100 Sheffield Shield
wickets in just sixteen matches to be a real chance. He too went
on the New Zealand tour, while Terry Jenner, the SA leg-spinner,
had headed the Second Eleven bowling averages in New Zealand,
taking 13 wickets at 18 runs apiece in the three internationals.

The Australian selectors would not have been pleased with the
Test team's showing in South Africa. When they looked at the
averages, their big black pencils would have been at work, crossing
out the likes of Eric Freeman and Laurie Mayne, plus erasing forever
the names of Jock Irvine, who had a horror run with the bat,

especially in India, and Ray Jordon who, somehow, it seemed, was never going to fit in. Freeman took 4/267 (average of 66.75) in South Africa and Mayne took seven wickets at an average of 44.85.

I didn't know it, but my spot was up for grabs, despite my having taken 28 wickets in the five Test matches against India at an average of 19.10 and six wickets in one Test against South Africa at an average of 34.16.

After a good tour of India Doug had a modest if not disastrous tour of South Africa—he was the second highest run-scorer (258) to Ian Redpath who scored 283 runs at 47.16. With an average of 32.25, Doug wasn't pleased with his form, but he would retain his Australian spot.

Doug's first match of the new summer was versus Queensland in Brisbane. He was bowled by 'Wild' Bill Albury for 12. Next game for New South Wales was against Western Australia at the SCG where Doug scored 25 in each innings, then he hit a marvellous 201 not out for New South Wales against MCC at the SCG.

It wasn't a very good innings. I struggled early on and continued to struggle throughout, but that wasn't greatly unusual for me because I have often struggled right through an innings and still managed a few runs. In South Africa we had lost a four Test match series four—nil, so you'd be struggling to find anyone who had done well. My own view was that it was the Australian batsmen, myself included, who had the most chance of being left out of the Brisbane First Test.

Our batting on that South African tour had created so many problems in not allowing the bowlers enough runs to play with against the opposition.

In that same match young NSW leg-spinner, Kerry O'Keeffe, was crazily being touted as the new Bill O'Reilly after his 6/69 off 28.3 overs against MCC. It was O'Keefe's accuracy which later won him a temporary Test spot. Bill Lawry was on a knife edge, for the Board would most certainly have been gunning for him to go. In those days a player who stood up to the Board was akin to Oliver Twist asking for more and the Board frowned upon any Australian Test player questioning its authority or asking for a better deal. However, Lawry kept his spot, so too did the bulk of batsmen, including Doug Walters. And although Greg Chappell was picked in the twelve, he was relegated to twelfth man.

Terry Jenner claimed a baggy-green cap, albeit as 12th man, and wicketkeeper Rodney Marsh and Alan 'Froggy' Thompson made their Test debuts.

Bobby Simpson warned of another batting debacle against England.

Doug Walters, very much an un-coached batsman, plays his defensive shots from a very open position. From this position he finds it difficult to combat short balls. Proctor and Pollock played successfully on this, and had him caught with monotonous regularity in the gully area.[1]

In addition, Simpson attacked Keith Stackpole's technique and wrote that Bill Lawry was a victim of getting too far forward too often.

Doug was typically realistic in his thoughts at the time.

I think all the Australian batsmen who came back from South Africa felt a bit under the pump. We simply had to perform or not stay in the side. It was as simple as that. But in the first five matches of their summer in Australia the Englishmen failed to dismiss the opposition in any of those games. Barry Richards, playing for South Australia in Adelaide, belted them for 224 and four of their five bowlers used in that game registered 'centuries' against their names.

The England team was led by the astute Yorkshireman Ray Illingworth, a splendid captain who was hard but fair. They had a couple of good fast bowlers in John Snow and Ken Shuttleworth, with the back-up medium pace of Basil d'Oliveira, and the spin of Illingworth and Derek Underwood.

Doug was surprised that the WA keeper Rodney Marsh was picked to replace his old mate and NSW gloveman Brian Taber.

True, Tabsy didn't have a great series with the gloves. He missed a few chances off (John) Gleeson, but he did so at a time when everyone was dropping them. We missed some 29 chances in just four matches. Taber didn't drop the 29 on his own in South Africa. If fielding had been the guide for selection, I don't think any of us would have got into the team.

Brian Taber had been having trouble with asthma in the republic and often had to take his puffer medication on the field at drinks breaks and during the usual lunch and tea adjournments. So when the side was being picked for this first Ashes Test, there was a huge cloud over Taber. The selectors went for Marsh and he was destined to stay for a marathon 96-Test match career.

The First Test was played at the Gabba. Lawry won the toss and batted. Stackpole, who was lucky to survive a run-out decision when he was on 18, became the first player to score a double century in an Ashes Test at Brisbane. Doug hit a brilliant 112 and with Stackpole (207) the pair put on 209 for the third wicket. After Doug was dismissed, Ian Chappell hit a solid 59, before the innings fell away alarmingly.

Snow's pace and fire on the relatively placid track was a pointer to things to come. The England fast bowler toiled through 32.3 overs to take 6/114. Despite the England reply being a mighty 464, Freddie came on to bowl all too infrequently sending down 5.5 overs to snare 3/12. In the Australian second innings Lawry hit a welcome-return-to-form 84, but the next best score was 36 by new-chum Rod Marsh.

England batted again, Geoff Boycott going for 16 and at 1/39 the game was over. A draw. On the rest day of the match, 30 November 1970, the players, the press and commentators banded together for a charity golf day under the management of the Sportsmen's Association.

Freddie was in a good mood, given his brilliant 112. His record at Brisbane also gave him many reasons to be buoyant. In three Test outings at the Gabba, he had scored a total of 422 runs in three completed innings; an average of 140.6. There was his debut 155 against England in December 1965; his 93 and 62 not out against India, after just leaving the army in January 1968, and his century in this match.

Just as I sat down to eat lunch before the hit-off, Frank Tyson, the great fast bowler, nicknamed 'Typhoon' came up to me. 'Walters, do you realise that your back-lift is crooked?'

I looked up from my plate and gave Frank a one word reply, 'Yes.'

'Aren't you worried about it?'

'No.'

'Well, you should be,' Typhoon said, 'because I reckon with that crooked back-lift, it would take me about three deliveries to put one through your defence.'

'That's one thing I won't have to worry about Frank. I don't have to face your bowling.'

Some hours later when all the players had trudged their way off the Indooroopilly Golf Course, I was presented with a trophy for being part of the winning team for the day.

As for Tyson, he spent most of his time in the rough trying to find his ball and in returning the day's highest score—a Bradman-like 125—

Frank was also presented with a trophy ... for the worst round of the day.
But Frank was happy with his prize and he returned to his drink sporting
a huge grin.

This was a chance not to be missed. I rushed over to Frank's table,
put my hand on his shoulder and said:

'Tyson, how could you possibly shoot 125 around here?'

'Quite easily, the way I play the game.'

'And what's more,' I continued, 'you seem pleased about your terrible
play. Aren't you worried about your golf?'

'No, why should I be? I've just won a trophy for my play.'

'Well, if I played golf like that I WOULD be worried about it!'

Frank Tyson played for England in 17 Tests taking 76 wickets at
an average of 18.56. He was one of the fastest bowlers of them
all and his fame hails from his explosive bowling during the
1954–55 Ashes series in Australia where he almost single-handedly
won the rubber by taking 28 wickets at 20.82.

Greg Chappell was picked in the eleven for the Second Test, a
great occasion for this was Perth's first Test match. The match
attracted more than 85 000 spectators, fetching £50 000 in gate
receipts and Greg Chappell became the sixth Australian to score
a debut Test century. Doug predicted big things for the young South
Australian.

Young Greg Chappell played a magnificent innings. It also stood him in
good stead for the rest of the summer because he didn't actually make very
many runs for the remainder of the season. I have always believed that
the best you see a player bat that is his standard, how good he can be. I
thought Greg would become a very good Test batsman, but I never regarded
him as an all-rounder, because he never really made any impression on
me as a bowler in his early years.

Doug at the age of twelve, the day he took a career-best 9/8.

Doug Walters, key member of the Maitland Police Boys Club, is pictured (wearing a handkerchief around his neck) second from left, front row.

A relaxed, upright stance.

Doug drives straight and powerfully.

Foot back and across and head over the ball, Doug is about to execute a late cut.

Always a straight shooter...Private Walters takes aim.

Doug takes time out for a drink and a sandwich during his time in the Nashos.

FAMILY

Doug about to get down the pitch to drive on the Walters' family backyard ant-bed pitch. May Walters plays a dual role: behind the stumps looking for a stumping and protecting the outdoor dunny. The picture was taken just days after Doug's debut century at Brisbane in December, 1965.

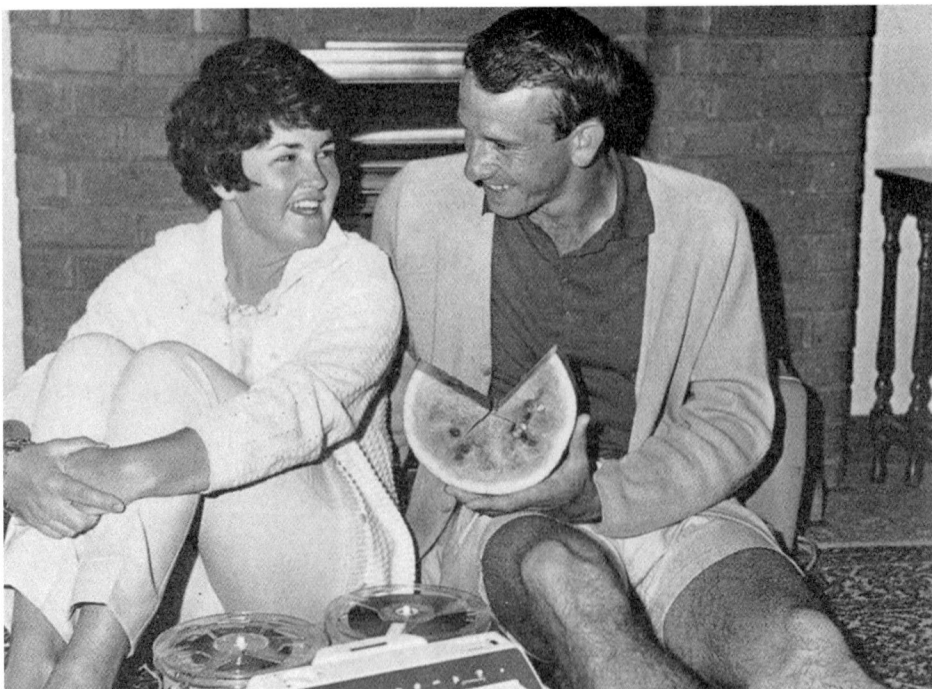

Caroline and Doug enjoy watermelon together as they listen to a recording of the radio coverage of Doug's debut 155 against England at the Gabba in December, 1965.

Relaxing after his brilliant Test debut century, Doug chats with cricket's greatest batsman in front of the Australian dressing-room at the Gabba.

Doug pulls powerfully during his epic century-in-session in the Perth Second Ashes Test of 1974–75.

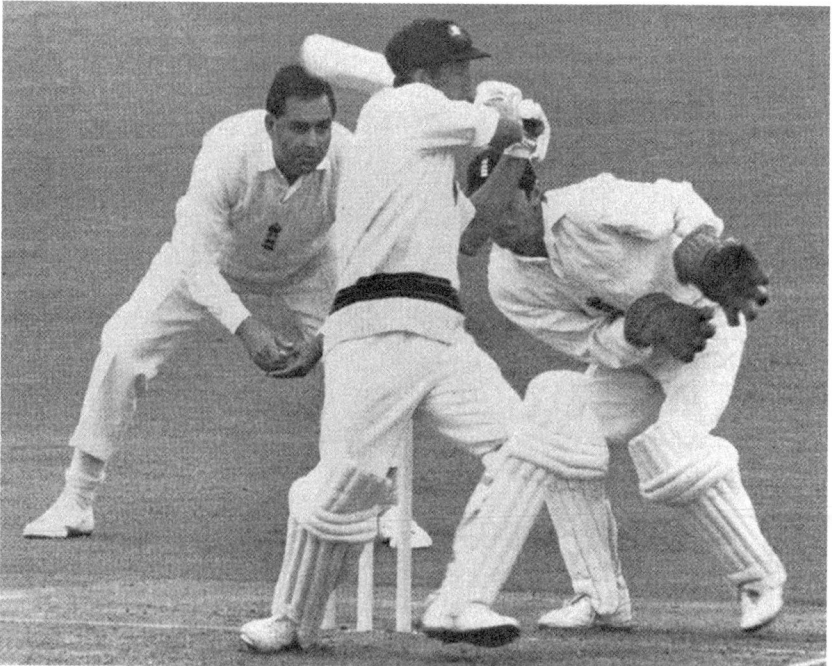

Doug flays England off-spinner Pat Pocock during his scorching 86 in the second innings of the First Test at Old Trafford in 1968. He hit 81 in the first innings.

Bob Willis clean-bowls Doug in his last Test innings in England, at The Oval in August, 1977.

Doug chops Derek Underwood on to his stumps and is bowled for a duck, second innings of the Second Test, Lord's, 1968.

Bill Lawry's Australians arrive in England, April, 1968.

The 1968 Australian and English teams give HRH the Duke of Edinburgh a resounding three cheers after meeting the Royals, Lord's, 1968.

Doug knows when to hold...and when to fold. Graham McKenzie is taking note of Doug's strategy.

And finally...to bed.

'Okay, Rowdy...that's got rid of the reds...now we start on the coloreds.'

'Old Golden Arm himself.'

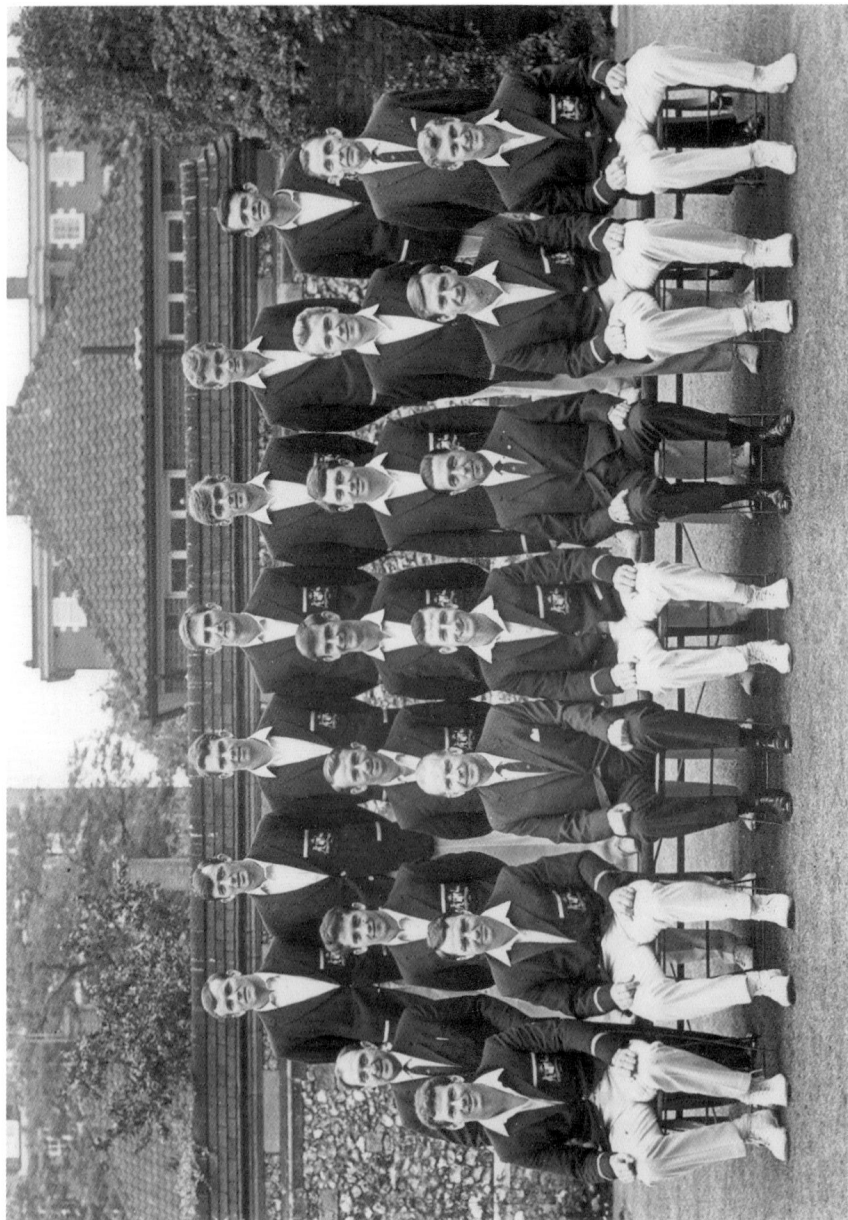

The 1968 Australian Touring team to England. This was the first of Doug's four England tours. He is pictured third from left, middle row.

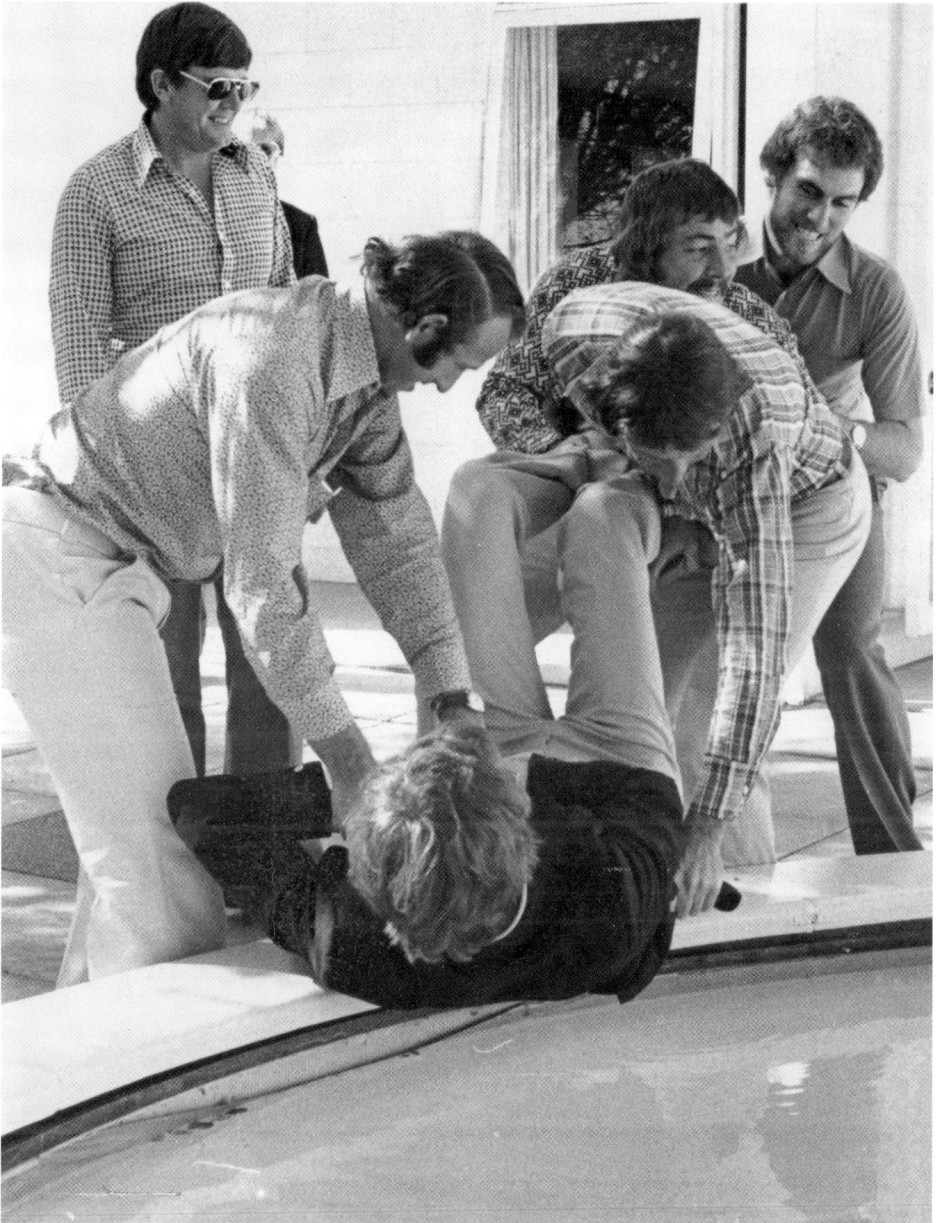

Doug (left), along with captain Ian Chappell, Rodney Marsh and Greg Chappell, about to throw the author into the hotel pool at Christchurch, 1974.

The cricketers who put their careers on the line, first summer of World Series Cricket. Doug is pictured second row, third from left.

The twentieth anniversary of World Series Cricket, December 1997. Doug is pictured front row, far right.

As the fans remember him, at the peak of his sporting powers.

Bruce Carter, Doug's plumber and good mate, drops in for a cold one.

Doug relaxes at home, surrounded by memorabilia, a television, bottles of cold beer and good reds, and the latest racing form guide. Life couldn't be any sweeter!

England batted first, scoring 397. Graham McKenzie returned to form with 4/66 and John Gleeson took 1/78 off 32 overs, with none of the Englishmen reading him very well. Australia replied with 440 with Greg Chappell (108) and Ian Redpath (171) leading the way. Earlier Ian Chappell scored an even 50 and Doug fell to Peter Lever for 7. He was bowled by the same bowler in the second innings for 8.

Ray Illingworth had won the toss, but there was no play and then four of world cricket's most influential administrators—Sir Donald Bradman, Australian Board chairman, MCC president Sir Cyril Hawker, MCC treasurer G.O.B. 'Gubby' Allen and the England tour team manager David Clark—decided that there would be a replacement Melbourne match to be played 21–26 January 1971. There was also a consensus between Messrs Bradman, Hawker and Allen that a one-day international was to be played on 5 January as a substitute for the washed-out Test match. Minutes after the ground announcer broadcast news of the game being abandoned, Sir Donald Bradman came into the Australian dressing-room. He stood on a bench seat in the players' locker area and told us that a one-day game was to be played. Sir Donald only spoke to us for a few minutes, not providing a lot of detail, other than to say that the match would be played with each side bowling 40 eight-ball overs and that a bowler was restricted to a maximum of eight overs. Twenty-one years later Sir Donald had more to say about that significant game.

I don't think any one person could be credited with the idea. Luckily the president of MCC, Sir Cyril Hawker, and the treasurer 'Gubby' Allen (not then knighted) were present. When it became evident that only one day remained, clearly it was useless trying to play a Test. A conference of all parties saw at once the problems. A huge financial loss to

Australia, loss to caterers and providers of drinks, no cricket over a holiday period, pre-sold ticket holders deprived of a Test, and sundry other considerations made the solution obvious—a one-day game and then substitute at a later date another Test. I do not take credit for the idea and neither should any other single person—it was a joint affair. And there was no thought at that stage of developing one-day games as they now exist. But the great success of the day and its obvious appeal to the public may have alerted somebody about future possibilities.[2]

As was the attitude with all of the team, the match didn't really mean a great deal at the time to Doug. Little did we realise, however, that we were about to play the very first one-day international.

I s'pose no-one felt as though this game was really special. One-day cricket wasn't a big thing in those days. Probably when we saw the size of the crowd we realised that this is the cricket the people really wanted.

Some 45 000 people turned up at the MCG that day, 5 January 1971. And they got what they were looking for—an Australian victory. Jenner played only one Test before I was back in the Australian Elevens. England won the toss and batted. There were no field restrictions, no coloured clothing, no player numbers. We wore creams and the field was set as if we were playing a Test match: three slips, a gully, third man, fine leg, that sort of stuff. England opener Geoff Boycott, who had batted brilliantly all summer, fell for 8 off 'Froggy' Thompson's bowling, John Edrich batted superbly for 82, before he top-edged a sweep against me and Doug cruised around from a backward square leg to take an easy catch. Next best scorers were Keith Fletcher and Alan Knott, both of whom scored 24 and England was all out for 190. Graham McKenzie took 2/22, Ashley Mallett 3/34, Keith Stackpole 3/40 and Alan Thompson 1/22. Alan Connolly, the clever Victorian medium-fast bowler, failed to take a wicket and conceded 62 runs off eight overs.

Ian Chappell (60) and Doug Walters (41) saw Australia to an easy five-wicket victory. Australia beat England by 45 runs in the first Test match, in March 1877 and here we were winning the very first ODI. The game was an experience, but few of the players fell in love with the concept.

The vital Fourth Test at the SCG saw Boycott (77) again in top form. He was unlucky in the first England innings, having smashed a Connolly long-hop with great power, but with the misfortune of hitting it straight down John Gleeson's throat at fine leg. It proved to be Connolly's last Test wicket, for he was dropped from the side after this match.

England scored 332, with John Gleeson (4/83) and Mallett (4/40) making most of the inroads. Doug only bowled three overs, but he did take a catch at point, off me, to dismiss Fletcher for 23.

During the Boycott–Edrich opening stand of 116, John Edrich (or Ede as we called him) waltzed down the wicket after playing the last ball of an over from Johnny Gleeson and announced to his batting partner: 'Boys, I've just worked out which way (John) Gleeson's going.'

Boycott smiled. 'Fook me, Ede, I worked out Gleeson two Test matches ago . . . but don't tell the others.' Boycott was so selfish that while he knew the method of how to 'read' the direction of Gleeson's spin and had worked it out two Test matches earlier, he was not going to reveal his method to the rest of his team.

Doug noticed a lot of grumbling and mumbling among a few players as soon as the Australian team arrived back in the dressing-room.

At the end of the England innings, just before lunch on the second day, I noticed Ian Chappell moving quickly through the dressing-room door, past me, and then he grabbed for his pads and thigh pad. 'What do you think you are doing, Chappelli?' Just then I heard the room attendant phoning through the Australian batting order to the scoreboard workers, with (Keith) Stackpole at number six. I said to Chappelli, 'Are you opening?' And he replied, 'Yeah, that's right.' This was the first I knew of Ian opening and I assumed that Bill Lawry had told Chappelli that he was expected to bat first. It proved a short-lived move. We were, I guess, worried about John Snow, but you don't normally change a batting order around one bowler. He was the one bowler in the side causing us problems. We thought that if we could see out Snow for the first five or six overs we would be okay.

I thought Stackpole had a good psychological effect on the rest of the team because if he got away with one or two attacking strokes early on, it got the pace bowlers on the defensive. As it turned out Chappelli was out in a flukey manner, with the square cut he intended being caught at third man. In the Perth Test he cut in the air in the third man area against John Snow where the ball landed some 30 yards over third slip. Ray Illingworth finally put a man at short third man, but without success in the Perth Test.

In Sydney the plan worked perfectly. Chappelli cut the ball over slips and straight to the man at short third man. I found Snow, and I know all the rest of the players did too, very difficult to cut. He was always climbing at you and you were never going to get over the ball and hit down on it.

Doug scored a solid 55 and Ian Redpath hit 64 in a disappointing Australian first innings of 236. John Snow bowled with hostility to grab 1/23 off 14 overs and Derek Underwood took 4/66 off 22 overs.

Batting a second time, England thrashed the Australian bowling. Sir Donald Bradman came quickly to my aid, indicating that I leave the area as he placed an arm on fellow Test selector Sam Loxton's shoulder to try to pacify him. The English press dubbed Rodney Marsh 'Old Iron Gloves' after he had dropped a number of easy chances.

Caroline Walters was intrigued by Rodney Marsh's nickname of Bacchus. And putting two and two together—the nickname and Rodney's missing chances—Caroline came to the only conclusion she thought possible: 'Do they call Rod Marsh Bacchus, Doug, because when Rod's wicket-keeping, he's always looking for someone to back him up? So back-us-up has been refined to Bacchus.'

And do you reckon Freddie let Rodney know about that one? Freddie and Chappelli liked to stir up Marsh early on saying things like 'Rodney, you are DUE to catch one.' But once Bacchus discovered that his mischievous team-mates were actually trying to help him relax, he lightened up and his wicket-keeping improved out of sight.

There is a certain collective parochialism about the SCG crowd, but they are mostly pretty knowledgeable. They voiced their opinion over Marsh replacing their home-grown keeper Brian Taber and gave Marshy a bit of a hard time. It was a nice gesture when Tabsy turned up in the Australian dressing-room to lend his support to Bacchus. England won the Fourth Test with a massive 299 runs, its highest win against Australia by a runs margin since 1936–37. Bill Lawry batted bravely to carry his bat for 60 in our second innings, the first Australian to do so at Sydney and the second after Bill Woodfull to achieve the feat twice. Freddie scored only 3 in the second innings. Freddie's mind was always on what was going on around him. When Greg Chappell came into the side he was given a go at second slip. There was Ian Chappell at first slip, Greg at second and Freddie at third. It was quite an experience fielding in slips with Freddie. And if someone asked him his estimate of the size of the crowd, Freddie would tell them soon enough. There was usually a long pause and he'd be asked again only to answer: 'C'mon, Greg, let a man concentrate...I was just counting them, then you interrupted. Now a bloke has moved in row 37 and that, combined with your interruption, I have to start again...One, two, three, four, five...'

The Fourth Test in Sydney was a triumph for John Snow, who took 7/40 in our second innings and shattered the face of Graham McKenzie with a ball which exploded off a length and hit him on the nose. McKenzie took 0/74 off 15 overs in the England first innings and 1/65 off 15 overs in the second. Both Connolly and McKenzie had played their last Test match.

Freddie's sense of fun was quite a contrast to the most staid of captains, Bill Lawry. The Phantom was incredibly conservative in his leadership, something which really belied his sense of fun and adventure away from cricket. He also possessed a keen sense of humour, he just didn't display it with a bat in his hand or when leading the Test side. But he was a fine opening batsman, one of Australia's best. At the batting crease, Lawry was a veritable corpse wearing pads; dour and deathly dull. As a captain, he hated a bowler giving away a single run. He wanted total pressure on the opposing batsmen and he achieved that with types of bowlers like Alan Connolly and John Gleeson, both tight bowlers who wore down a batsman. On a placid wicket in Adelaide in the South Australia versus MCC match, South Australia amassed 8/648 before Ian Chappell called a halt to the slaughter. I scored 42 and told Snow that he 'wasn't quick enough to bowl a bouncer'. Snowy never forgot and he gave me a fair workout as I jumped about, ducking and weaving for an hour over six runs. Not long afterwards, a photograph of my way of handling Snow's short-pitched stuff arrived in the dressing-room. It showed my legs in a tangle and the bat being knocked out of my hands. Someone had written: 'To Rowdy,

All my love, Snowy'. But I don't think it was John Snow who penned the words. Guess who?

I asked Freddie.

I honestly can't remember whether it was me or not. It is something I would have liked to have done . . .

Every one of the Australian batsmen was intent upon finding his own method of playing Snow. He had our batsmen very worried. Doug remembers the difficulty in facing the fast bowler.

With an ordinary bowler this doesn't matter so much, but I found myself trying to get back on the back foot to him straightaway and it was obvious the two Chappells had tried to devise a method of going across the crease to play him. Both Ian and Greg Chappell had close shaves with Snow narrowly missing bowling them around their legs. Indeed Greg Chappell was bowled around his legs in the Sydney Fourth Test match.

For the Fifth Test match the Australian selectors brought back Alan Thompson and included Queensland swing bowler Ross Duncan to replace the axed pair McKenzie and Connolly. And NSW spinner Kerry O'Keeffe was brought in to replace me—I was relegated to carry the drinks.

Australia made a good fist of its first innings scoring 493; Lawry (56), Ian Chappell (111), Ian Redpath (72) and Doug scored 55. Rodney Marsh, who played magnificently down the order, was deprived of becoming the first Australian wicketkeeper to score a Test hundred because Lawry declared the innings closed at 9/493 with Marsh stranded on 92 not out.

It was the most ludicrous call by Lawry because we took drinks with Marsh needing about 10 runs for his century and the drinks interval took some ten minutes. The wicket was a beauty and we didn't exactly have much of an attack. England replied with 392; Froggy Thompson took 3/110 and Ross Duncan, the Queensland swing bowler, struggled in excruciating pain with a badly bruised heel over 14 overs for his 0/30. It was destined to be Rosco's only Test match, but he has always maintained that he did the right thing by himself.

> We all play the game to reach the highest level we can achieve and it was my aim to play Test cricket. Had I ruled myself out of this match I may not have been given another chance. So I played with an injury and I have never regretted it.[3]

Young spinner Kerry O'Keeffe bowled a long and tidy spell of 31 overs, but failed to get a wicket and conceded 71 runs. Johnny Gleeson toiled away, getting 3/60 off 25 overs and Freddie chimed in with 1/7, clean-bowling Brian Luckhurst for 109. England's Boycott (76 not out) and Edrich (74 not out) crawled to 161 without loss in a boring last day's play.

A financial world record was achieved on day three—gate receipts of £25 070. But world record receipts didn't affect the players. We were still on $200 a game.

I got back into the side for the Sixth Test match in Adelaide, O'Keeffe being dropped for this fixture. However, the big news was the debut of Dennis Keith Lillee, the young firebrand fast bowler from Western Australia. Lillee took the new ball with Alan 'Froggy' Thompson. England batted first and when John Edrich was on 7, Doug Walters produced a nice little delivery which cut off the track and Edrich edged it straight to me in the gully: straight in and straight out. It was a sitter. Poor Freddie was downcast, but he didn't say a word. But I knew what he would have said had I held on to that easy catch in the gully. Whenever he broke a partnership, as he invariably did after a long one, Doug would hold court as the players gathered around and he always said: 'Bloody beauty ... one for none!' This time, however, Freddie was left to ponder what might have been and I was banished to the outfield. Edrich edged one again, this instance off Dennis Lillee and Keith Stackpole at slip accepted the chance. Edrich made 130.

The game was memorable because of Lillee's debut bag of wickets. He was a sight to behold as he stormed in from his long run, impressing all and sundry with his stirring haul of 5/84 off 28.3 overs. The rest of the attack looked decidedly pedestrian and, despite Boycott being run out when he was on 58, the Englishmen made run-getting look easy and they compiled an impressive 470.

We replied with a pathetic 236, Keith Stackpole hitting a terrific 87, but Lawry looking ordinary getting only 10. Doug fell to Peter Lever again, this time scoring just 8. Rather than enforce the follow-on, Illingworth decided to bat again and this let us off the hook. Lawry bowled Thompson and Gleeson almost exclusively and England declared at 4/233, leaving Australia with a near impossible target of 469.

Lawry fell again cheaply for 21, but thanks to intelligent and capable batting by Stackpole (136) and Ian Chappell (104), Australia saved the day. The changing of the guard was already happening with the bowlers. It was a sort of musical chairs for the attack, but the knives were now out for the Australian captain. Lawry was seen as a liability which the nation could no longer afford to head its cricket team. The side for the Seventh Test match in Sydney was the last Test Eleven Sir Donald Bradman ever presided over. Bradman had first become a Test selector while captaining Australia in the 1936–37 Ashes series against an England team led by Gubby Allen. Australia made wholesale changes, axing Lawry, Froggy Thompson, Gleeson and me. The bombshell was the sacking of Lawry and he had to find out about his axing through his opening partner and friend, Keith Stackpole, who heard the news over the radio.

Ian Chappell was made captain and in came big Queensland left-arm Tony Dell, SA leg spinner Terry Jenner, the reinstated Kerry O'Keeffe and Victorian opening batsman Ken Eastwood. England were bowled out for a paltry 184, after Chappelli sent them in, emulating P.S. McDonnell, George Giffen and Bob Simpson when he invited the opposition to bat in his first Test as captain. O'Keeffe and Jenner both grabbed three wickets and Tony Dell bowled with pace and fire to take 2/32 off 16 overs. In reply the Australians got 264: Redpath (59), Walters (42) and Greg Chappell top-scoring with 65. An 80-run lead was useful, but England in a very even second-innings batting performance managed 302, leaving Ian Chappell's men needing just 223 runs to win.

It should have been a cakewalk, especially after John Snow was injured, but the England team rallied brilliantly. Illingworth bowled his off-breaks with steady precision and arty craft to take 3/39 off 20 overs; d'Oliveira got 2/15 and Underwood claimed 2/28 off 13.6 overs. It was a brilliant performance by England which was clearly the better of the two sides. Snow, who took 31 wickets for the series, and Boycott, who was injured before the Seventh Test, ironically having a bone in his arm broken by a rising ball from Graham McKenzie, were the stand-out performers for the winning team. Boycott scored 657 runs in the series at an average of 82.13, with two centuries. Doug hit 373 runs at 37.30 for the series, moderate by his standards at home. So after the series and with winter approaching, Doug returned to working full-time with Rothmans.

During the off-season there was much speculation about whether or not the South Africans would tour Australia. A Springbok rugby tour Down Under was put under intense pressure by protests and the authorities believed that a cricket match could be far more easily disrupted by protestors than a rugby match. There was a sustained campaign by protest groups and political pressure finally convinced the Australian Board of Control for International Cricket that the proposed South African tour of Australia in 1971–72 should be cancelled. As Board chairman, Sir Donald Bradman announced the cancellation of the tour and then began hastily setting up an alternative event: a tour by a World Eleven to play Australia in a series of five internationals. The games would not be awarded Test match status, but the side the Board put together was a formidable one indeed: West Indian champions Garry Sobers, Rohan Kanhai, and up-and-coming Clive Lloyd; the great South African Graeme Pollock and his brother Peter; Hylton Ackerman with Indians Sunil Gavaskar and Bishen Bedi; and Pakistani batting maestro Zaheer Abbas. They formed the nucleus of this team of champions and Australia would have to play well to match them. Ian Chappell had the chance to work closely with the team for there were bigger fish to fry in the near future, with the 1972 tour of England close at hand.

Doug began the summer well, hitting 158 against Victoria in Melbourne and then he smashed an even, unconquered century against the World Eleven for New South Wales in Sydney. He had made a habit of thrashing visiting touring teams for New South Wales at the SCG. Doug played in four of the internationals against the World Eleven, hitting 355 runs in five completed innings for an average of 71.00, but it was his second innings hundred in the MCG match which lifted his performances out of the ordinary.

That was the celebrated match 6 January 1972. Sobers was out first ball in the World Eleven first innings. He played too soon to a Lillee short ball and edged it to second slip where Keith Stackpole took the ball neatly. Triumph for Lillee; a first-ball duck for Sobers. Batting in the second innings Sobers flayed the Australian attack unmercifully, scoring 254; an innings which prompted Sir Donald Bradman to say that it was the best he had seen in Australia. The World Eleven scored 514 runs in its second innings after being dismissed for 184 in the first. Dennis Lillee had taken 5/48 first up, but with Sobers in full flight Lillee suffered to the tune of 133 taken from his 33 overs. Left with 414 to win the game, Australia was 4/157 when Doug Walters came in.

It was one of those occasions when everything went right. I felt good and the ball was meeting the middle of the bat, but after Garry Sobers' amazing 254 no-one really remembers any of the other scores. I guess I now know how Arthur Morris felt when Don Bradman played his last Test match. Arthur is often asked if he played in the celebrated match when Bradman got a duck in his final innings. 'Oh, yes, indeed I played in the game. In fact, I was at the other end when Eric Hollies bowled Bradman with a wrong'un.'

'And did you get any runs?' they ask.

'Yes, I did. I scored 196!'

I have been asked if I played in the match when Sobers scored that amazing 254 and only recently one of the blokes who played in that match with me, SA's leggie Terry Jenner, said he had only just realised, after watching a documentary on the game, that I scored a century before lunch on that last day.

Despite Sobers stealing the show, the Sydney newspapers acknowledged Doug's effort.

An amazing century before lunch by Doug Walters highlighted an exciting two hours' play on the last day of the Australia–World XI cricket match at the MCG today.

Walters' 102 in the first session was the first century before lunch ever hit at the Melbourne Cricket Ground. Walters, who was two not out overnight, reached his century with a slashing cover drive in the last over before lunch off Tony Greig.

Although Australia had little chance of winning the game Walters attacked all morning and his 100 came up in 132 minutes with 14 fours. The last Australian to score a century before lunch in this country was Arthur Morris who hit 108 not out (for NSW) against Queensland on the third morning of the match in 1948–49.[4]

The previous night before Doug's historic knock, he attended a show with his skipper, Ian Chappell, and NSW wicketkeeper, Brian Taber, who was in Melbourne for some coaching business. Chappelli says, 'I remember saying to Herbie (Brian Taber), "Keep an eye on Freddie will you, I don't want him up all night." Herbie forgot all about Freddie and he left the show about 3 a.m. Doug walked outside and was surprised by the glare of the sunshine.'[5]

Doug is unlikely to forget what happened that day.

The sun was so bright it made you squint. 'I have to play a match tomorrow,' I said.

'No,' said the host, '. . . you have to play TODAY.'

When I got back to the team hotel, I asked the receptionist if she could put through a wake-up call to my room at twenty to nine.

'Certainly, Mr Walters. That would be 8.40 tonight.'

'No . . . make it this morning . . . twenty to nine.'

'But sir. It is now 8.30 a.m.'

'Yes, I know. I've got to play cricket today and you wouldn't want me to turn up to the match without having had any sleep, would you?'

Doug headed the Australia first-class batting averages in 1971–72, with 895 runs at an average of 68.84 and a top score of 163 not out for New South Wales versus Western Australia in Perth. In that match Walters mauled the WA speed battery of Dennis Lillee (19–0-119–0); Bob Massie (22–2-106–2) and Graham McKenzie (27–1-109–1).

People often ask whether I played against Dennis Lillee much. Well, I did play against Dennis Lillee a fair bit, for in those days we played most of the Sheffield Shield matches and the clashes were heated. There were no beg-pardons and matches were fought out fiercely.

Doug was, over the years, a prolific scorer for New South Wales against Western Australia. He seemed to lift when playing the better bowlers, especially Lillee. And Dennis Lillee holds a special place in his heart for the Doug Walters batting magic.

I place Doug Walters in the same class as Viv Richards in the context of taking an attack apart. With Viv it was a brutal assault, but with Freddie it was more touch and placement. But both Richards and Walters were ruthless in their execution. During my time with Western Australia we won a lot of Sheffield Shields and we beat New South Wales often, but Doug always seemed to score against us. He played the swing of Terry Alderman and Bob Massie well, and it was always a great challenge to bowl to him. He would thrust that angled bat at you and you always thought of an outside edge, but the ball which swung away seemed to suit him best. Doug was the most laid-back of characters. Whether he got a duck or a hundred, he was the same. He never complained about a bad decision. I consider myself having been very lucky to have played cricket in the same era as Doug Walters. A short time back I caught up with Doug and do you know the bloke hasn't changed a bit. He's still wearing the same tight-fitting, light-blue Rothmans Sports Foundation tracksuit he was wearing in 1971.[6]

The series against the Rest of the World was hard fought and it gave the captain, Ian Chappell, and the Test selectors scope to access the players before the vital tour of England. Doug balled brilliantly throughout the summer, not only his century in a session in the Melbourne international. In Brisbane Walters hit 75 not out; in Perth, 125; in Melbourne 16 and 127; in Sydney 8 and 4 and in Adelaide he was rested to allow the selectors a chance to see John Benaud in action. Walters in four games scored 355 runs at an average of 70. Freddie was eagerly looking forward to his second England tour.

chapter nine
the
AGONY

The 1972 tour was a low point for me...I expected to be dropped for the previous Fourth Test at Headingly (Leeds). I wasn't hitting the ball as well as I would have liked. However, when you get dropped it makes you bite the bullet. It makes you more determined to come back and prove them wrong.

Doug Walters was among only seven Test team-mates who had toured England before. The others were Ian Chappell, Paul Sheahan, John Inverarity, John Gleeson, Brian Taber and me. The Australian selectors were brutal in axing three stalwarts in Bill Lawry, Graham McKenzie and Ian Redpath from the 1972 tour of England. NSW opening batsman Bruce Francis controversially took Lawry's spot; NSW pace bowler David Colley replaced McKenzie and WA batsman Ross Edwards, who was second to Walters in the first-class averages with 773 runs at 64.41, toured ahead of Redpath. Doug and Test captain Ian Chappell flew out of Australia ahead of the rest of the team to play in a two-day testimonial match for Garry Sobers in Kingston, Jamaica. They flew in to London twelve hours ahead of the bulk of the tour party which had spent a few hours in San Francisco. Doug dearly wanted to assert his authority on the cricket grounds of England.

On Thursday, 28 April, the Australian team had a 60-over practice match at The Oval. We played through the English rain, which the locals called 'drizzle', with our manager Ray Steele umpiring, his assistant, Fred Bennett, and the perky physiotherapist Dave 'Doc' McErlane helping out in the field.

Even our English-based baggage-master, A.T. Tony Smith, in those days a man of enormous bulk, ever sporting a bright-red nose, fielded.

E.W. Swanton observed in his column next day.

Surrey provided an excellent pitch over on the Harley-ford Road side, where the trams used to run. They are said to be quicker on this edge of the square, and this one had pace and a generous bounce. Walters, for instance, to whom the 'keeper stands back only by courtesy', got two or three ones up head-high.

Walters made batting look very easy until he was caught driving with his front leg so far from the ball that Arthur McIntyre, Surrey's coach and cricket manager, averted his offended eyes.[1]

Swanton made another astute observation.

The traditional 'baggy-green cap' might have been specially designed for the Australian hair-styles of the seventies.[2]

The England captain, Ray Illingworth profiled every member of the Australian touring team; a different profile every day in his column in the London *Mirror.* About Doug he wrote:

We all knew Doug Walters' weakness during the tour of Australia (1970–71). And Doug knew we knew...the cry of 'Up periscope!' told him often enough. The cry would coincide invariably with a bouncer from John Snow, pitched around off stump. And Doug would drop to his knees, duck his head and leave his bat stuck vertically in the air. It was a comical sight, but unfortunately, Walters is one of those rare characters who forgets a mistake the instant he makes it and is just as likely to clout the next ball for four. He is a marvellous improviser—possibly the best in the game—a natural striker of the ball and temperamentally sound, once he has shaken off his early stage fright.

He always will be a bad starter. He can't bear to watch the game from the players' balcony and will play cards and smoke countless cigarettes to take his mind off things. This is why you have to catch Doug quickly because as soon as he has got the feel of the game his awkwardly angled bat is compensated by a good eye and the will to give the ball a crack. He is particularly strong on the on-side and probably scores more runs through mid-wicket than any other Australian. For all the ugliness of his technique, the proof of the pudding is in his Test aggregate of 2623 (runs). And, remember, he is the only Australian, after Bradman, with a Test average of fifty-plus. He was even called another Bradman six years ago when, as a raw 20-year-old, he carved hundreds in his first two Tests against England. Facts never supported the prophets, but it is true that, on occasions, Doug will make mincemeat of the best bowling.[3]

Doug Walters played 19 first-class matches in England in 1972, hitting 935 runs at an average of 38.95. He was fourth (to Greg Chappell, 1260 runs at 70.00; Keith Stackpole 1309 runs at 43.63 and Paul Sheahan 788 runs at 41.47) on the tour averages. Doug hit three centuries—154 versus Warwickshire at Edgbaston; 150 against Kent at Canterbury and 109 versus Derbyshire at Chesterfield. But in the Test matches he had a disastrous time of it. He scored 17 and 20 in the First Test at Old Trafford; 1 at Lord's in the Second Test match, where Bob Massie took a debut 16/137 to steer Australia to its first Test match victory in 11 games; 2 and 7 in the Third Test at Trent Bridge, Nottingham, and 4 and 3 in the Fusereum pitch at Headingly, Leeds, and Trent Bridge in the Fourth Test: a total of 54 runs in seven completed innings at an average of 7.71.

However, Doug never lost his sense of fun. Australian journalist Mike Coward, who was covering his first international tour with the Test team, was greatly taken by Freddie's laid-back attitude and his wonderful sense of humour.

> I have a clear recollection of an amusing interlude at Southampton on the 1972 tour. These were the days when journos could fraternise with the players and I was in a group led by Doug in search of the local casino. There were three or four of us and I think Doug and I were accompanied by Ross Edwards and Graeme Watson, who had a sensational match at Southampton. We were making our way through a maze of one-way streets and across round-a-bouts away from the hotel when a good-sized lorry pulled up and asked for instructions to a specific address. Before anyone could mutter that they had no idea, as we were visitors in town, Doug leapt forward and reeled off a dizzying set of directions. It was a priceless performance. He maintained a

straight face and intoned the instructions in the most serious and authoritative manner. It was 'first right, second left, through the set of lights and then second left and then right at Barclays Bank'. That sort of stuff. The driver left with a wave and a honk of his horn, oblivious to the fact that one of the game's greats had done him cold. It was quite a side show—more memorable than anything on offer at the casino![4]

Illingworth's team was, like Ricky Ponting's men in 2006, a fine team, but getting a little long in the tooth. Ted Dexter, writing in the *London Daily Express,* under the heading 'DAD'S ARMY GOES BARMY', may have inadvertently hit upon a tag for the band of British cricket supporters we see at grounds throughout the world today. Dexter wrote:

A fifty-five minute barrage by fast bowlers John Snow and Geoff Arnold on a grey Old Trafford morning did everything to alter this England team's elderly Home Guard image.

Dad's Army went barmy. They suddenly looked more like a Panzer Division as the last six Australian wickets were demolished for a mere 23 runs . . . Doug Walters could easily have set a record for the highest number of 'air' shots, although a claim by Jim Laker to sixty-seven misconnections in an innings of 22 not out at Melbourne in 1958 sets a very high standard . . . After three dropped catches in three balls off Arnold on Friday, they were flinching visibly at every ball.

They knew a lot depended on getting Walters out early. They suspected the pitch would become more friendly, as it actually did. Arnold bowled to Walters, who angled his bat awkwardly across the line of the ball and Illingworth acted out his lines by dropping the chance. I never believed

I would see nine catches go down in succession in one Test match. Yes nine! And it looked like being ten when Greg Chappell edged Snow fast and low between Luckhurst and Friday's chief butterfinger, Tony Greig. This time, thank goodness, England's new all-rounder had other ideas. And after a spectacular dive and roll he came up smiling with the ball held high. The spell was broken and England's confidence surged. Snow started to hit poor Walters up and down the legs as he bowled a good yard faster. Colley and Gleeson heard their off stumps go clattering back one after another.

Two wickets in three balls to Snow. The remaining obstacle, however insubstantial, was Walters, who by this time was barely able to hobble his runs. Finally Snow let him have a bouncer and a vain attempt to hook lobbed gently to a grateful Illingworth.[5]

The Australians' home away from home in London was ever the Waldorf Hotel, a grand old Victorian building set smack in the middle of London's West End, built along the semi-circular Aldwych, a Keith Miller drive from Australia House. Captain Ian Chappell straight away set the pattern for team morale, which was so much higher than it had ever been under Bill Lawry's leadership. The Waldorf public bar became our lounge room, although we also had a team room on the first floor of the hotel. But it was in the front bar that you'd find Chappelli and Herbie Taber, the Fox, David Colley, Beatle (Graeme Watson), me and, of course, Freddie. Some nights we'd be joined by FOT (Dennis Lillee) who was sometimes accompanied by Mick Jagger, who had taken a shine to the way this Australian team under Chappelli played the game and particularly loved the pace and fire and rhythm of Lillee. There Doug would sit at the bar with team-mates quietly chatting away between sips of beer and a drag on a cigarette. But Doug's

England trip wasn't going that swimmingly; runs weren't exactly coming at a rush, so in a cricketing sense he could identify with Jagger's hit, 'I Can't Get No Satisfaction'.

Within a few yards of where Doug sat on the bar stool, would be Jagger, leaning up against the wall. He usually wore very casual gear—blue jeans, a sloppy joe windcheater and sandshoes—and in his hand would be a half-handle of Double Diamond. He would often be in earnest conversation with the young Dennis Lillee, who, in those days, rarely partook in the demon drink. Actor Ed Devereaux, who starred in the long-running TV series *Skippy the Bush Kangaroo*, was also a regular. Devereaux was a dinky-di Aussie, with language to match. Whenever Doug asked him to have a pint, Ed would enthuse: 'Shit a brick, would I ever love a beer!'

So we seemed to have a constant stream of visitors to the Waldorf bar, but still the wives of the players were 'banned' from the team hotel. Caroline Walters stayed at a hotel nearby and Doug could visit her there. Doug and Caroline frequented the London Cricketers' Club, hosted by Frank and Sheila Russell and they sometimes stayed with the Russells.

Frank Russell was ever the life of the party. A huge man with a booming voice, Frank often hosted touring parties to go and watch Test cricket, be that in Australia or the Caribbean. He wore foreboding-looking horn-rimmed glasses and whenever you saw him he'd be at the bar or about to launch into another session at the bar, with the question, 'Well, now Freddie, what will it be, a Fosters?'

One night, my wife Christine and I dined with Doug and Caroline at the Russells' home in London's fashionable Knightsbridge. Earlier that day we used one of the team cars and I had a spot of bother when I parked too close to the kerb in Bayswater Road.

I pinched the tyre and let all the air out of the front left-hand side wheel. I couldn't drive the vehicle back to the Russell's place, so I left the car on the side of the road. 'Good, God, Rowdy. You left the car at Hyde Park Corner!' I can still hear Frank's booming indignation. 'C'mon Freddie, we'll have to salvage the bloody thing.' So at 1 a.m. early on a Monday there were Freddie and I and Frank changing the tyre of one of the team cars right on Hyde Park Corner, near the rear of Buckingham Palace, one of the busiest little traffic zones in London.

After batting failure in all four Tests, Doug's cricket was at such a low ebb, there was no alternative but to look for a replacement. His performances in England that summer were so poor even captain Ian Chappell decided that the little bloke needed a rest from the Test Eleven. It wasn't an easy decision for Chappelli because he believed in Freddie. When he first took over the Australian captaincy he went to Doug and told him that he wanted him to continue batting in his natural, attacking way. After the disappointing First Test loss at Old Trafford, Chappelli called a team meeting. Our manager, Ray Steele, held up a newspaper which carried the headline: 'AUSSIES TAKE LOSS LYING DOWN'. Ray looked over his rimless glasses and cast his eyes about the room, '... Pig's bloody arse we take it lying down!'

With Walters out of the Fifth Test at The Oval, the team for that Test in 1972 was the first occasion in Australian Test cricket history that there was no NSW player in the eleven. As Paul Sheahan said, Doug would have died for the Australian team, a trait which was belied by his relaxed and seeming casual air. Freddie was, as everyone knew, deeply hurt by his axing from the side, but he swept away his disappointment by showing how much he cared for the team.

Freddie waited for the perfect timing, then he stood up to address the players. He had covered his hair with a wad of cotton wool to mimic Ray Steele's bald head and he looked over the borrowed rimless glasses in the true style of our manager. 'Take this lying down... pig's bloody arse we will!'

Chappelli believed that Doug's words had an uplifting effect on the team.

We did win the match. It was an enthralling game, which ebbed and flowed. The pitch was a beauty, very much like the tracks at home. We won the game okay and I always regard Doug Walters' comments as part of the reason we won that game. After Doug's comments there seemed to be a 'let's do it for Dougie' attitude amongst the team. He was a hugely popular member of the Test squad and his actions that night helped lighten the mood. He did us proud.[6]

The Fifth Test was very much a make or break game for the side. To have lost this match we would have returned home a failed team. Winning the game would not only square the series one–all, it would help erase the disappointment of having been 'done' on a terrible wicket at Leeds; one tailor-made for 'Deadly' Derek Underwood.

The win in the Leeds Fourth Test ensured England's 'Dad's Army' retained the Ashes. Freddie spent the entire six days of the Fifth Test match playing cards, drinking tea and smoking cigarettes. He probably didn't see a ball bowled, but that was his way. When the side was batting, Freddie never watched the game. He was always sitting at a table playing cards with whoever happened to fancy a game.

Australia won the last Test, thanks to some brilliant bowling by Lillee and centuries to Ian and Greg Chappell. All the blokes felt for Freddie, yet somehow we all knew that he would bounce back when the new season began in Australia. Doug was determined to fight his way back.

The 1972 tour was a low point for me. I guess after my poor Test form my cricket career was at its lowest ebb. It was disappointing to be dropped, but to be perfectly honest I expected to be dropped for the previous Fourth Test match at Headingly (Leeds). I wasn't hitting the ball as well as I would have liked. However, when you get dropped it makes you bite the bullet. It makes you more determined to come back and prove them wrong. It's all a matter of confidence. The following year was an amazing turn-around for me. I had a very good tour of the West Indies.

Whatever his form with the bat on tour, in the Australian team bus he found plenty of time for mischief. Doug was always up the back of the bus playing cards, having a beer with a cigarette in his hand. He never changed. After one or three beers the 'boys at the back of the bus', led by Freddie, got a bit raucous and loud. Sometimes the coach wouldn't have a toilet, so often there would be the cry, 'Hey, driver, stop for a piss!' Freddie never let it pass. 'Hey, driver. Don't stop for a piss, let's stop for some PISS!'

The cassette recorder at the front of the bus was often playing the popular songs of the time, such as Helen Reddy's 'I Am Woman', Roberta Flack's 'The First Time Ever I Saw your Face', Billy Thorpe's 'Most People I Know Think That I Am Crazy' and John Lennon's 'Imagine'. Doug always sang along to renditions of such songs as 'Sweet Caroline', 'Sad Movies', or 'When the Lights All Went Out in Massachussetts'. And if those songs were on board, Doug would get them played very regularly; too frequently for some of the blokes trying to sleep at the front of the vehicle.

After a game against the Minor Counties at Stoke-on-Trent, we boarded a coach bound for Hove to play a three-day match against Sussex. An hour or so into our journey, the bus slipped off the motorway and stopped at a large restaurant and a group of shops and a service station. Ray Steele sat alone. He wore his almost prerequisite dark-blue pin-striped suit, and peered over his horn-rimmed glasses, focusing his gaze on the bulging leather briefcase before him in the middle of the table. Scattered about the eatery were other members of the touring party. At one of the tables, team physiotherapist Dave 'The Doc' McErlane held court with a collective of players. Doc loved to tell stories tall and true and he always came up with some beauties. Thankfully, some were true, but Doc always gave them that special touch he would call 'embellishment' and we would call 'bullshit'. When not on tour with the Australian cricket team, Doc was the resident masseur at the Harbord Diggers' Club in Sydney.

Darkness had descended by the time Doc took a breather from another tale of life as a POW. He caught a waitress's eye. He winked, and blurted: 'See that bald-headed bloke sitting over there on his own? He's got a bomb in his bag!' The waitress got Doc's message okay. She realised it was a joke, but unfortunately for Dave and for the Australian team, the manager behind the counter overheard the bit about the bomb and saw nothing funny in that at all. The stern-faced boss saw it as a terrorist threat and rang the police. In 1972 terrorism in the United Kingdom was rife. The IRA was setting off bombs in London, almost on a daily basis. The entire United Kingdom was on high terrorist alert, and people found nothing funny about terrorist bombs or a terrorist threat. Those working in industries where there were large gatherings of people were understandably nervous, and this particular motorway complex was always busy. Within minutes of the manager's SOS telephone call, the place was surrounded. Armed police and army commandoes wearing flak jackets and brandishing machine pistols burst onto the scene.

Within minutes the entire complex was cordoned off—this was the real deal. By the time the commandoes were convinced they had any potential threat covered, Doc had removed his own horn-rimmed glasses and was sitting in the team coach, a picture of middle-aged bliss. There can be no guarantee that he was not uncomfortable and that his guts weren't churning, but Dave McErlane was a survivor. The leader of the action squad was leading the restaurant manager, the man who rang for help, through the team bus.

'A grey-haired man with horn-rimmed glasses, you say?'

'Yes.'

At that, the leader stopped at the seat occupied by our team assistant manager Fred Bennett. Grey hair, horn-rimmed glasses. Fred was frog-marched off the bus to the accompaniment of some light-hearted barracking from the boys. Ray Steele, the man who was sitting alone with the bulging suitcase, negotiated a 'deal' with the action team leader. Good thing the bloke liked cricket. Twenty-five autographed sheets went the way of the commandoes along with a profusion of apologies. Steele proved a master of diplomacy. He talked the action team leader around, but he didn't mind the leader giving us all a bit of a dressing down. The words 'irresponsible' and 'a night in jail' spring to mind. In hindsight, of course, there can never be any fun when you are talking about terrorism and the loss of innocent lives.

'We learnt right then and there that it was high time we stopped making jokes about bombs. "The Doc" owned up to police,' Chappelli recalled.[7]

The action team leader graciously accepted, but we could all see that he and his men were suitably pissed off with the Aussie cricket team. In 1972 terrorism of the IRA kind was a constant threat and had been long before Ian Chappell's men had landed at Heathrow. Little wonder the manager rang the riot squad when Doc made his ill-timed joke. We escaped jail, but not a defeat at the hands of Sussex.

Chappell declared our second innings closed at 2/262 with Stackpole unbeaten on 154 and Walters on 42. Doug got 58 in the first innings. Sussex then got the required runs to beat Australia for the first time since 1888.

During the tour we had been invited along to the Anglo-American Association for a boxing match-cum-banquet at the London Hilton Hotel. As we sipped and supped at that lavish table, we watched a huge Scotsman unmercifully thrash a little Englishman in the ring which had been set up in the middle of the room. It reminded us of the Second Test at Lord's when Bob Massie's 16 wickets tore the heart out of our English opposition. I sat near to one of the guest speakers, a man named Clement Freud. He was the proud grandson of Sigmund Freud, the famous psychologist who had some interesting theories on human sexual activity.

We learnt that Clement Freud disliked smoke as much as he loathed Australians. Freud had parachuted into Germany at the height of an Allied bombing raid. He was badly shocked and burnt by exploding shells as he floated down to earth and therefore hated smoke and detested anyone smoking.

This night Freud made the great mistake of getting stuck into the Australians. He talked of how our team had 'chips on their shoulders...' and the theme of his talk was generally degrading to all things Australian. We were most unimpressed. When we discovered Freud's aversion to smoke, I called upon the assistance of that master smoker, Doug Walters, and Paul Sheahan, whom I had noticed had just lit up a huge cigar. Freddie got on one side of Clement and Timbers on the other. Combined they blew a blanket of smoke over our table and Freud stood, staggered and fell backwards near the stage. Then he cleared out and could not be pacified until an official assured him the smoking team had left his table.

We left the London Hilton Hotel at midnight and drove to a record studio where we recorded that great hit song, 'Here Come the Aussies'. British pop singer Daniel Boone, who had an international hit with 'Beautiful Sunday', co-wrote 'Here Come the Aussies', which reached the Top 40. We also recorded the flip-side special, 'Bowl a Ball, Swing a Bat', the lyrics of which were supplied by a professional song-writer. Mercifully, the lyrics were not the work of our Messrs Edwards, Chappell and Sheahan, who collaborated to pen a naughty team sing-along entitled 'The Rain Is Pissing Down on Me'. We drank beer and sang for some three hours until 'Here Come the Aussies' was successfully put right.

The song got more airplay than Freddie got runs in the Test matches and was the number one popular song in Perth for a whole week. We made the record for Penny Farthing Records, appropriate for this international sporting team which played Test cricket for peanuts.

chapter ten
the
ECSTASY

Chappelli was calm, but he indicated that I should take up the third man position. And for the rest of the session until the drinks break he ran me from third man to fine leg. As the players gathered around to grab a drink, Chappelli spoke to me. 'That won't happen again, will it Doug?'

Back in Australia after his horror tour of England, Doug did as he always did regardless of his form, he looked forward to the new summer. But the new season didn't start brilliantly for him. Far too soon the critics were calling for his head after a string of early-season batting failures. Doug scored a duck against Queensland in Brisbane; six and 106 against Western Australia in Perth, after being dropped before he scored in the second innings; 14 and 0 against

South Australia in Adelaide and a duck and 10 against South Australia in the return match in Sydney. Then came the NSW second innings against Western Australia at the SCG. Doug hit a brilliant 159, belting Lillee and Bob Massie into submission to hand New South Wales a four-wicket victory over the Sheffield Shield holders.

Cricket writer Phil Wilkins wrote of Freddie's innings:

> Once a champion, always a champion—Doug Walters demonstrated it to a host of disbelievers as NSW beat the Sheffield Shield holders, Western Australia, by four wickets at the SCG yesterday.
>
> Walters was master of ceremonies in an innings of 159 as NSW made 6–325 in the fourth innings to erase the season's memories of pitiful collapses and his team's succession of three outright defeats. 'I told you anything could happen while the little bloke was out there,' NSW triumphant captain Brian Taber said amid a welter of champagne bottles in the team's dressing-room after the game. Walters, composed, sat back with a beer and the ever-present cigarette, and agreed without feeling that now he would be everybody's darling.[1]

Doug's 159 against Western Australia silenced his critics and put him right back in the frame to be recalled to the Australian team. The first two Test matches against Pakistan saw Australia win easily, with Rod Marsh becoming the first Australian Test keeper to hit a century in a Test match in the First Test in Adelaide. I got 8/59 in the second Pakistan innings in Adelaide, which turned out to be the best innings bowling analysis by any Test bowler at the Adelaide Oval in the twentieth century, but Freddie wasn't there to see it. He was busy getting 133 versus Victoria in Melbourne.

We were again without Freddie when we played the Second Test at the MCG, where Jeff Thomson on debut won a remarkable game despite Pakistan declaring its first innings closed at 8/574. Doug was busy elsewhere, scoring 43 and 176 for New South Wales in a return game with Victoria at the SCG.

He was now ready for a Test return.

Before the Third Test Paul Sheahan and I were dropped, because we both had opted out of the West Indies tour, which was only a couple of months away. Sheahan was a teacher and he was hell-bent on building his teaching career. There was no money in cricket, so his academic career had to pay the way. I was just getting into journalism and I had a chance to get on a local newspaper, rather than stay selling advertisements. In retrospect I should have gone because a 25-wickets-plus series would have really gone down a treat. Doug was still working for Rothmans. Ian Chappell was working with another cigarette company, WD & HO Wills; Greg Chappell worked for Coca-Cola; Bob Massie was in the Commonwealth Bank, so too Dennis Lillee; and Rod Marsh was a school teacher, but he later turned to promotion for the Swan Brewery. Not everyone got paid while they were away. It was usually leave without pay. Doug was among the lucky ones in the Australian team and he was paid during his absences, thus his eagerness to please his bosses by seemingly always having a packet of Rothmans within camera range. Ian Chappell wanted Walters and he got his man. Freddie was picked for the final Test match against Pakistan at the SCG. NSW batsman John Benaud, who had scored 24 in his Test debut in Adelaide and 13 and 142 in the Second Test at the MCG, was dropped.

The selectors went for the tangle-footed Victorian medium-pacer Max Walker to replace Jeff Thomson, whose 0/110 wasn't an ideal start to his international career, though we soon learnt that the bloke had played the match with a broken bone in his left foot.

NSW leg-spinner John Watkins came into the side to replace me because I was unavailable for the Windies tour and the Test selectors wanted to take a look at the mettle of Watkins.

The Third Test was very much the great escape for Chappell's team, the second match on the trot where the odds were on a Pakistan victory.

Thanks to a last wicket stand of 83 by Watkins (36) and Bob Massie (42), in the Australian second innings, Chappelli's men were able to set the visitors a bit of a score to chase. Dennis Lillee bowled his heart out for 23 overs straight for a return of 3/68 and Walker took an amazing 6/15 off 16 overs. Our actor mate Ed Devereaux, who spent many enjoyable hours drinking with us at the Waldorf Hotel bar in London, sent Chappelli a telegram.

It was simple, to the point: 'MAX WAX PAX'.

Freddie was back on the big stage, but at the SCG in the Third Test he was very much a bit player. Freddie scored only 19 and 5, but Chappelli wanted him for the important tour of the Caribbean. He was fully aware of Doug's genius on slow, turning pitches. And he was due to get some Test runs.

NSW leg-spinner John Watkins hailed from Newcastle, where his family ran a green-grocery. John, or 'Wok', as he became known, bordered on the naïve. His first over in Test cricket—the only Test he ever played—versus Pakistan at the SCG in January 1973 threatened to go for hours had Umpire Tom Brooks not been inclined to let half a dozen very wide balls go through down leg-side to a diving Rodney Marsh without calling them wides.

We took off from Sydney bound for the West Indies in the early evening, about 6 p.m. There was the usual pre-tour excitement, the gathering of family and press before we boarded the aircraft and, after the plane levelled out, we decided upon a few drinks and a game of cards. About five hours

after take-off, Johnny 'Wok' Watkins turned to me and said, 'Well, Freddie.
I'm ready for bed ... when do we get into our pyjamas?'

The Australian Test cricketers in that time could be a bit hard on a naïve bloke. You either sank or swam. In Wok's case he probably sank. In one early match, Wok was observed by the players who were standing in the bar at the ground after play, enjoying a few well-earnt Red Stripe beers. He was dashing about the oval after play, running lap after lap. Freddie and the lads were a little amused by Wok's show of enthusiasm. After Wok had showered and joined the team at the bar, Doug had a quiet word.

'Now, Wok. What was that all about ... running laps after play?'
'Well, Freddie. I want to be fit enough to continue bowling at my best after twenty-odd overs.'
'Wok, have you considered that the most important thing is to be skillful enough to GET twenty overs in the first place? And another thing. I noticed your action in running. You were pumping your arms up and down and some of the more radical locals might think that you are taking the piss out of the black power sign. You'll have to appease them somehow.'
'How do I do that, Freddie?'
'I think things could be worked out in about a week during this match. May I suggest that you leave a carton of Rothmans cigarettes outside your hotel room every night after 10 p.m. Oh, and you'd better also leave a carton of Benson & Hedges outside with the Rothmans. Wouldn't do to upset any of them that prefer another brand.'

Trouble is Wok didn't quite cotton on.

Doug began the Caribbean tour with a solid 38 in a light-hearted 40-over match against the University of the West Indies at Mona Campus, Kingston on 1 February 1973. Watkins and Max Walker took two wickets apiece. The first important match was against Jamaica at Sabina Park.

Doug fell for 5 in the first innings and had to settle for a quiet game of cards, cups of tea and a truckload of cigarettes while Greg Chappell (106), Ross Edwards (44) and Rodney Marsh (45) made merry run-making in the sun. But in the second innings, Doug steered Australia home by five wickets with a good knock of 64 not out. It was a vital innings for Freddie in the eyes of his skipper.

> The most heartening of all the performances in the second innings was that of Doug Walters. Doug went in at a critical stage. With Keith Stackpole batting down the list because of a stomach upset the situation was quite tense, but Walters rose to the occasion and played a very disciplined and pleasing knock as far as the Australian selectors were concerned.[2]

In the First Test at Sabina Park, Jamaica, Australia declared at 7/428, with Freddie hitting a solid 72. Rod Marsh hit his wicket in trying to hook a bouncer off Uton Dowe, the fast bowler. Keith Stackpole had butchered the bowling of Dowe and the fast man's first six overs cost some 60 runs. Light relief came from a wag in the crowd.

> As soon as the crowd saw the West Indian captain Rohan Kanhai throw Dowe the ball and they recognised the big man measuring out his run-up, a bloke in the crowd yelled out, 'Hey, Kanhai. Have you not heard of the Eleventh Commandment—DOWE SHALT NOT BOWL!'

In the lead-up match to the Second Test, against a Youth Eleven, Doug hit a whirlwind 81 and an unbeaten 102 in a 193-run unbeaten stand for the third wicket before his partner, Ian Chappell

(106 not out) declared. Doug also chimed in with 4/9 in the Youth Eleven's second innings.

But the match was drawn.

The vital Third Test was played at Queen's Park Oval, Port-of-Spain, Trinidad, on a wicket that traditionally favoured spin bowling. Australia batted first. Ian Chappell had turned his ankle playing tennis a day just before the game and Greg Chappell batted three, Walters, four. Ian Redpath scored 66 and Greg Chappell 56 after a disastrous start when Stackpole smashed a Keith Boyce short ball straight to Maurice Foster at square leg and Australia was one for none. Straight after lunch on that first day Doug Walters produced another innings of pure genius, belting a glorious 112. Ian Chappell believes it was the best innings he had ever seen in a Test match on a turning wicket.

Doug walked out to bat at Queens Park Oval and hit the first ball from Lance Gibbs through the covers for four. I believe the drive through the covers against an off-spinner on a turning pitch is one of the most difficult shots in the game. There was a spot on the pitch—very powdery stuff—outside off stump on a perfect length for Gibbs, but that didn't deter Doug. Greg Chappell had just fallen to Gibbs a couple of balls before lunch. Doug tucked into curried goat and immediately after lunch he proceeded to take the West Indians apart. At one stage Gibbs had six men on the on-side and only three on the off. Doug belted a Gibbs delivery over mid-wicket, one bounce into the advertising hoardings, so Gibbs took the man from point and placed him on the mid-wicket boundary. It was a seven–two field. The next ball landed in an identical spot to the one Doug hit over mid-wicket, only this time, he backed away and cut it past point to the boundary. The frustrated bowler waved the man from mid-wicket to point and the next ball was round the same spot. And Doug proceeded to hit Gibbs over mid-wicket for four. Gibbs shrugged his shoulders, threw up his hands and walked away, a disillusioned man. Doug went from nil to 102 in that session: the finest innings I've seen on a pitch taking turn.[3]

There was more than a little of the Bradman killer instinct in Walters' batting. I have seen glimpses of it when bowling to him and certainly it was there against the World Eleven at the MCG in 1971, again at Queens Park Oval on 23 March 1973.

Doug sometimes targeted a bowler. He'd go after him and take twenty or so quick runs off a bowler, just as a Sobers or a Richards or a Graeme Pollock would do.[4]

Phil Wilkins in the Sydney Sunday newspaper, *The Sun-Herald*, lauded the Walters' knock:

PORT-OF-SPAIN (Trinidad) Saturday—The magic of Doug Walters returned with a rush yesterday—to the delight of a record crowd of drum-beating, whistling Trinidadians.

The 30,000 spectators greeted every incident in the tension-packed first day of the Third Test with shouts and whistles, and many danced in the dust of the outer as Walters carved out a memorable 112 in 148 minutes, putting Australia in the happy position of 6–308 at stumps. When his swashbuckling innings ended, he had hit 16 fours, a six and much of the venom from the West Indies attack.[5]

Thanks to Doug's brilliant 112 and Ian Chappell's gutsy 97 in the second innings, Australia won the Test match by 44 runs.

While his team-mates raved about Doug's first-innings knock, he has never put that innings at the top of his career list.

Chappelli has always said that was a special innings. You know the West Indies didn't have anyone very quick in that game and although the ball was turning at right-angles I didn't think it was too bad a wicket to bat on. I don't rate that hundred at Trinidad as highly as I do a few others, especially the one at Perth a year or so later.

Doug had his highs throughout the Caribbean tour ... He also had the odd low point.

During one of the Tests Terry Jenner and I went to the Rothmans Ball. It was the night before the last day of the Test and we made sure we'd be up in the morning by booking an early morning call and breakfast. Terry had a bloke picking him up very early that day to take him shopping before the game. I was awake when Terry left, but then rolled over and went back to sleep. The early morning call didn't come and breakfast didn't arrive. Terry phoned me from the ground at 10.40 a.m. The hotel was some twelve kilometres from the Test venue and I had about twenty minutes to get there. I dressed in double quick time and grabbed a cab. I told the driver to hightail it to the ground, telling him I was an Australian player and was running very late.

That morning I experienced first hand what it must have been like making those mad-cap Keystone Cops movies. Cars were queued up for miles back from the ground's entrance, so my cab driver immediately took to the footpath, scattering pedestrians all over the place. By the time I got there the players were on the field. By the time I had dressed and went down to the gate, they had bowled a couple of overs. I couldn't attract anyone's attention in the break between overs, so they bowled another one before I walked on. I've never felt such an idiot as I waited to go on. Chappelli wasn't overly impressed. He didn't say much other than, 'Down there, you,' as he sent me from fine leg to third man for the rest of the session. As we came off for lunch, he said. 'It won't happen again, will it Doug?'

'I hope it doesn't happen again, Ian. But I can't guarantee it.'

During the time he served as a boundary rider that day, Freddie noticed a bicycle leaning up against the fence at third man and for some time he was of a mind to hop on the bike and ride across the ground and down to fine leg at the opposite side of the oval.

While that thought definitely crossed my mind and it might have been a hoot for the crowd, I thought I might have pushed my luck a bit far already.

The Fourth Test in Georgetown, Guyana, begun on 6 April 1973. On the first morning of the match, Freddie surprised everyone in the Australian dressing-room when he downed his cup of tea, stubbed out his cigarette, stretched his arms in an upward movement and said: 'Ah, well I think I will get warmed up for the battle.'

The players all knew that Freddie simply didn't warm up on the morning of a match. He didn't go to the nets or even pick up a bat and play a shadow drive. All eyes were on the little batting maestro. He strolled over to the dart board hanging by a single nail on the wall, plucked a dart and moved back to the mark whereupon he fired a dart at the board. 'That's better . . . I'm ready to go now.' No-one remembers where the dart struck, all they do vividly recall is what happened next.

The West Indians batted first and they compiled a significant 366 in their first innings. Clive Lloyd played a magnificent innings of 178, but even before Lloyd's onslaught the opening partnership of Roy Fredericks and Gordon Greenidge was looking threatening. Jeff Hammond and Max Walker had both bowled well, but it was Doug Walters who made the breakthrough. His 'warm-up' worked. He had Fredericks caught at slip by Ian Chappell, then he clean-bowled Greenidge. Freddie finished with a career-best 5/66 off 18.2 overs.

> *And I have to say I must put that performance down to my warm-up in the dressing-room.*

Australia replied with 341, Doug hitting a brilliant 81, then the West Indians collapsed in their second innings to be bowled out for 109. Hammond (4/38) and Waler (4/45) were the stars, but Freddie also chimed in with a share of the spoils, getting 2/23 off 13 overs. Thanks to a brilliant, unconquered opening stand of 135 by Stackpole (76 not out) and Ian Redpath (57 not out), Australia romped home by ten wickets.

The Fifth Test at Queens Park Oval, Port-of-Spain, Trinidad, was drawn. Doug got 70 in Australia's first innings of 419. And he scored 27 in the second innings. Chappelli's men won the series two–nil and much of that victory went to Walters' amazing ability to bring his genius to the fore when it counted. Lion-hearted Max Walker grabbed 26 wickets on the sluggish wickets and Jeff Hammond performed well, as did—at times—the spinners in Kerry O'Keeffe and Terry Jenner. Ian Chappell enhanced his standing as an outstanding captain and the likes of Keith Stackpole, Greg Chappell, Ross Edwards and Ian Redpath were all good contributors. Rodney Marsh kept splendidly and his batting, at times, was crucial to the cause. Back trouble to Dennis Lillee was a real dampener and Lillee would face a long stint of rehabilitation after a back operation to fix some hairline fractures before he could once again bowl in the Test match arena.

For Freddie, life was good. He enjoyed himself on the tour of the Caribbean, whether in the middle belting the hell out of the West Indian attack, playing cards, fishing, or breasting the bar enjoying a quiet drink. That's where Freddie is in his element, having a drink and socialising with his mates.

Doug leapt back into favour with his stunning tour of the Caribbean. It wasn't just the volume of runs he scored, but the manner in which he flayed the opposition. Doug led the tour averages with 834 runs in ten matches at an average of 69.5, just pipping Greg Chappell who scored 110 runs at an average of 69.3. In the Tests, Doug scored 497 runs at an average of 71.00. When he returned home NSW cricket did a back-flip and he was again offered the State captaincy for the 1973–74 season.

It was a hugely popular move with NSW fans. Here is a typical congratulatory telegram Freddie received:

Telegram 28 AUGUST 1973, Guildford, NSW
MR D WALTERS
C/O ROTHMANS
STRAITS AVE
SOUTH GRANVILLE NSW
(GUILDFORD)
CONGRATULATIONS ON YOUR APPOINTMENT
AS CAPTAIN OF NSW SHEFFIELD SHIELD SIDE
STOP LOOKS LIKE 1973–74 HAS PROSPECTS OF
BEING YOUR BEST SEASON EVER
HAROLD GOODWIN

The newly installed NSW captain began the summer of 1973–74 in fine style, hitting 67 and 59 in the first Shield match in Brisbane and 24 and 110 against Western Australia in Perth. Boy did Freddie love playing against Western Australia. He stumbled against South Australia in Adelaide with 1 and 8, then 30 and 19 not out against South Australia in the return match in Sydney. Then came Western Australia again in Sydney and Freddie hit a first-innings 114.

His sparkling form prompted a young fan to pen these words:

MY HERO
DOUG WALTERS

Out to the field the great Walters strides,
Bat in one hand and ready to ride
Ride on his bat, smash the poor ball,
Flying, flying, over the wall.
Cheers are so loud and long,
As nothing he does is ever wrong,
How's that he crys [sic] as he bowls the ball,
He always makes the wickets fall.
Walters, Walters, they chant.
Let him bowl, bat, rave and rant,
Ah here he comes the great wonder one,
He lets the crowd have all the fun.
Kerrie Sharpe

It was in this summer of 1973–74 that Sir Donald Bradman instigated a change in the name of the Board. From the Australian Board of Control for International Cricket, it became The Australian Cricket Board. The word 'control' had some damning connotations about it.

Since the Board's formation in 1905, the Board assumed 'control' over the players, which, by the time Doug Walters began playing Test cricket, had assumed ridiculous proportions, such as the wives having to travel and live separately on any overseas tour. Perhaps Bradman sensed revolution in the air in the wake of the tour to

India in 1969–70 and the players refusing to play a Fifth Test match in South Africa at the end of that gruelling six-month excursion.

The next summer would be a historic one, for Australia had finally relented to allow Test matches between Australia and New Zealand to resume. The only Test ever played before 1973–74 was in Wellington in 1945–46 when Bill Brown's team thrashed the Kiwis in two days by an innings and 103 runs. It proved to be Bill O'Reilly's last match. After taking 3/19 off seven overs in the second dig, following his 5/14 off 12 overs in the first, the Tiger ripped off his boots and hurled them through the open dressing-room window.

'That's it, I'm done,' he said, his wobbly knee had finally given in after a 27-match Test career that yielded 144 wickets at an average of 22.59 and a Test best innings bowling performance of 7/54 versus South Africa in 1935–36.

Doug continued his good form into the First Test against New Zealand at the MCG. He scored 79 out of Australia's 462 for eight declared. Keith Stackpole got 122, Ian Chappell 54 and Greg Chappell 60. It was NSW all-rounder Gary 'Gus' Gilmour's debut Test match and he bowled beautifully in the NZ first innings, taking 4/75 off 22 overs and he belted a quick-fire 52 coming in at number nine. New Zealand scored only 237 in its first innings and were bowled out for 200 in the second. Doug (3/26 off 13 overs) and I (4/63 off 24 overs) enjoyed bowling in tandem. The Second Test played in Sydney saw New Zealand outplay us to a large extent. Batting first the Kiwis scored 312, then, thanks to the young tearaway Richard Hadlee, who took 4/33, Australia was bowled out for a paltry 162, with Walters getting 41 and Ian Chappell 45.

Batting again, New Zealand hit 305 for nine wickets declared, leaving Chappelli's men with a massive 456-run victory chase in little more than a day's play. At stumps on day four, we were 2/30 and looking down the barrel. Stackpole and Ian Chappell were out cheaply, both lbw to Richard Hadlee and Paul Sheahan (14 not out) and Greg Chappell (8 not out) were the overnight batsmen. I was staying with my uncle, Bill West, who lived in Castle Cove. He loaned me his car and I had instructions to keep to the left lane on the Cahill Expressway lest I end up in the centre of town and miss the start of the match. So I ensured that wouldn't happen by taking off very early.

When I got to the ground I got the shock of my life, for there in the dressing-room helping himself to a cup of tea was none other than Kevin Douglas Walters.

'You're here early, Freddie. Looking for a bit of net practice, eh?'

'No, Rowd. I went to the Bridge Hotel last night for a meal and a drink and when it became too late to go home, I thought I'd get Caroline to drop me off at the cricket ground.'

Freddie was still dressed to the nines: resplendent in his dark suit and tie. He didn't look the worse for wear, but you could tell he had had a few drinks. He was the next man in. We'll never know whether Freddie could have turned in another great batting performance after a big night out. On that last scheduled day of the match the cricket gods ordained that New Zealand would have to wait a while for its first Test victory over Australia with a rain deluge which continued for the entire day. It was the weather that beat the Kiwis that day. And when the umpires—Max O'Connell and Peter Enright—finally called off the match, Freddie pulled the top off a coldie and his team-mates joined him.

We had played against the Kiwi left-arm spinner, David O'Sullivan in Melbourne. He had a bit of a jerky action, but no-one bothered about him. After all, his 23 overs at the MCG had cost 80 runs and he didn't get one off line let alone past the bat. Jack Collins, one of the umps for the Adelaide Third Test, approached Ian Chappell and said, 'We are concerned about the action of one of the New Zealanders ...'

'If you mean David O'Sullivan, Jack, don't call him. We want him to continue bowling,' Chappelli laughed.

O'Sullivan did keep bowling and ironically he took 5/148 off 35.5 overs and one of his 'bag' was Doug Walters, clean-bowled for 94. Six Test matches were to be played, three in Australia and three in New Zealand. In the lead-up to the New Zealand Tests we played a match on the spin-friendly Eden Park pitch in Auckland. The Auckland team had a useful batting line-up including Mark Burgess, who was also a superb cover fieldsman. Doug tells the story of the day I batted with Kerry O'Keeffe.

Our intrepid last man was Rowdy Mallett. He did a fine job keeping the bowlers at bay while O'Keeffe got to 99. Kerry struck what should have been a single, but Rowdy was busy practising his defensive shots and he didn't back up as well as he might and got run out, leaving Skull high and dry 99 not out. I don't think Kerry was terrible impressed.

That's Doug's version. When I went to the wicket, O'Keeffe was on 71. I sacrificed many singles to allow him to farm the strike and was very alert at the non-striker's end in the over in question. O'Keeffe, on 99, blocked three balls in a row. I sensed he was going to go for a suicide run. I called him down the track before the fourth ball was to be bowled and told Skull to be very wary of any silly singles and don't, 'whatever you do, run if you hit one to (Mark) Burgess at cover point.' The very next ball—the fourth one— Skull hit straight to Burgess and took off.

I was a bit slow off the blocks and dived, my bat got stuck in rough ground in front of the popping crease and thus failed to slide over the line. I had skinned my right elbow in the process of diving and to add insult to injury I had been given a run out. Skull was fuming. After a deathly silence in the dressing-room, Walters and Marsh led the laughter. The salve for Skull was a red-ink (not out).

The Wellington First Test was drawn after a runs-fest. Both Chappells scored a century in each innings and Greg Chappell hit 247 not out and 133, emulating Doug's double century, and a century in the Fifth Test against the West Indies at Sydney in 1968–69. Basin reserve was a huge ground in those days and the wind swept that wide expanse for every second of the game. Freddie missed the party, getting 32 and 8. Then it was on to Christchurch for the Second Test, where New Zealand finally beat Australia for the first time. Kiwi opener Glenn Turner hit a century in each innings to hand the hosts their first Test win over the baggy-green. There was a flair-up when Ian Chappell had a few verbals with Turner over a disputed umpiring decision. New Zealand batsman Brian Hasting hit a ball from me over mid-on. The ball clearly bounced in the field of play before it went over the fence, but Umpire Bob Montieth signalled a six, when he should have waved a four. Turner was at the non-striker's end and when he interrupted Chappelli's questioning of Umpire Montieth, who changed his signal from six to four, Ian gave Turner both barrels. Doug remembers the heated confrontation between Chappell and Turner.

The air turned blue with Chappelli telling Turner where to get off and Kiwi skipper Bevan Congdon told Ian after the day's play that Glenn Turner had demanded an apology. Ian's never been very good at apologising and he didn't even try on this occasion. He said whatever was said on the field was left on the field and that was the end of it. I didn't agree with Chappelli over this incident. I thought Chappelli was wrong and I felt he should have apologised to Turner.

Australia was hell-bent upon winning the Third Test match in Auckland. Water got under the covers and at one end of the Eden Park Test pitch there was a huge wet patch. Kiwi captain Bevan Congdon sent Australia in to bat and Stackpole was out first ball of the match, caught at slip off Richard Hadlee. Wickets tumbled until Doug Walters came to the crease and he played a wonderful knock. Doug was in the seventies when I came to the wicket at 9/191. I wanted to be there for him to get his hundred. Hadlee was bowling fast and moving the ball off the seam and I figured that if I upset him he might try to knock my block off rather than the stumps. As he was about to deliver, I pulled away from the wicket feigning that there were people moving behind it. I asked the umpire if the sightscreen could be moved a fraction to the right. Umpire Frank Gardiner stood upright and replied: 'I am sorry, but the sightscreen is fixed and cannot be moved. Can we get on with the game?'

It had the desired effect. Hadlee did try and decapitate me but I survived, long enough for Freddie to get his hundred. He scored an unbeaten 104 out of an Australian total of 221. Doug played brilliantly. He blasted the hell out of Hadlee. When he pitched up, Doug smashed through the covers or mid-off.

Whenever he strayed onto Walters' pads he was dispatched through mid-wicket and anything remotely short was mercilessly smacked square of the wicket, either past point or mid-wicket, by a cut or a pull. This was vintage Walters and of all the players I've seen on the Test stage perhaps only he could have played that well on such a wicket.

At the end of the day New Zealand was reeling at 8/80. Gus Gilmour had starred, taking four cheap wickets. Max Walker and I had grabbed a couple each.

Gus led us off the field. He had bowled beautifully and set us up for a Test win. Out of the shadows ran big Alan Davidson, the ex-champion all-rounder. Alan saw Gus as the new 'Davo' and he was probably something of a Davo protégé. Davo rushed up to Gus and wrapped his arms around him.

'Well done, Gus. Magnificent stuff. Do you know, Gary. If I had been bowling out there today . . . I would have bowled them out twice.'

Right throughout the tour Freddie kept an eye on just where Caroline was sitting in the grandstand. He'd count the crowd and note when Caroline moved to another spot in the stand. My wife, Christine, had accompanied Caroline on the tour and the girls stayed at a hotel or an apartment as close as they could to the team hotel wherever we were in New Zealand. Freddie knew the instant the girls arrived at the game . . . 'The girls have arrived. They are in row twenty-two of the Members' Stand.'

On the night following Freddie's brilliant century at Eden Park, Richie and Daphne Benaud were invited to join Caroline and Freddie, Christine and me for dinner. Daphne, Caroline and Chris cooked a lovely meal and in after-dinner conversation, Richie suggested that I bowl over the wicket to the right-handers, rather than go around.

'From around the wicket you are spinning in to hit the middle of the bat,' argued Richie.

'Well, I think I have a better chance of getting an lbw from around the wicket and I am going to stick to bowling around on this track,' I replied stubbornly.

Freddie found our debate very amusing.

Richie seemed far from impressed with Rowdy's stance on his bowling strategy. Anyway, next morning Rowdy was on straightaway, bowling to Glenn Turner. He immediately proceeded to bowl over the wicket to the New

Zealand opener and on the fourth ball Turner edged one onto his pad and Greg Chappell took the catch at short leg. Rowdy turned to the press box, where Richie sat, and gave him the thumbs up.

I am not sure Richie has ever forgiven me for that little episode, but, in my defence, I guess I eventually took his advice . . . and it worked.

Caroline and Chris were two cricketing wives thoroughly sick of the way the Australian team officials treated them. Our manager in New Zealand, Frank Bryant, was a good bloke, loved a beer and a chat, but he had been conditioned in the ways of the Board. Wives were on the outer. At Wellington, the girls snuck into the back area where the players were watching the game. They came in from the biting cold—windy Wellington really stood up to its name in that match. I recall Frank Bryant was sitting near me and he said quietly: 'I didn't notice those two women behind. As far as I am concerned they are not here . . .'

It was tough enough for an Australian cricketer in those days to try and hold down some sort of job, or get a company to agree to your having time off without pay, then be paid the pittance of a rank amateur and be expected to perform like an elite professional.

We duly won the Auckland Test match, Ian Redpath getting a grand unbeaten 159 in our second innings, putting the game beyond the Kiwis' reach. Australia drew that sector of the series one–all and in the overall six-Test rubber we won three and lost the Christchurch encounter.

A late tour highlight was Freddie scoring a remarkable century in a session against Northern Districts. The most extraordinary aspect of that knock was his running between the wickets, because Doug did not hit a single four. Ian Chappell has never forgotten Freddie's batting that day.

We were playing in Hamilton and I got a hundred before lunch. The field was up for a lot of that time. Doug hit a century in the final session with the field well-spread and he did it with fabulous running. He had to do a lot of running because he only hit one four. Doug had the ability to hit the ball at just the right speed to pick up twos where a ball hit harder would realise only one run. Michael Bevan and Steve Waugh were also good at doing that. Doug was terrific to have batting at number six because he could keep the scoreboard ticking over and bat really well with the tail.

Doug was a brilliant judge of a run and his running between wickets was exceptional.[6]

I have to refute Chappelli's claim that I hit one four. We did RUN a four, but I didn't actually hit a four in the entire innings. The grass was so long that it was almost impossible to hit the ball along the ground for a boundary.

Imagine. A hundred in a session of first-class cricket without one single boundary hit. That must be some sort of record in world cricket history.

I did a lot of running that day ... and worked up a healthy thirst.

Rodney Marsh believes he learnt a lot about the game of cricket from Doug Walters.

I was very close to Doug. He batted six, I batted seven. He liked a beer and a smoke, as I did in those days and he liked playing cards and he probably taught me how to play cards. Doug was always good company because of his sense of humour. He was a pretty simple bloke; he didn't expound too much on the state of the world or things like that, but he was always a man's man. I think he enjoys the company of men perhaps more than in mixed company. He's got a wonderful memory for humour. He'll store things up and bring it out many years later. In 1972, when Ian Chappell was in his first tour captaincy stint, he said to the Australian squad, 'I am happy for you blokes to come to my room anytime day and night, so long as it is before 3 o'clock in the morning.' Of course, first night, Freddie kept me up drinking with him until 2.59am and that's when we knocked on Chappelli's door. That was typical of Doug.[7]

chapter eleven
a TOUCH
of BRADMAN

How sweet the feel and the sound of my bat striking that short Willis delivery. It was one of those times when the bat hits the ball at precisely the right moment. I hit it right in the screws.

The ball sailed away, neatly bisecting the two guys at backward square and thudded over the boundary line.

Six! You bloody beauty!

With the New Zealand tour over, we now had the chance to play England in Australia and regain those elusive Ashes in 1974–75. Early in the new summer Freddie struggled for runs. He scored 10 in Brisbane, before getting clean-bowled by the latest fast-bowling sensation Jeff Thomson. Thommo played for New South

Wales in the last match of the summer against Queensland and he bowled like the wind, so that Queensland bent over backwards to get him to shift States. Freddie didn't last too long in the NSW second innings. Thommo bowled him all ends up for a duck. He took 4/65 and 2/7, helping Queensland to an easy outright victory. In that match, Martin Kent hit a debut 140 to immediately earn the sobriquet 'Super', derived from *Superman*. Against Western Australia at the SCG, the visitors smashed the NSW attack. Wally Edwards got 153, Bruce Laird, 117 and Rodney Marsh, 168. Doug scored 48 and 6 and NSW batsman Rick McCosker began a great run of scores with 138 and 136 not out in that drawn match. Against MCC (England) at the SCG Doug had a double failure (16 and 4), while McCosker hit 52 and 56 and then Doug failed again (11) against Victoria at the SCG, while McCosker hit 164.

At least Doug did well with the ball, taking 4/23 off 10 overs in the Victorian second innings. Freddie didn't consider he was a certainty for the First Test.

I felt a bit under pressure. I needed runs in the Test match and while I felt as though I was hitting the ball well in the nets I had to take that form into the middle.

Fellow NSW batsman Rick McCosker was striking the ball beautifully and had already passed 500 first-class runs when the First Test team was named. McCosker missed selection, but not so WA opening batsman Wally Edwards, who came into the eleven to replace Keith Stackpole who retired after his last Test pair in Auckland. Ian Chappell won the toss and batted.

Chappelli used a Gray Nicholls 'Scoop' bat first up and hit 90. Greg Chappell scored a confident 58, Ross Edwards 32, then there was a string of moderate to low scores, including Doug's contribution of 3, before he fell to the gangling Bob Willis. A flurry of strokes from Max Walker (41 not out) and Jeff Thomson (23) gave Australia a handy total of 309.

Ian Chappell had thoughts of opening the bowling with Dennis Lillee, who had fully recovered from his back ailment, and bringing Walker into it, but instinct took over from the skipper. He chucked the ball to Thommo, wished him luck, and then spent the next five minutes wondering how anyone on earth could bowl so fast into the wind.

'I watched in awe,' Chappelli says, 'He was the quickest into the wind bowler imaginable.'

Thommo's breakneck speed erased memories of his first Test effort against Pakistan two years before when he got 0/110 and played despite having a broken bone in his left foot. The Englishmen could not believe it. Jeff Thomson was a human catapult.

Here was a bowler that eased himself to the wicket with a casual sort of shuffling gait and then let fly. Perfectly side-on at delivery, Thommo had the ball in his hand only inches from the ground as he leaned back ready to transfer his weight to the front foot. Thommo—surely the fastest bowler to draw breath—was a sight to behold in full flight. He took 3/51 off 21 terrifying overs in the first innings. While all the talk was Thommo, Doug felt as much under the pump as he had ever been.

This may well have been the most nervous I had been leading up to an important innings. I had failed in the first dig and there was little decent form coming into the game. I simply had to fire.

And fire he surely did, hitting a delightful cameo of 62 not out. Rodney Marsh (46 not out) helped Freddie carry the team to 288 for five down before Chappelli declared. He could then unleash Lillee and Thomson to wreak havoc on the hapless Poms.

Thommo gave Australia 17.5 overs of pure, unadulterated pace in the second innings, taking 6/46. When he clean-bowled Tony Greig for 2 in the England second dig, the crowd went berserk. It was the famous 'sandshoe-crusher', his first yorker that Thommo used to break toes and shatter stumps.

Australia was one up and on the way to winning back the Ashes.

By the second Test match of the 1974–75 summer all cricket lovers knew that every now and again Doug Walters could throw us a glimpse of his batting genius. Australia also had the two most fearsome pace bowlers in world cricket—Dennis Lillee and Jeff Thomson—about to be set loose upon the Poms on the fast and true WACA wicket in Perth. Hand injuries to Dennis Amiss and John Edrich in the Brisbane Test resulted in the England selectors calling for dear old Colin Cowdrey, who was, no doubt, at the very time they decided to call him up, sitting by a roasting fire in his Kentish home in Canterbury enjoying a buttered crumpet and a piping hot cup of tea. The rotund and ageing Cowdrey made the rushed trip to Perth. He was then pushing the age of 42.

The hard-and-fast Perth track was very much a death-trap for the faint-hearted. England batted first, and while the likes of David Lloyd ducked and dived and froze before the fearsome attack of Thomson and Lillee, when Cowdrey waddled to the crease he stood proud and tall.

After copping a pounding in one over from Thommo, Cowdrey was struck a number of telling blows to the chest and right forearm; the plucky England batsman wandered down the pitch at the end of the Thomson over and approached the fast man.

Cowdrey put out his hand and said, 'Hello, Jeff. My name is Colin Cowdrey. So nice to meet you.' Thommo was a bit non-plussed, so too the nervy David Lloyd who found Cowdrey coming up his end after another Thomson barrage and saying, 'I say, David. This is all rather fun, isn't it?'

You couldn't help but admire Colin [Cowdrey]. He made only 22 and 41 but he batted at number three and took the full brunt of Lillee and Thommo at their fiercest. I reckon he finished that Test with as many bruises as runs.

Freddie chimed in with 2/13 off his 2.3 overs to help our attack rout the England team for 208. Cowdrey got 22, going too far across to cover Thomson and lost his leg stump. Lloyd played bravely after having a Thomson delivery smash his little pink protector, which split, causing him no end of discomfort. Lloyd often regales the agony of that time when 'everything that should have been inside the box had found its way through holes and was trapped on the outside'.

Lloyd got to 49 before he snicked Thommo to Greg Chappell, at second slip, the first of a record seven catches Greg would take in the match. The first ball Doug Walters faced in Test cricket was from little Fred Titmus, the Middlesex and England all-rounder, who suffered a nasty accident in the Caribbean a couple of years before this Perth Test. Titmus lost a couple of toes in a boating accident when his foot got accidentally tangled in the boat's propeller. Fortunately the big toe of his right foot survived and it is the big toe that maintains a person's balance. When Titmus reached the crease at the fall of the sixth wicket with England in dire straits having scored 132 runs, Doug broke into song, a take on Leo Sayer's 'Long Tall Glasses (I can dance)':

You know I can't dance . . . you know I can't dance . . .

You needed dancing feet to evade the missiles from Thommo and Lillee. One ball from Thomson took off from just short of a driving length, cleared Marsh's head by a mile and hit the bottom of the sightscreen at the Members' End on the full pitch. Freddie had

Titmus caught by Ian Redpath for 10 and only the pluck of keeper Alan Knott (51) helped England to limp past 200. The Australian first innings began steadily, with Ian Redpath (41) and Wally Edwards (30) getting Chappelli's men off to a fair start, then Ian Chappell fell for 25 and Greg Chappell and Ross Edwards put on 79 for the fourth wicket before Chappell fell to a lazy shot off Bob Willis, caught in the slips cordon by Tony Greig for 62. It was only a few minutes before the tea break, but Doug walked out as he always did, seemingly totally at one with the world, with not a care. He was the epitome of calmness. Viv Richards would say, 'Here's one cool dude.'

As the incoming Walters passed the outgoing batsman Greg Chappell on his way off, Greg said: 'This time I've given you a bit of a sighter,' a reference to what happened at Queen's Park, Port-of-Spain, Trinidad, in 1973 when Greg had fallen to Lance Gibbs right on lunch. Doug was 3 not out at tea. The Perth wicket was not a raging turner as he experienced in Trinidad, where he had played an extraordinary, Bradman-like innings, but it was a hard-and-fast track, which also provided the pace-men, such as Willis and Chris Old, with lots of bounce. There was good carry through to the wicketkeeper, but, however quick the wicket was, the bounce was even and true, unlike the wickets in Adelaide and Melbourne when even on the first day the bounce can be variable.

Right from the start I middled the ball and felt in total control. I'd look about the field and visualise the gaps, then I found myself placing the ball almost to perfection. Round the time I was in the 60s I thought I had a realistic chance of scoring a hundred in a session. I was seeing the ball that well. I felt so good, so confident that I believed I could make somewhere in the vicinity of 130 in the session. I was on three at the resumption after tea and in the 60s when drinks were taken.

Australian captain Ian Chappell thought the way Doug was hitting the ball reminded him of his sensational knock in the Trinidad Test a couple of summers back, and that he had a real chance of doing it again. At drinks Chappelli said to twelfth man, Terry Jenner: 'Check with the little fella and see what his chances are.'

When Terry handed Doug a drink, he asked, 'How's it going?' 'I think I've got a chance.'

That was the extent of the conversation. Doug knew exactly what those in the dressing-room were thinking. How could they have known that he was a little frustrated in the middle? There he was in the midst of the best batting form of his career, in with a real chance of 'doing a Bradman' for the second time with a coveted Test century in a session, only to have Rosco at the other end unintentionally stealing the strike.

Ross Edwards was trying to give me most of the strike, but the more he tried, the more he grabbed the strike for himself. A century in a session was very much on my mind. My form was too good to miss this chance. I felt as though I played only one false shot in the entire knock, and that was in the last over when I was on 93. I needed 10 runs to complete the hundred in a session, so if Willis was going to bounce me I was going for the hook. I hooked at the first bouncer and got a glove, the ball careering over Alan Knott's head for four. It was the only ball I played in that session which missed the middle of my bat. I guess I was feeling like Don Bradman must have felt when he played that great innings at Lord's in 1930.

In that match, Bradman strode to the crease with the score at 162. Bill Ponsford (81) was out and Bill Woodfull, who went on to hit 155, welcomed the young Bradman to the crease.

In that game, the Second Test match of the tour, traditionally held at Lord's, Ponsford fell immediately after play was stopped briefly for the teams lined up in front of the Lord's Pavilion to meet King George V. Bradman went on to score 254 out of 423 runs made while he was at the wicket...

Every ball I faced in that innings I played exactly as I wanted. It was the nearest thing I had ever come to batting perfection. Even the ball Percy Chapman stood on his ear to catch me off (Jack) White at cover I had hit sweetly and it was only an inch or so off the ground.[1]

Doug had one over in which to forge his name indelibly in the record book, a second Test match hundred in a session.

I had six balls to go to score ten runs. Willis had been bowling two to three bouncers an over, so I would be looking for more of them. I decided to be looking to get on to the back foot, looking for a pull or a cut. Willis' deliveries three, four, five, six and seven (eight ball overs in those days) were well up and on the stumps. There was no joy for me there.

At the other end, Ross Edwards was almost beside himself with anger and frustration.

As we approached stumps, Doug's positive attitude and stroke-play didn't decrease. In fact, if anything, he got increasingly flamboyant. At this stage it occurred to me that a touch of discretion was called for considering the state of the match. So I engaged Doug in conversation, sagely and sensibly pointing out the logic of batting out the final over, so as to be not out at stumps, regrouping the following morning and burying the Poms next day, thus putting the match out of their grasp.

I also pointed out the certainty of Willis bowling short balls and bouncers, which had caused Doug some difficulty on previous occasions. Doug nodded slowly, apparently absorbing this patently obvious wisdom and he ambled back to take strike at the Pavilion End.

So much for logic and wisdom. Along came the (inevitable) short ball which he tried to hook.

Doug reached up, jumped and slashed at it, got a top edge and it just beat the leaping keeper's gloves and raced to the boundary for four. For a number of balls I had been walking down the wicket, swearing at him. I had virtually given up trying to talk sense into him. I ended up yelling out, swearing, calling him an idiot.[2]

Thankfully, Doug Walters, at the other end, was completely oblivious to Rosco's pleas for restraint. Ross Edwards was an accountant. He thought logically and clinically, but like most accountants, he figured that a successful outcome could only be achieved by a careful and pragmatic approach. Edwards was promoting the strategy of playing each ball on its merits. Nothing silly. But it focused on surviving to fight another day. Doug's thoughts were the complete opposite.

I had one ball to do this thing. It had to go for six for me to get to 103, and get exactly 100 in the session. I decided that I would give it everything on that last ball. Chances were Willis would drop short. I figured that he'd do that in the hope that I would play a rash hook and get a top-edge. And I was keen to take the bait. I was hitting the ball so well and seeing it so early I reckoned that I could do it.

Back in the Australian dressing-room, the players were having little side bets. We all thought as one. If any mortal in cricket history could do the seeming impossible, to hit the last ball of a day's play for six to notch a hundred in a Test match session, it was Kevin Douglas Walters. Somehow, we all thought, Freddie would find a way.

Willis was about to turn at the top of his bowling mark. What was going through Willis' mind? Would he pitch the ball short and try me out and would I be game enough to hook and risk holing out to either of the two men stationed on the backward square boundary?

Bob Willis had already decided to bounce Doug on that last ball.

Dumb fast bowlers can't help themselves. In 1970–71 we got Dougie on a number of occasions with the short ball, either caught pulling or at third man. The one earlier in the over which just cleared Knotty's head could have gone anywhere and, yes, I was going to bounce him on that last ball. When the popcorn's boiling in a heated fast-bowler's mind they, we, simply go berserk. I believed he would go for it, and let him have it and did he respond...[3]

Willis charged in with his bustling approach, arms and legs flailing; his fuzzy hair dancing in the wind as if chased by the Fremantle Doctor.

Willis dropped short alright and I was already in position to pull the ball. How sweet the feel and the sound of my bat striking that short Willis delivery. It was one of those times when the bat hits the ball at precisely the right moment. I hit it right in the screws. The ball sailed away, neatly bisecting the two guys at backward square and thudded over the boundary line.
Six!
You bloody beauty.

It was a brilliant shot. I guess one of the great individual strokes in Test cricket, given the circumstance. One other stands in my memory, when Steve Waugh hit Richard Dawson for four to bring up his hundred off the last ball at the SCG in 2003–4. But Dougie's shot was fantastic. Remarkable stroke and what a fabulous bloke.[4]

In the Australian dressing-room there was a sort of stunned silence.

While we had witnessed this freakish cricket first hand there was a surreal feeling to it. You had to pinch yourself to believe what you just saw. We all knew that Freddie had the temperament and skill to do what he had just done, but to execute such a stroke on the last ball of the day to bring up an extraordinary milestone was little short of a miracle. He struck the ball with amazing force, the ball took off like a jumbo jet and I swear it didn't get above 3 metres at any time in its rocket-like journey just in front of the square, landing over the rope in the lengthening shadows of the WACA scoreboard—the stroke of a master batsman; a shot that would have thrilled such players as Viv Richards and Don Bradman. The crowd rose as one to welcome the conquering hero as Doug meandered off the ground and, back in the Australian room, there was more than a hint of mischief in the eye of our captain, Ian Chappell. He ushered us all to the showers at the back of the dressing-room, indicating that we should be deathly quiet. The shower-room door was slightly ajar and we all clamoured for a look.

The crowd gave me great applause. Many youngsters—and not so young— spilled onto the ground, slapping my back sore and I was looking forward to the sanctuary of the dressing-room. Ah, yes, the dressing-room. The guys would mob me, they'd pump my hand and say, 'Beauty, Doug' and all that sort of stuff. They would probably douse me with champagne. I would be the hero of the hour.

The dressing-room was empty. Doug wandered through the door, a look of mild surprise sweeping momentarily over his face. But he acted as he normally did, whether he scored a duck or a hundred; calmly and slowly he removed his baggy-green cap and his gloves. He lit up a Rothmans filter with his beloved gold Dunhill lighter, mopped his brow and sat down. Then he looked about him. There was a long moment of total silence. The master practical joker was the target this time.

'You bastards,' I thought. Here's a man hitting a six off the last ball to complete a century in a session and you haven't got the decency to be there to hero-worship me when I get back. You probably didn't even watch the last over. 'Where are you, you bastards?'

Then Ian Chappell burst through the door to the showers and gave me a blast.

'You dopey bastard. What do you mean by playing that totally irresponsible shot and getting out on the last ball of the day? Haven't you learnt anything about team first, individual second?'

Jesus, that's lovely. Not only had Chappelli not seen the last over, but he's stuffed up what happened anyway.

Chappelli glared at me for a couple of seconds. Then he broke into a huge grin and gave me a hug—the pre-arranged signal for the rest of the guys to emerge from hiding in the showers.

Doug didn't have to raise a finger that night (except to light another cigarette). The beers flowed. The boys opened the cans for him. All he had to do was to sit back and enjoy. We were all thrilled for Doug, but moreover, we knew (and Freddie's performance confirmed it yet again) that we were in the company of someone very special. On this day Doug Walters proved to all and sundry—though no proof was required for those who had seen him a lot at close quarters—that this batsman in full flight was a genius. Poor Rosco. He'd just completed an unconquered 79 and was in line for a Test century in front of his home crowd, but was very much an afterthought to the blokes swarming to congratulate Doug. Edwards recalls:

Such an expression of his talent had generated a thirst in Doug; and he wasn't in his best condition next morning. As it happened, next day in the middle I had most of the strike and I was looking to push the ball into the gaps and run like hell. This was not at all to Doug's liking and after running all those twos and threes for me he wasn't in the best condition; and the first ball he faced, he weakly hung his bat at one outside his off stump and he was caught behind.[5]

In reality Doug copped a brute of a ball first up from Willis. It rose like a striking brown and Doug was simply good enough to get a touch to it, the ball ballooning to a grateful England first slip fieldsman, Keith Fletcher, who accepted the catch gleefully. So ended one of the very great Test match innings.

Edwards regards himself fortunate to have been there.

How lucky was I to have seen the entire innings from 22 yards! But how sad that the footage of this great hand seems lost. It happened that Channel 7 had telecast this match and for some time retained the old two-inch tapes. Channel 7 chief executive Brian Treasure contacted the Australian Cricket Board asking if they would like to take a copy of Doug's special innings on a more permanent and convenient tape format.

Astonishingly they (the Board) were not prepared to pay for the tapes, so all of the taped footage of Doug's great innings and all else in that match was wiped.[6]

Not surprisingly the old Bradman tag reared its head again, but Doug Walters always handled the tag well. He simply ignored it and played his own game. I once asked Sir Donald Bradman whether it concerned him when people tried to compare him with the likes of Victor Trumper. He replied in writing:

> No, it never irked me when older players spoke so highly of Trumper and their views did not have any influence whatsoever. You ask did it give me greater resolve to become the 'greatest batsman of all time'.
>
> I never set out to become the 'greatest batsman of all time', nor did I ever have such an ambition. I merely tried to play as best I could and any comparable judgement of skill was for others to determine. I think I also had enough sense to realise that each individual has his own particular skill and style and that you have to make the best you can of yourself. It is usually hopeless to try and copy others.[7]

Doug never tried to copy anyone else and no-one could possibly have emulated Doug, on or off the field. He was, and is, unique. But in many ways he was like Bradman. They had similar upbringings. Country lads. And there was a naïve and likeable boyishness about them which captured the hearts of a nation, The Don in the 1930s and Doug in the 1960s. On most days, Bradman could destroy an attack and Doug, in his day, could also tear an attack to shreds, very much in the ruthless Bradman vein. E.W. 'Jim' Swanton, who for more years than the locusts have eaten was the cricket correspondent for the *London Daily Telegraph*, watched a lot of Test cricket, covering every England tour of Australia from 1946 to 1975. In the wake of Doug's century in the session in Perth in December 1974, Swanton wrote: 'Who better than Walters when the mood is on him?'

Over in New Zealand, the Bracewell family were listening to Alan McGilvray auding the innings of Doug Walters in the Perth Ashes Second Test match. Brendon Bracewell, who played five Tests for the Kiwis in the 1978–81 period, tells of the family's love for Freddie.

Doug Walters was certainly a hero in the Bracewell household, right up there with Don Bradman, Clarrie Grimmett, Stan McCabe and Keith Miller. You can't get any higher than those blokes. Dad would come in from laying bricks all day and fiddle with the nobs on the wireless; simultaneously attaching wire to the aerial with the iron or hair clippers affixed until the crackle subsided enough for us to pick up the long-distance voice of Alan McGilvray. Dougie's hundred against the Poms in Perth was one of those great occasions around the Bracewell family wireless. Mum finally had enough, saying 'Can't you turn that racket off so we can have tea?' We all looked at Dad. And there he sat blissfully in his chair, tears were running down his cheeks and at that moment he uttered his first words for two hours.

'Jeez, that was beautiful...'[8]

Brendon's brother, John 'Braces' Bracewell, was a fine, attacking off-spinner for New Zealand and now the national coach of the Kiwis. Braces loves to talk of 'Dougie Walters'.

For years in the backyard I would always 'bags to be Doug Walters'. I think the kids today say 'shotgun Doug'. Dad spent hours telling us tales of Miller, Lindwall, and all the greats of the past and we'd hear the stories after dark when we couldn't get out in the backyard and do the real thing. Doug was playing when I was a kid so it all seemed more real. I had his style of walk, style of play and would try and hunt in the covers, pretending to be him.

I'm just pleased I didn't know he smoked.

I played my first Test in 1980 against Australia in Brisbane and during the first innings had to bowl to the man I used to pretend to be. Dougie was one of the reasons I was doing what I was doing. After the match Lance Cairns shoved a six-pack under my arm and marched me into the Aussie dressing-room and sat me down next to Doug and himself. He said, 'Drink up and listen.'

I must have looked a real dick as I just sat there and never said a word for about four hours. After that time I couldn't speak anyway. It is always such a relief if you get to meet your boyhood hero and find he lives up to the high expectations of a schoolboy dreamer. He scored 100 against us in the last Test (at the MCG) and I enjoyed being able to return the story of it to Dad.[9]

Doug Walters had done the batting genius hat-trick: he had scored a century in a session, scored a hundred before lunch versus the World Eleven at the MCG in 1971, he hit that hurricane ton against the West Indies in Port-of-Spain in the period between lunch and tea and, in Perth in December 1974, Freddie hit a hundred between tea and stumps. There was something surreal about the way he brought up the hundred in Perth. Few people who were there could believe the skill and the nerve required to execute such a shot at that stage of the match: it was to Doug very much a matter of six or out. That attitude or crude philosophy, if you will, endears Freddie to the people. He is like them, salt of the earth, a good bloke who, in between having a bet, having a drink or smoking a smoke, belts the hell out of all the leading cricketing nations in the world.

That fabulous Trinidad knock came less than a year after his disastrous 1972 tour of England, when Doug was dumped from the Test team for the Fifth Test at The Oval. Earlier in that tour his failure in the Lord's Test had a cricket fan and long-time friend of Bradman questioning his form.

Rohan Rivett, for many years editor of *The News* in Adelaide, developed a close relationship with Don Bradman. The Don had resigned as a Test selector in 1971, but he kept a close watch on all things cricket.

When Rivett questioned Doug Walters' indifferent performance in the Second Test at Lord's (caught Illingworth bowled Snow for one), Bradman said: 'Marvellous ability, but lack of application.'[10]

Was Bradman out of touch here? Walters might have not practised too hard on the morning of any match, but to accuse him of a lack of application. Nonsense.

There is no doubt that Bradman had a soft spot for Doug. Of course, he identified with Doug's NSW country upbringing, but he also liked Doug's natural friendliness and genuine modesty.

—⁓—

Doug first met Bradman as a youngster, after walking from the Gabba in the wake of a century on his Test debut in December 1965. At stumps Doug was 119 not out.

> He [Sir Donald] was sitting on the first chair near the entrance to the Australian dressing-room. He stood with his hand out to congratulate me and suddenly Richie Benaud jumped in front of me. He'd rushed down from the commentary box, pushing in front of Bradman, thrust out his hand and said, 'Congratulations Doug, don't sign a thing until you see me.' And away he went. Sir Donald shook my hand and said, 'If you ever need my advice, come and see me.'
>
> I guess Bradman said that to a lot of people.

I'm not sure if I know of anyone who has ever taken his advice. We all need advice, but Bradman was then chairman of the Test selectors and the icon of cricket that he was, I guess at that very time, the last bloke you'd ever go to with a problem with your game was Sir Donald Bradman.

Doug had good reason not to seek advice from any Test selector, as he explains:

I am an advocate against a Test team coach being part of the Test selection committee. Imagine going to Bob Simpson, when he was the Australian coach and a Test selector, with a problem about your technique. I am sure he would have advised your going back to grade cricket or Sheffield Shield cricket to sort the problem out. I think most coaches would think along the same lines.

Over the years Doug spoke a number of times with Sir Donald. He would visit the Australian dressing-room on the morning of matches, especially the first day of a game, wish the players well and enjoy a cup of tea. But it was after Doug had retired that he got to know The Don a whole lot better.

In December 1982, on the eve of the Australia–England Third Test match at the Adelaide Oval, Doug was in town attending a pre-Test function. He found himself within earshot of Sir Donald, who was asking the manager of the England team what the players were doing on the following day.

He told Sir Donald that they had nothing planned until 3 p.m. when they would practise at the Adelaide Oval nets.

'Well then,' said Sir Donald, 'I'd like to invite them to my place for morning tea.'

The manager was understandably delighted and jumped at the opportunity to spend time with the Bradmans. Then Sir Donald looked around and he saw me standing there. 'Oh, Doug. If you are not doing anything tomorrow, you are welcome to also come for morning tea.'

'Thank you very much, Sir Donald. I'll be the first one there.'

And I was.

It was absolutely sensational. I walked into Bradman's place. Lady Jess had the tea and the scones ready. Ten minutes later the England team's bus pulled up and, within moments, three or four fast bowlers baled him up in a corner and quizzed him:

'How would you go in today's cricket, facing these four or five West Indian fast bowlers?'

Sir Donald answered their question brilliantly.

'Look, a lot of things have changed in cricket since I played. We have restrictions on the leg-side. Captains do their homework. The wickets are nowhere as good as they were when I was playing and there is a good deal less overs bowled in a day's play today than there was in my time...'

I'm looking at these Pommie fast bowlers and you could sense that they were rubbing their hands in glee. They've got the great man in a corner in his own house seemingly admitting that he wouldn't be as good a player in their era.

Bradman continued: 'No, I wouldn't have scored anywhere near the amount of runs I scored those days...'

There was a long pause and the Poms were looking smug.

'... But I would have scored a lot more runs than the bloke who came second!'

Doug Walters had the temperament and the raw skill to draw closer to being 'another Bradman' than any other batsman of my time. To me, Doug's Perth epic came with more than a touch of Bradman. And even Freddie, who is quiet, reserved and genuinely a modest bloke, thought his Perth innings was a special knock:

Just like what I read of Bradman's knock at Lord's in 1930, that century in the session in Perth was, I felt, the closest I ever came to playing the perfect innings, where every ball I played went exactly where I intended. I guess it gave me an idea of how Don Bradman must have felt as he blasted his way to all those centuries.

In the Perth Second Test, England opener Brian Luckhurst copped an injured hand in the first innings. As a result of the injury Luckhurst came in at the fall of the fifth wicket and as he walked to the centre, Umpire Tom Brooks spoke to Ian Chappell reminding him that there was to be no short stuff bowled at Luckhurst. Chappelli was unimpressed. 'I told Tom I didn't agree with him, but he was in charge and so there wouldn't be any bouncers bowled at Luckhurst.'

The Englishmen were shocked by the speed and ferocity of Thommo. They thought it was good old Aussie propaganda when they first heard about this so-called new speedster. Before the series began we had Lillee talking about where he wanted to hit batsmen with his bouncer and Thommo appeared in print being quoted as having said that he liked to hit batsmen and wanted to see blood on the pitch.

There was a lot of talk about bouncers in this series, especially from the English journalists, who screamed about intimidatory bowling and made a big thing over a television interview in which Dennis Lillee pointed to his body to show where he aimed his bouncer. The English press wanted the Australian Cricket Board to officially censure Lillee for having the audacity to say what he did. However, I can't see much sense in trying to hide the fact that a fast bowler naturally aims for a part of the batsman's body when he bowls a bouncer. Let's face it, the bouncer is used to menace the batsman. It is a legitimate delivery and the only time there is an outcry over bouncers is after a batsman is hit. A batsman gets hit by a bouncer either by bad batting or he is beaten by sheer speed. There was an awful lot of bad play by the Englishmen in this series.

Thanks to the exploits of Lillee and Thomson and the fabulous century in a session by Freddie, we found ourselves two–nil up going to Melbourne for the Third Test. Doug was in the best form of his career, but the sluggish Melbourne wicket was a far different prospect than the hard, fast and bouncy Perth track. We suspected that the Poms, despite their battering at the hands of our demon fast pair, would play better on the more sluggish Australian wickets. As it tuned out the game was tight and hard, with Australia 8/238 with one ball to go and seven runs to win. Freddie scored 36 and 32 in a match that proved very tight bowling and scarcely any runs to play with for the fielding side. The match finished in a tight, hardly contested draw. There was no room in this match for the buying of any wicket.

I got a couple of wickets in the first innings and I had a partic-ularly tense period in the second dig.

Fred Titmus ran the ball to point off my bowling and the ball scurried along the turf to Doug. He collected the ball and appeared to be shining it; I thought, contrary to the rules, but I said naught to the umpires. The instant I caught the ball I knew there was something wrong—there was a gigantic spider on it! I threw the ball high in the air as if it was a live hand-grenade.

As Freddie and everyone else knew, I was not too keen on spiders. Spiders and snakes weren't my cup of tea. A deadly brown or red-bellied black was unlikely to invade the hallowed turf of the MCG, but a spider? It was one of Freddie's favourite ploys to stick a plastic spider onto the ball with chewing gum. I always played the straight man and made a scene ... Sometimes I left the big wad of chewing gum on the ball and bowled it. Imagine if it had stuck on the bat.

Rowdy was always fair game. He had an aversion to snakes (as we discov-ered in Bangalore) and he didn't like spiders. There was also the cigarette

*butts. Rowdy used to wander about the change-room barefooted and I'd
toss the live butts in his path.*

*At times he'd be totally oblivious to it, but on occasion he side-stepped
them brilliantly, only to fall away and land seated on the bench in front
of his locker only to find he had sat on his boots which were usually lying
upside down, with the spikes sticking straight up.*

Australia probably should have won the drawn match in
Melbourne, but Chappelli's men were confident of a win at the
SCG to seal the Ashes. NSW opener Rick McCosker came into
the side. A good move, as Wally Edwards, the WA left-hander, looked
out of his depth at the international level. McCosker had been
selected because of an amazing string of big scores in Sheffield
Shield cricket. He was ready.

*The team, inspired by Lillee and Thomson, was the best Australian team
I have played in.*

For the Sydney match we had our best eleven out there for the
series. Rick McCosker fitted in brilliantly and clearly was a far
superior player than Wally Edwards. The eleven for the SCG Fourth
Test (in batting order) were: Ian Redpath, Rick McCosker, Ian
Chappell (captain), Greg Chappell (vice-captain), Ross Edwards,
Doug Walters, Rodney Marsh, Max Walker, Dennis Lillee, Ashley
Mallett, and Jeff Thomson. Australia batted first and McCosker
opened with Ian Redpath. Redder (33) was out hit wicket, trying
to blast Fred Titmus to the mid-wicket fence, but Ian Chappell
(53) and Greg Chappell (84) helped McCosker along the way. The
tall, angular debutant hit a glorious 80. He played some delightful
drives and cuts and was good off his pads. Doug went, lbw to
Geoff Arnold for I. Seems it was a flood or a drought when it
came to Walters. The tail wagged and we got to 405, then bowled

the Poms out for 295. Batting again Greg Chappell got an unbeaten 144 and Redpath also starred, hitting 105. Freddie was bowled by Derek Underwood for 5. Australia declared at five down for 289, leaving England to score exactly 400 to win. There was only 4.3 of the mandatory last 15 overs to spare when I had Arnold caught at short leg by Greg Chappell to ensure a 171-run win. It was my 100th Test wicket, coming in 23 Tests.

The Ashes were ours because we were three up with two to play. The Adelaide Test was memorable for the batting of Doug Walters (55) and Terry Jenner (74). They came together at the fall of the fifth wicket and really took to the bowling of Underwood, who had threatened to go through our line-up like a dose of Epsom Salts. Walters and Jenner put on 80 runs for the sixth wicket, then Max Walker, 41 not out, Dennis Lillee, 26 and me, 23 not out, helped us limp to a respectable 304. England scored only 172 in its first dig; Lillee 4/49, Thomson 3/58 and me 3/14, the main wicket-takers.

In our second innings Freddie hit a fabulous 71 not out and along with Rodney Marsh (55), the scoreboard rollicked along until Chappelli called a halt to the slaughter by declaring at 5/272. England was set 405 runs to win, but again Lillee (4/69), backed by Max Walker (3/89), with some help from me (2/36), dominated and Australia sailed to a 163-runs victory. The final Test match was played at the MCG. Thommo was missing, courtesy of a shoulder injury sustained when he was serving during a rest-day tennis match at Yalumba in the Barossa Valley, and Lillee bowled only six overs in the first innings before he limped off with a foot injury. I shouldn't have played in the match for I got my heel caught between a couple of rocks where I was building a path at home and had a huge blood blister. The blister was drained but fluid built up again because the doctor in Adelaide drained it with a syringe. All that was required was a tiny cut each side of the blister. It was red raw by the start of play. Ian Chappell had had a major victory over the usually intransient Australian Cricket Board by having the players' pay for a Test match doubled—from $200 to $400.

So like Thommo in his first Test match at the MCG against Pakistan, I decided to tough it out. At a civic reception the night before I was trying hard not to limp, but Test selector Sam Loxton spotted my hobbling gait.

'Ohhhhhhooo … you're limping.'

I told Sam my foot had gone to sleep listening to his speech.

We were heading for certain defeat, when at tea on the second last day, we received a pleasant surprise. Into our dressing-room walked the famous entertainer, Shirley Bassey. We took tea with the singer, although there wasn't a lot of good cheer among the troops. We led four–nil coming into the match and didn't want to concede a game to the Poms. Shirley couldn't understand why we weren't in a more buoyant mood.

'Why so glum, chaps? After all you are winning,' she laughed.

Freddie twigged.

I have a feeling that you are in the wrong room, Shirley. This is the Australian dressing-room.

Initially Miss Bassey looked quizzically at Freddie, until one of her minders whispered in her ear.

'I think we are in with the Aussies.'

'Oh, Good Lord. I am sorry. I need to be in the England dressing-room.'

England won the final Test, but we won back the Ashes we lost to Ray Illingworth's men back in 1970–71.

The English cricket writer, E.W. 'Jim' Swanton, who had watched every Ashes Test series in Australia since Freddie Brown's team toured in 1946–47, was amazed by the Australian fielding.

It was easy, watching this series, in frequent dejection at England's batting frailties to overlook the excellence of the Australian close catching. Granted that the batsmen generally gave them every cause to keep the sharpest lookout, the standards of such men as the Chappells, Mallett, Redpath and Walters were marvellously high. It was true enough that the fast bowlers won the series, but what extraordinary support they had![11]

Round this time cartoonist Paul Rigby turned up a wonderful image of a battered English lion in a coffin being swept through a field of beer cans, images of Lillee and Thomson bowling together in the shadow of the old SCG Members' Stand. The cartoon carried the tag-line: 'Ashes to Ashes, dust to dust—if Thomson don't get ya, Lillee must...'

In the Sydney Test match a big group of people carried along a huge banner, and emblazoned across it were the prophetic words 'The Doug Walters Stand'. The sign was fixed at the Randwick end and some time later Doug did have a stand named after him at the SCG.

chapter twelve
a TEST
in ASHES

Doug go and put the fucking pads on...I'm going to bat
you next. You go in next and get a bit of a hit against the
old ball. You get a good start—I've seen you get hundreds
on worse pitches than this one. It's a fucking good pitch...[1]

The Ashes in safe hands again, Doug Walters went back for a brief
stint with Rothmans before the Australian team headed off for
England for the inaugural World Cup and while we were in England,
four Test matches after the Cup final. Two weeks in Canada
preceded our tour of England in 1975. The Australian Cricket Board
decided that the team be billeted with local families during our
fortnight in Canada, in Vancouver for one week and again for
another week in Toronto. We didn't for a moment think that the

Board could not afford to put us up at a hotel, however, it was another way of saving money while at the same time putting across the line that it was good PR to mix with the local community. A match in Vancouver and another at the Curling and Skating Club in Toronto and we were off to the World Cup. The 1975 Australian captain Ian Chappell recalls Freddie's performance during a practice match in England before the World Cup matches began.

We had sixteen men—eight a side. And there was Doug opening the bowling with Dennis Lillee and he knocks over 'Stumpy' Laird straightaway. I walked to the wicket and Doug gets me caught behind off his out-swinger. And there I am in the grandstand thinking 'this is supposed to be good batting practice and here I am sitting idle in the stand'. So I got Stumpy to put his pads on again and go in at the fall of the next wicket. When Laird got to the crease, Freddie, at the top of his bowling mark, yelled: 'Haven't I seen you somewhere before, batsman?'

Well, you wouldn't know it, but Freddie knocked Stumpy over again straightaway and I walked in on a Doug Walters hat-trick. I hit Freddie's first ball straight over his head for four and he said, 'Hey, Chappelli, isn't this supposed to be good batting practice?'[2]

We played Pakistan at Headingly, Leeds, in our first game of the preliminary round of the World Cup and beat them by 73 runs. Doug got a wicket, a good one in Mushtaq Mohammad, but the star of our attack was Dennis Lillee, who took 5/34 off his 12 overs. Umpire Harold 'Dickie' Bird kept chirping to me at mid-off, extolling the excellence of Lillee's bowling, especially the leg-cutter. When Lillee clean-bowled the Pakistani skipper Asif Iqbal with a superb leg-cutter, Dickie Bird did a little victory jig of his own, dancing about the wicket as if his admiration of Lillee's bowling came to fruition with that one stunning ball. I thought then that Dickie had his index finger at the ready for an lbw appeal. Doug scored only 2, but Ross Edwards (80 not out), Greg Chappell (45) and Alan Turner (46) combined to ensure we got a reasonable total: 278 for the loss of 7 wickets. We then played Sri Lanka on the flattest of flat tracks at The Oval. Rick McCosker (73) and Alan Turner (101) set the pattern for a big total with an opening stand of 182 and we reached 328 for the loss of five wickets. Doug scored 59.

Opening batsman Sunil Wettimuny played a Jeff Thomson thunderbolt on to his body. Wettimuny was given a thorough going over by Thommo, who had by then completely recovered from the tennis court shoulder injury he sustained in Adelaide during the Ashes series against England. Then little Duleep Mendis, now the chief executive of the Sri Lankan Cricket Board in Colombo, was struck on the head by a climber from Thommo. He was knocked out cold and took some time to come round.

We gathered around the bloke on the ground. He was lying on his back looking up at the heavens and when Chappelli asked him if he was okay, Mendis, tears rolling down his cheeks, said, 'Please Mr Thomson, I (am) going now . . .'

Both Sri Lankan batsmen hit by Thomson that day spent the night in a London hospital. There was a brave face to the Sri Lankan batting effort. Their bravery in the heat of battle, however, was not matched by their ability to combat genuine pace. Freddie's six overs cost 33 runs and no wickets. They batted pretty well and got to 276 for the loss of four wickets, but there was no sense of urgency in the Australian attack. We knew we had enough runs and we won easily by 52 runs.

Then we came up against the West Indies at The Oval. Freddie was run out for 7, both openers McCosker (0) and Turner (7) failed and so it was left to Edwards (58) and Rodney Marsh (52) to put some semblance of respectability into the innings and we finished with a moderate 192. The West Indies passed our score with just 3 wickets down, but we had done enough to win a place in the semi-finals. We were scheduled to play England at Headingly, Leeds. Gary 'Gus' Gilmour, the talented NSW all-rounder, was selected for the game as the wicket was a sward of green. Gus proved the difference between an Australian win and a big loss. The left-hander bowled magnificently like his mentor Alan Davidson, curving the ball in late or pushing the ball across the right-handers at just the right pace, just the right length. He took an incredible 6/14 off his 12 overs and skittled England for 93. Then Gus top-scored with an unbeaten 28 to see Australia home by four wickets. His not-out partner was Doug Walters, on 20. Before the World Cup final against the West Indies, Freddie got some good news from home.

I learnt, to my surprise and delight, that I had been awarded the MBE,[3] for services to cricket. It was a great surprise, totally out of the blue, because I thought that if ever I was going to get an award like that it wouldn't come until after I retired.

The World Cup final at Lord's on 21 June was the longest day of the year in Britain. It also felt like the longest day in cricket history. The Australian team got to the ground at around 8.30 a.m. and we left long after the pubs had shut. It was a glorious day; one of those typically brilliant English summer days when you convince yourself that it is never-ending. Some 26 000 people packed into Lord's for the World Cup final and the receipts topped a whopping £66 950, a record purse for a one-day match in England.

The match was the best one-day game I played in and I am sure it put one-day cricket on the map. Clive Lloyd hit a magnificent 102 to spearhead the Windies to an impressive tally of 8/291 off their 60 overs.

Freddie's boyhood hero Rohan Kanhai scored a solid 55, helping Lloyd to put on 149 runs for the fourth wicket after the Windies were looking down the barrel at 3/50. But it was Lloyd who stole the show, consistently smashing the ball straight past the bowlers to the boundary fence. He hit with tremendous power, waving that three-pound lump of willow as if it were made of balsa wood. In the wake of Lloyd's crushing stroke-play, Gilmour, who on one occasion was almost decapitated by a fierce Lloyd straight drive, was asked how do you bowl to Clive Lloyd? Gus replied: 'How do I bowl to Clive Lloyd? . . . with a helmet on!'

Australia, batting second and chasing a formidable 292 runs for a win, suffered five devastating run-outs. Alan Turner (40), Ian Chappell (62), Greg Chappell (15), Max Walker (7) and Jeff Thomson (21) were run-out, mostly due to direct hits by the mercurial Viv Richards. Doug batted fluently for 35 before he was bowled by Clive Lloyd's medium-pacer. Lillee and Thomson put on 41 for the last wicket, a final ditch effort to make up for four extraordinary run-outs which preceded their partnership.

Late in their stand, Thommo hit a ball to mid-off where it was caught. The crowd rushed onto the field as they thought the game was all over, a Windies win, but the umpire had called 'no-ball'; the fieldsman threw at the stumps and there was Lillee and Thomson charging up and down the wicket trying to run 17 over-throws to claim victory. Never missing an opportunity, Lillee yelled to Thommo, 'C'mon, mate, we can win this.' In all the confusion, with the crowd flooding the field and our last pair running up and down the pitch, we had a faint hope that the impossible could be achieved. During the 1868 Australian tour of England, another fast bowler,

Twopenny, hit a ball so high in the air that he ran 9 runs and that record has stood the test of time.

The day Thommo and Lillee tried to run away with cricket's first World Cup, Umpires Dickie Bird and Tommy Spencer allowed only 3 runs to be added to the Australians' total before the ball got swallowed up by the crowd. Soon after that, Thommo became the fifth Australian batsman to be run-out in that innings, the total standing at 274—18 runs short of victory.

In the lead-up games before the First Test against England, Freddie got 10 not-out in the one-day (35 overs a side) friendly against Middlesex at Lord's. The match was played as a boost to J.T. Murray's benefit year. Murray, a long-serving Middlesex and England stalwart (wicketkeeper/batsman) was known as the gentleman cricketer and he showed his class with a gem of a 27 not out after stumping Greg Chappell (105) with painless precision. Doug then hit a brilliant 50 against Kent at Canterbury, where the tree on the ground reminded him of the tree just backward of square leg at Dingadee. After the Kent match, we played Hampshire at Southampton, winning by four wickets. Doug was rested for this game, but he returned for the match at Lord's against a much-vaunted MCC Eleven where he hit his only century (103 not out) on that famous ground. Doug and Greg Chappell (86 not out) helped to set up an Australian win. Walters and Chappell put on a stirring 166 runs in two hours for the fourth wicket to hand Australia an emphatic seven-wicket victory.

A three-day match at Swansea preceded the First Test. Doug scored only 18, but Australia got its revenge of the Welshmen, who had won convincingly against us in 1964 and in 1968. Ian Redpath always said that it was worth the loss in Wales, given when the County team wins at home, the entire crowd stands and sings a stirring rendition of 'Land of Our Fathers'. The First Test was at Edgbaston, Birmingham, and England captain Mike Denness effectively signed his own death warrant that day, 10 July 1975, when he won the toss and invited Australia to bat first. Under leaden skies and on a decidedly green-tinged pitch, which was always going to help the England seamers, we managed to get to a very useful 359. Rick McCosker (59), Alan Turner (37), Ian Chappell (52) and Ross Edwards (56) all got good starts but failed to go on to hit a big score. It was one of those pitches where you were never really ever 'in' on it. Greg Chappell, who had been in superlative form in the lead-in games, his 144 against Glamorgan at Swansea was a cracking knock, was lbw to Chris Old for a duck and Freddie fell to the gentle medium pace of Tony Greig for 14.

It was left to the belligerent Rodney Marsh to belt his—and Australia's—way out of trouble and into a reasonable position with 61 out of 79 runs for the sixth wicket. Then he fell, ignominiously, after a break in play. There is an art to the Englishman's manner of understatement: 'Marsh showed much displeasure at his dismissal which followed next ball after a delay of five minutes when the ball had lost its shape within eight overs of coming into use.'[4] Freddie saw the whole thing through an Australian realist's eyes:

> Rod Marsh top-scored for Australia with 61 and was far from happy with his dismissal. John Snow, recalled belatedly by the England selectors, complained to Umpires Arthur Fagg and Dickie Bird about the shape of the ball. The Umpires decided to replace it but then Mike Denness and the officials haggled for seven minutes over a replacement. They even sent three Warwickshire cricketers into the nets with a new ball with (strict) instructions to thrash it for 48 deliveries. But before the Warwickshire trio returned, Umpire Fagg threw a 20-over-old ball to Denness—the same ball Denness had refused to use seven minutes earlier—and told him to use it.
>
> After the break in play, the first delivery from Geoff Arnold found the edge of Marsh's bat and Keith Fletcher held the catch in slips. Marsh stormed off the field and slammed the door of the dressing-room. Unluckily for

Rodney, there was glass in the upper part of the door and it broke. On the 1975 tour we had a team song along with lyrics devoted to players' exploits on and off the field. Each played had a verse devoted to him. Rodney's verse went like this [to the tune of 'Bad, Bad LeRoy Brown', Jim Croce, 1972]:

'Bad, bad, Rodney Marsh, slammer of doors and breaker of glass.
Peace will come to stay, when Rodney goes away . . .'

I won't tell you any of the other verses lest I run foul of the libel laws. Mind you, we later heard that Rodney wasn't the only Test cricketer in that game to show disdain over an umpiring decision. Apparently John Snow, unhappy at being given out lbw to Dennis Lillee in the England first innings, returned to the home dressing-room and thrust his bat through the television screen.

The English bookmakers were lengthening the odds on Mike Denness' chances of retaining the England captaincy, while the odds shortened considerably on the man most likely to replace him, the gangling Tony Greig. Back in 1972 Doug was among a number of Test players who bet on our team, taking five wickets in a session. The money was laid at Ladbrokes, the betting firm which had a betting tent near the boundary rope at mid-wicket on most county grounds. However, we took six wickets, not five. Ladbrokes were specific. We took one wicket too many to collect.

After our experience in getting those six wickets in a session in 1972, when we should have only taken five to collect, no-one was interested in having a bet on Greig, as we already had our betting fingers burnt.

Tony Greig was like a giraffe, tall and gangly, but he made the absolute most of his ability and he had the passion and combative nature to take on the captaincy. When bowling at Edgbaston he hung on to the ball too long for the batsman, and too late for Dickie Bird to avoid it. Greig let the ball go behind him and Dickie copped the full force of it on his right knee. Dickie cried out in anguish, hopping about and putting on a magnificent show for all and sundry. That afternoon he hopped and squealed some more. Next morning, Dickie turned up in the Australian dressing-room to announce: 'I'm fooked...I can't go on. Mi back's fooked. I can't stand straight and I can't stand out there today...'

Predictably Greig got the England captaincy for the Second Test at Lord's. England batted first and Dennis Lillee made early inroads, Barry Wood lbw for 6 before in sauntered the bespectacled, grey-haired Northamptonshire batsman David Steele. At the age of 33 Steele probably had to pinch himself when he discovered that he had made the Test side. As Steele recalls, reality hit as soon as he reached the crease.

> I floated out through the Long Room. People were looking at me. I could hear them muttering, 'Who's this old grey bugger?' as I walked past. Thommo stood with his hands on his hips, I said, 'Good morning, Thommo.' He said, 'Bloody hell, who've we got here? Groucho Marx?'[5]

But Steele showed his mettle. He hit a good debut double of 50 and 45, was bowled by Thommo in the first dig and caught and bowled Doug Walters in the second. John Edrich hit 175 to save the game for England. Doug bowled only 2 overs for the match and got 1/6. He failed with the bat on a very flat track and Ross Edwards fell for 99. Dennis Lillee (73 not out) and I put on 69 for the last wicket and I became Steele's only Test wicket. It wasn't a memorable Test for Doug, but he remembered, in detail, one particular incident.

> *The Second Test at Lord's was graced by Her Majesty, Queen Elizabeth and the Duke of Edinburgh and a certain Michael Angelow. The Queen*

and the Duke were introduced to the players during the tea break on the first day. Angelow introduced himself late in the Test when he ran on to the field naked, hurled both sets of stumps, without dislodging a bail and rushed headlong into the waiting arms of the law. Lord's had its first streaker and an MCC official commented royally: 'We were mildly amused.'

Fleet Street won the day when all the morning newspapers published that superb photograph of Angelow's nether region being politely covered by a policeman's helmet. It was precisely 3.20 p.m. when Angelow ran across Lord's and preceded to leap-frog both sets of stumps. The famous BBC broadcaster, John Arlott, gave a legendary description of the event.

Ah, we have a freaker…the old ladies in the crowd are seeing what they haven't seen for years. He's masculine, well built, wearing plimsoles and I'm sure if his mother is watching television she'll recognise him.

Arlott, a former policeman, famously forgot the term for unclad runners at sporting events, calling Angelow, a cook in the British Merchant Navy, a 'freaker', instead of 'streaker'.[6]

Years later the quick-thinking bobby in question said he had placed his helmet over the man's privates out of sheer embarrassment.

I said to Angelow: 'You are not required to say anything, unless you wish to do so'…and Michael (Angelow) turns around and says, 'Give us a kiss!'[7]

Angelow didn't get his, but he was fined £25 next morning when he was confronted by the Beak (Magistrate) in the St John's Wood Magistrates Court. He had bet his friends the very same amount, £25 to streak at Lord's.

Doug hit a hurricane 103 not out in our next match against Somerset at Taunton, enough good form for Freddie to miss the following game against Northamptonshire, the game before the vital Third Test match. Freddie made good use of his time off.

The day before the Northants match, Ian Chappell and I took on Rodney Marsh and Rick McCosker at golf. Marshie isn't at all like his famous brother, Graham, especially when he has a golf club in his hand. Bacchus plays golf right-handed and that's where the resemblance to his brother ends. But on this day Marshie fired his head off and for the first and only time he broke par with a round of 69. Only trouble was, Chappelli and I still took the money. I don't think that put Rodney in a great frame of mind for the next four days. Rodney showed displeasure when given out bat-pad to Bishen Bedi and as he walked through the crowd, a Northants fan yelled, 'Don't smash the pavilion down.'

When Max Walker batted, the Pakistani import Sarfraz Nawaz told Max he'd phoned up the local funeral directors and they had room only for one more body in the cemetery. Sarfraz then proceeded to bowl two short-pitched deliveries in a row to Thommo, who was caught off the second. Unlike the MCC official over the streaker at Lord's, Thommo was not even mildly amused. Sarfraz told the press that Thommo had told him he would 'see him later'. Sarfraz, in his usual modest way, continued, 'I told him (Thommo) he should give me his bat and pads and I would face him straightaway. I could not wait to bat against Thommo after that. I asked the skipper if I could open the batting.' A glutton for punishment, Sarfraz had a go at Chappelli when a caught behind decision went against the Pakistani. 'You should be ashamed of yourself for not walking. You make the umpire's job harder.'

On the eve of that final day's play, rotund Colin Milburn, the former Northants and England opening batsman, who tragically lost an eye in a head-on motor accident in 1969, strode into the

Australian dressing-room and declared: 'I think I should take the Australian captain and his wicketkeeper out for a big drink.' Marsh noted that 'Ollie' (Milburn) was already a bit under the weather and he thought that this might be his big chance. 'Milburn, tonight's the night I am going to drink you under the table.'

But Milburn stayed on his feet, occasionally getting the odd comment when he dropped his glass eye into Ian Chappell's half-filled pint of lager.

The next day Australia needed 318 to win the match and Chappelli and Bacchus made it look easy. They raced to the victory target in just 214 minutes, fuelled by Sarfraz's caustic comments and the after-effects of what they had been up to the night before.

Ian Chappell hit 116 not out (in 115 minutes) and Marsh an unconquered 65. Their fifth wicket partnership of 107 came in just 54 minutes of explosive batting. So the big drink helped their batting, just as Freddie knew it surely must.

Headingly was the venue for the Third Test. It was in Leeds in 1972 that the Poms prepared a wicket for Derek Underwood and we lost the match that cost us the Ashes. Seemingly, Headingly was a ground that would always provide Ian Chappell's men with something odd or bizarre. It was on this famous ground in the heart of Yorkshire, where Don Bradman hit a hundred before lunch in 1930 to emulate Charlie MacCartney's effort in 1926. Gary Gilmour starred with the ball for Australia, getting 6/85, and England were all out for a modest 285. Then Chappelli's men collapsed to be all out for 135. Ian Chappell (35) and Rodney Marsh (25) were the only Australians to get more than 20 runs. Doug fell for 19 and Phil Edmonds, the new England left-arm spinner, took 5/28. His haul of wickets comprised Ian Chappell, Greg Chappell (13), Ross Edwards (0), his third duck in a row in Test matches at Leeds—Doug Walters, and Max Walker (0). Incidentally, it was at Leeds in 1972 that Greg Chappell was so frustrated by his own dismissal on top of his anger over the state of the 'Fusereum' wicket that he drove his bat handle into the door of the drying cabinet and exclaimed, 'There's no fucking justice in this game,' before sitting down next to Doug Walters. No-one said a word.

Three years later, in the 1975 Leeds Test match, Freddie was given out lbw to Edmonds for 19. Walters came in after being dismissed, whacked the same drying cabinet, then sat down next to Greg Chappell and declared, 'There's no fucking justice in this game.' Again, no-one uttered a word.

England batted again and, although we dismissed them for 291 (Gilmour took 3/72 and I took 3/50), because we batted so poorly in our first dig, their lead was seemingly unassailable. Ian Chappell had shown fierce intent, hitting a brilliant 62, with 11 fours and one six, before he fell victim to a dodgy lbw decision. But he still believed Australia could win the match.

> I had a premonition that (Doug) Walters was going to get a century. Rick McCosker was batting well and just before I was given out, I was starting to think, 'If Rick and I are here at stumps we'll win this match.' Then I got the decision and when I got in the dressing-room ... I am swearing and throwing the soap at the shower wall and I suddenly thought, 'Shit, hang on Ian, there's a Test match going on and it's a Test match we can win.' I thought that if Doug gets in before the new ball is due and has ten or twelve overs, he can make a hundred on this pitch ... easily. I went straight out onto the balcony, draped in a towel, dripping wet. Greg [Chappell] was in and Rosco [Ross Edwards] was padded up to go in next, and I quietly said to Dougie, 'Go and put the pads on, Doug.'
>
> 'Chappelli, I'm not in next!'

'Doug, go and put the fucking pads on.' And I followed him into the room, saying, 'I'm going to bat you next. You go in and get a bit of a hit against the old ball. You get a good start—I've seen you get hundreds on worse pitches than this one. It's a fucking good pitch.' When he was padded up, I went to Rosco and said, 'Take 'em off Rosco, Dougie's going in next.'[8]

Greg Chappell (12) was the third man out with the score at 174, when in strolled Freddie. The phlegmatic Walters hit four telling fours in his 25. By the close of play on the fourth day, the match was amazingly evenly poised.

We were 3/220, chasing a historical victory. In 1948 Don Bradman's 'Invincibles' scored 404 in a day to win the Test. We had to get 445 runs for a win. At stumps Rick McCosker was unconquered on 95 and Doug Walters was not out 25.

A great day's cricket was about to unfold.

History was made alright on that fateful day, 19 August 1975, but alas it wasn't cricket history. In the dark of night, vandals sneaked into Headingly and, stealthily avoiding security personnel, they crawled under the covers and wreaked havoc with the Test match pitch. Doug remembers seeing the damage.

The vandals dug holes in the pitch near the popping crease and poured oil on the wicket in the region of a good length. The Headingly pitch had been sabotaged by four people, who were campaigning to free a Londoner serving seventeen years' jail for armed robbery.

One of the four, Peter Chappell, was sentenced in the Birkenhead Crown Court to 18 months' jail in January 1976, for his part in the vandalism of the Headingly pitch. The match ended up in a draw, the last day being abandoned due to the defacement of the

Test pitch. Loss in gate receipts and the sale of scorecards was estimated upwards of £8000. Victorian leg-spinner, Jim Higgs, the best of the Australian leggies after Richie Benaud and before Shane Warne, broke a long-standing batting record in England by going through the entire tour and failing to score one single run.

In fact, the only ball Glad (Higgs) faced, he was bowled by Yorkshire's Chris Balderstone; the ball coming from the face of his bat and running back on to the stumps.

Higgs took the record from Sundown, an Aboriginal cricketer who toured England with the first Australian cricket team in 1868. Sundown (tribal name, Ballrinjarrimin) played only a couple of matches on the 1868 tour before he took ill and had to sail home (with Jim Crow) ahead of the rest of the touring party. A specialist batsman, Sundown scored just one run on the 1868 tour.

Perhaps it was Sundown who inspired the immortal line about the batsman 'who scored only one in the first innings, but was not quite so successful in the second'. Jim Higgs did improve his batting and some five years after the 1975 tour, Higgs became a key figure in helping Kevin Douglas Walters complete his fifteenth— and last—Test match hundred.

The Oval Fourth Test—the last of the 1975 series—was played over six days; the longest game of cricket played in England and Australia fielded in more than five of those days. Receipts were £63 705, the attendance 78 000.

In the Test matches Freddie was fifth in the averages with another modest return, this time 125 runs (highest score 65) at an average of 31.25. However, he led the Australian batting averages in all first-class matches with 784 runs at 60.30. He hit three centuries: 103 not out against MCC at Lord's; 103 versus Somerset at Taunton and 102 not out against Leicestershire at Leicester. The Fifth Test at The Oval proved to be Ian Chappell's last as captain. It was also Ross Edwards' last Test match. Chappelli hit an Ashes-high 192 and Rick McCosker, who was stranded on 95 in the abandoned Leeds Test, scored his maiden Test hundred (127) and Doug came good with a dashing 65. England followed on after its first innings 191, scoring a laborious 538. Bob Woolmer hit a painstaking 149, the slowest, most boring innings imaginable. Woolmer batted for eight hours, nineteen minutes over his innings, which was nothing short of torture and sacrilege for red-blooded batsmanship. Yet, Woolmer's innings effectively saved England from outright defeat.

Chappelli's regular bowlers trundled themselves into exhaustion: Lillee bowled 52 overs; Thommo, 30; I bowled 64 and the Chappells bowled 29 overs between them. Very late in the proceedings along came Doug Walters. He bowled a mixture of long-hops, full-tosses and little late out-swingers to collect 4/34 off 10.5 overs. It was a lovely cameo performance that was so typical of Freddie, whose immortal words haunted us yet again when he slipped one past Woolmer, trapping that slowest of slow batsmen, lbw.

'Bloody beauty . . . one for none!'

chapter thirteen

SWORN
to SECRECY

'Righto, how many renegades have we got on this plane?'
We all knew what Skull was talking about, but no-one said
anything. Sworn to secrecy, a rebel didn't even know a
fellow rebel.

The Australian cricket public eagerly awaited the arrival of Clive
Lloyd's West Indian team for the 1975–76 summer. And Freddie
was keen to make amends for yet another dismal Ashes series in
England. In New South Wales' first couple of matches Freddie got
45 and 7 versus Queensland at the Gabba and 13 and 17 against
Western Australia in Perth. Then came the fateful Sheffield Shield
match against South Australia in Adelaide. Freddie got a solid 56
in the NSW first innings. Set 266 runs to win, New South Wales
probably would have cruised to victory had not fate taken a hand.

When Doug was on five in the second dig, SA fast bowler Wayne Prior dropped one short.

The ball blancmanged, much slower off the pitch than I anticipated. I just went to hook Fang [Wayne Prior] and my springs somehow got caught in the cracks in the wicket.

My foot stayed still and my knee kept going. In trying to stop the shot, I lost balance and I crashed heavily into the stumps. There was a loud cracking noise and excruciating pain. I thought a stump had broken off and had gone through my leg. The pain was so intense. Both ligaments had snapped and my kneecap had fallen out of place and was round my shin bone. When Robin [Haskard], the SA physiotherapist, straightened my leg he was able to manoeuvre the kneecap into place and strap it. Because both ligaments had snapped, there was nothing to hold the kneecap in place.

In 1975 rehabilitation for such an injury was pretty slow. At first the injury seemed relatively minor. When Doug fell on his stumps, the SA players celebrated another NSW wicket, not knowing the extent of his injury. South Australia won the match by 21 runs, but the cost to the NSW captain and Test batsman Doug Walters was far worse than a Sheffield Shield loss in the City of Churches.

I came back to Sydney from Adelaide that night and went to see the doctor next day. I found Doc [Brian] Corrigan in good spirits. He had not been to bed and the party was still going when I arrived at 11 a.m.

He said, 'C'mon in, Freddie. Let's have a look at that knee of yours.' The doc had a look at it and said that it would be okay in a fortnight. He wanted to see me again in a couple of days.

By that time I was black from my hip to my big toe and the knee was very swollen. He told me that's how the knee should have looked when he first saw me a few days before. Doc Corrigan's initial estimate of recovery within a fortnight had suddenly blown out to two months. Actually, it was three months before I played cricket again.

Freddie was destined to miss the changing of the guard. Greg Chappell took over from Ian Chappell as Test captain and he began his Test leadership with a century in each innings against the tourists in the Brisbane First Test match. Gordon Greenidge padded up to the first ball of the series from Dennis Lillee and was given out lbw. At lunch on that first day the Windies were 6/125. That set the tone for the way they played that series. Their reckless attacking batsmanship came off once, in Perth when Roy 'Freddo' Fredericks thrashed 169, setting up the only West Indian Test win of the summer. Australia won 5–1. Doug Walters missed the party. He was fated to play just nine Tests against the West Indies—four in Australia and five in the Caribbean—scoring 1196 runs in fourteen innings for an average of 92.

While I didn't play in any of the Test matches against the Windies, I had another view of the game by doing some television commentary with the ABC for three of the Tests. I also reported on the games for Sydney radio station 2UW. It was, I found, much easier handling the West Indies fast bowlers from in front of a microphone rather than at the wicket.

—∞—

May 21, 1976 was a big day in the Walters household—the happy day when Caroline and Doug's first born—Brynley Douglas Walters—came into the world. Doug well remembers the occasion:

You've no doubt seen those cartoons showing the chain-smoking expectant fathers pacing up and down waiting for news of the new baby. Well, that wasn't the case with me. Caroline had the baby at the Sanitarium Hospital in Wahroonga and there they have a very strict no-smoking policy. Every now and then I'd duck outside for a puff or two.

When the doctor came to announce the birth of a bouncing boy, he said, 'C'mon, Doug. We'll both sit down and have a Rothmans now!'

Caroline and I were convinced our first born would be a girl and we had plenty of girls' names picked out, but not many for a boy. In her work as a school teacher, Caroline said there was a boy in her class who was always on his best behaviour and his name was Brynley. All the other boys' names I picked out had, at some stage, been the worst kid in her class. I liked the name Brynley too, so we agreed and Brynley Douglas Walters he became.

Doug's injury slowly healed and he returned to play in the last three Sheffield Shield Matches, scoring 8 (run out) and 0 against Victoria at the SCG; 102 against Western Australia at the SCG and 50 and I against South Australia at the SCG. The good news was that Freddie's knee withstood long days at the crease and in the field, and he was raring to go for the 1976–77 season.

Doug didn't start the summer in a blaze of glory, hitting only 139 runs in six completed Sheffield Shield innings at an average of 23.17. But he was still selected in Australia's team for the First Test match against Pakistan to be played in Adelaide.

The side took on a whole new look after Ian Chappell had retired, and without stalwarts Ian Redpath and Ross Edwards, the batting line-up looked entirely different. Pakistan batted first and the day was marred by a terrible injury to fast bowler Jeff Thomson.

Zaheer Abbas went to hook and the ball came on quicker than he expected and he knocked it straight up in the air. Turner, with his eyes only for the ball, moved underneath it. Thommo raced in too. I thought it was Alan's catch, but Thommo didn't want to take any chances. Thommo finished with a dislocated collarbone in his right shoulder and he missed the rest of the

Pakistan series, as well as the short tour to New Zealand and the Centenary Test. I think quite a few batsmen all round the world breathed a sigh of relief when they read over their cereal the next morning that Thommo was out of action for the rest of the Australian season.

Adelaide had not been kind to Thommo. He hurt his shoulder playing tennis on the rest day of the Test there in January 1975, and now a dislocation in the shoulder of that same lethal right arm.

Australia needed the experience of Walters, probably more than ever. If Doug was nervous he didn't show any outward signs. He wore the face of a poker player as he walked to the crease at the fall of the 3rd wicket. Ian Davis hit a fine 105, and Alan Turner (33), Rick McCosker (65) and Greg Chappell (52) all got good starts. It was all paving the way for Doug Walters to cut loose. Doug grabbed the Pakistani attack by the throat and shook it: he cut and drove with great power, his triumphal 247-minute return to the Test batting crease realising 107 runs in 247 balls with 9 fours. There was Doug's old mate Sarfraz Nawaz opening the bowling with Salim Altaf and the pacy emerging star Imran Khan, the first change pace-man. All three suffered at the hands of the Australian batsmen and Doug was most severe on Salim who conceded 71 runs off his 15 overs. The Pakistanis fell for 272 in their first innings, but batting a second time they plundered the Australian attack, Zaheer Abbas scoring 101 and Asif Iqbal, a superb, free-stroking unconquered 152. Dennis Lillee bowled magnificently on that dead, flat track, taking 5/163 off a marathon 47.7 overs. Spinner Kerry O'Keeffe also bowled well, with 3/166 off 53 overs. Pakistan hit 466 in its second innings, leaving Australia to score 284 runs for victory. Turner (48), McCosker (42) and Greg Chappell (70) paved the way for what should have been an easy Australian win.

Then Doug cruised to 51 in 95 minutes before he edged a ball from the left-arm spinner Iqbal Qasim into the waiting gloves of keeper Wasim Bari. Gary Gilmour (5) tried to hit Qasim out of the ground and was bowled, but with only six wickets down Australia was just 56 runs away from victory when the first of the mandatory last 15 overs began. Gary Cosier and Rodney Marsh, both hard-hitting batsmen, were at the crease and a win was, seemingly, within easy reach. But both batsmen played dull, boring cricket. It was a dreadful spectacle with half-volleys being patted back to the bowler and a thorough lack of urgency in the running between wickets. When the overs ran out Australia was 6/261, 24 runs short of a win. Cosier scored 25 not out in 83 minutes, with four fours and Marsh 13 not out in 71 minutes with one four. Doug didn't say much about the Cosier–Marsh display, but felt the injury to Jeff Thomson cast a cloud over the Test match.

My innings was overshadowed by the incident when Thommo and Alan Turner collided with a sickening thud when they both went for a skied catch off the speedster's bowling.

Australia won the Second Test of the series by a whopping 348 runs, with Greg Chappell (121) and Cosier (168) playing superbly. Doug hit 42 before falling again, caught behind to Qasim, and Lillee took match figures of 10/135 to complete the rout. In the Australian second innings Doug was bowled by Imran for a duck. It was Imran Khan who starred in the Third Test at the SCG. The speedster took 6/102 and 6/63 to defeat the Australian batsmen and set up an eight-wicket victory for his country. Doug was out for 2 and 38, both times the victim of Imran, caught behind by Wasim Bari.

—◠◠—

The Australian captain, Greg Chappell, had lost the core of the Australian team. There needed to be a new and immediate strategy for this new-look Aussie outfit. Greg decided that he needed the support of his two most senior players—Doug Walters and Rodney Marsh. They would help him by introducing early morning fitness runs at the start of the Australian tour of New Zealand in February 1977.

Perhaps Freddie wasn't the man for the job, for he was the last to rise in the morning and joined the gang wearing three-toned boxer shorts and a T-shirt emblazoned with Dukes, a new brand of cigarettes. Freddie soon dropped off the pace and was not seen again until he rejoined the squad 200 metres from home. He careered past the front-runners and dashed straight to his motel room, whereupon he collapsed in a heap on his bed. The next morning, as if almost on cue, Freddie arrived with a new *Playboy* T-shirt, which carried the all-important message on the back, 'JOGGING CAN KILL'.

That was Freddie to a tee. He always had the last laugh.

Freddie always reserved something special for the land of the long white cloud. In 1974 he hit a century in a session against Northern Districts without hitting a single boundary and then he savaged the New Zealand attack, including Richard Hadlee, with a brilliant hundred at Auckland out of an Australian total of 220. Would the Christchurch Test of 1976–77 provide a Walters special? The Australian manager was Roger Wootten, 'Wotton as in cotton, not Wootten as in rootin' ', he'd often say in introduction and he was, like all Australians, a Doug Walters fan. The team was staying at the Avon Motor Lodge in Christchurch and the night before the Test match the drinkers in the side usually had a few beers before retiring. Roger stayed with Doug for a couple of hours after the traditional team meeting, then called it a night, fully expecting Doug to also go to bed.

At 5 a.m. he banged on vice-captain Rodney Marsh's door. 'Let me in, Bacchus, let me in!' The bleary-eyed wicketkeeper opened the door and Roger blurted, 'He's still in there.'

'Who's still in where?'

'Dougie's still in the bar.'

Rodney assured the team manager that Doug knew exactly what he was doing and that sometimes he would have a big drink the night before a day's Test cricket. He could cope, but Freddie admits he was worse for wear the next day and he struggled to see the ball.

> *Richard Hadlee bowled a few to me early which I hardly saw. I either missed the ball or somehow negotiated it with my bat away from my body. I had a few anxious moments in that first half hour. Gradually, I managed to get bat on ball, for it was only during my struggle in the first 20 or 30 runs that my timing was totally astray. At the end of the day I was something like 20-odd.*

Roger Wootten turned up at Rodney Marsh's door the following morning. Yes, it was 5 a.m.

'He's still there!'

Rodney didn't even bother to open his door and told Roger to go back to bed, saying something along the lines of, 'Freddie knows what he's doing.'

This time in the bar Freddie found an able ally, in the personage of Gary Gilmour. Gus was known to be partial to the odd glass of Galliano and on this night he stayed the distance with Freddie. Some of the journalists on tour were sharpening their poison pens for they witnessed two Australian cricketers drinking beyond the norm before batting in a Test match. Freddie and Gus were the overnight not-out batsmen. Next man in, Kerry O'Keeffe, who seemed to take himself altogether far too seriously throughout his playing career, was in a state, saying that the pair were totally irresponsible.

Next day Freddie continued on as if he'd had a full night's rest. He scored a Test high of 250 and Gus hit his maiden Test century (101). The pair put on a record 217 for the eighth wicket and Freddie hit a total of 30 fours and one six in his 250, which took 390 minutes.

The pitch in Christchurch was a bit dicey, with some uneven bounce. I didn't hit the ball well for the first 20 runs, but after that initial stutter I played as good an innings as I've ever played to notch my highest Test score.

That night everyone joined Freddie for a drink. It was a time of great celebration.

Australia drew the Christchurch match but, thanks to Dennis Lillee's double of 5/51 and 6/72 at Eden Park, Auckland, Greg Chappell's men won the Second Test by 10 wickets. Freddie scored 16. And despite his lack of runs at Eden Park, Freddie did have cause to celebrate. Not just the Australian victory, but his invitation to sign up for the new revolution that would become known as World Series Cricket.

I first heard of World Series Cricket in Auckland. It was during the Second Test match and I met John Cornell, who was staying at the same hotel as the Australian cricket team. He was then better known as comedian Paul Hogan's off-sider, Strop.

But Cornell had another task at the time. He was busy signing up players for WSC with former Australian Rules star, Austin Robertson. Dennis Lillee mentioned that Cornell and Robertson wanted to see me in one of the bottom dressing-rooms at Eden Park during the lunch break.

Freddie wandered down to one of the vacant dressing-rooms. He must have looked a little intimidated, for Cornell broke the ice with a statement that Freddie says really took him aback.

'Look Dougie, I'm going a bit bad. Can you lend me a few bucks?' Obviously they hadn't heard of my reputation for not putting my hand in my kick, but I said, 'I've left my wallet in our dressing-room, but I'll see you right.' Strop couldn't help having his little joke, even without his lifesaver's cap. They both had a chuckle, then they put to me a proposal to join WSC on a three-year contract. I was guaranteed $75 000 over the three years. They didn't have to talk too long to convince me. I said to count me in. The guaranteed money for three seasons had plenty to do with my decision, because cricket had become a professional game in everything but the players' payments. The players were the poor relations.

At the same time my decision to join WSC was a lot easier than it would have been for some of the young blokes, like David Hookes. I was 30 years of age and the best part of my Test career was behind me. Robertson and Cornell did not hide the realisation that whoever signed up for WSC was likely to be banned from playing Test cricket by the Australian Cricket Board. It must have been a huge decision for the young-sters. When they spoke to me, no other players' names were mentioned and I was told the matter had to proceed with the utmost secrecy.

Doug knew other players had also been sworn to secrecy.

On the aircraft from Sydney to Melbourne, the five NSW representatives for the Australian team were settling down as the plane levelled out when Kerry O'Keeffe turned around and said, 'Righto, how many renegades have we got on this plane?' We all knew what Skull was talking about, but no-one said anything. Sworn to secrecy, a rebel didn't even know a fellow rebel.

The Australian team returned home to prepare for the game of the century, the Centenary Test. The first of these matches was played at the MCG in March 1877, and Australia won by 45 runs. In 1977 Melbourne really turned it on. The old Test cricketers were invited to the match and all the functions and there was much fanfare to celebrate 100 years of Test cricket between Australia and England.

The Melbourne officials provided a special room for the old cricketers: free drinks all day every day. And could some of those blokes drink. Poor Freddie. Had he not been sweltering out in the middle of the MCG, he would have loved to have been drinking with the old hands in that special room. But for once Doug Walters had more important things to do than drinking. It was during that celebratory Test that Doug Walters signed on the dotted line for WSC.

I signed my contract in the dressing-room at the MCG during the Centenary Test. What a game that was: the best Test match I played in. It had everything: brilliant bowling, superb batting, great fielding and a fairytale finish.

Doug remembers a heated confrontation between the England captain and David Hookes, who made his international debut in the 1977 Test after a naming run of five centuries on the trot for South Australia in the Sheffield Shield competition.

Hookes was young and brash and dashing and if someone had a verbal 'go' at him on the field, he wasn't afraid to retaliate.

Tony Greig felt the full weight of Hookes' bat when the youngster hit five successive fours off the England captain in the second innings. I don't know if the MCC would have approved of some of the language Mr Greig used, but his remarks to Hookes went along these lines, 'Why don't you fuck

off. You're just another fucking Aussie, who can't fucking play.' Hookes,
brought up in the tough Shield competition, had the perfect reply.

'At least I'm an Australian playing for Australia. Not a fucking South
African playing for England.' I think Mr Hookes won that one.

At the Test match Sir Donald Bradman was in raptures about
Hookes' batting and he was moved to say, 'I've just seen in Hookes
the reincarnation of Frank Woolley.'[1]

The Australian team had great belief that they could win the
match, despite being bundled out cheaply in their first innings. Doug
fell to Bob Willis for 4 and only Greg Chappell (40) and Rod
Marsh (28) got more than 20 among the batsmen.

*Greig won the toss and sent us in to bat. It seemed he had made the right
decision when we were bundled out for just 138. The English press who
had labelled us the 'Ugly Australians' from the last tour, could hardly control
themselves, and their poison pens worked overtime about how the arrogant
Aussies had been cut down to size. Unfortunately, the Aussies were
arrogant enough to believe they still had a chance to win the match. We
bundled out the Poms for 95, with the remarkable Lillee taking 6/26.*

*In our first innings Rick McCosker played a ball from England fast
bowler Bob Willis into his face and he suffered a broken jaw.*

The SACA doctor, Don Beard, a cricket fanatic and the official
medical man at Adelaide Oval for more than forty years, was the
first man on the scene, attending to the injured Test batsman. 'My
colleagues at the conference would have been surprised to see
images of me running on to the MCG while they watched the
cricket on TV during a lectures break,' the doc laughed, 'but I was
glad I was there and glad to help Rick.'[2]

Doc Beard once cut out cancerous tissue from Ian Chappell's
chest only days before Chappelli led his country on the 1972 tour

of England, and he served in medical teams in the battle grounds of Korea and Vietnam.

Doug was concerned for his team-mate when he saw McCosker walking out to join him in the middle of the MCG. McCosker resembled an Egyptian mummy, his head and face swathed in bandages.

I was surprised to see Rick padded up to go in our second innings. Greg Chappell told the press he would have sent McCosker in earlier, if a wicket hadn't fallen. 'I was going to put him in after Rod Marsh, but the second new ball was taken and I didn't want him to have to face that, so I put Dennis Lillee in. When they did so well and Rod was in sight of a hundred, I thought that was the time for Rick to bat. It gave Rod his chance of a century. Rick was at the ground before play and he wanted to bat. It was largely his decision. I don't know whether he was putting on a brave front, but I think he wanted to bat for his own sake and the team's.'

McCosker told reporters, 'I told Greg I could bat and he let me pad up. It looks a lot more painful than it is. When I got to the centre I was sorry I wasn't there earlier. The wicket was a pleasure to play on.'

I don't know about all of that; all I do know is that innings of 25 by McCosker was the bravest thing I've seen on the cricket field and I'll never forget the sight of him with his bandaged head ducking the bouncers, for Tony Greig showed him no mercy. Rod Marsh probably summed it up best when he said, 'I knew McCosker would bat at some stage, but when our lead went to 400 I thought he probably wouldn't. Then out he came and I was a bit worried it would be hurting him a lot. I said to him after three balls. "How are you going, pal? You know you can just walk straight back whenever you like." He told me to mind my own business and get on and make a hundred. The pain from a broken jaw is excruciating. It made me realise what Test cricket is all about.

Who would have believed that the game ended with a 45-run victory to Australia, the same result as the very first Test match played at the MCG exactly 100 years before?

Who can forget the brash, young Derek Randall doffing his cap and bowing after a Lillee bouncer? Randall won the Man of the Match Award of $1600 with his second innings of 174, but I thought the award should have gone to Lillee who took 11/165 for the game. We chaired Dennis off the ground at the end of the match, but I think he would have much rather have pocketed the $1600.

chapter fourteen

PACKER *really* did CARE

Packer turned up a few minutes later. Kerry threw off his suit coat, rolled up his sleeves and proceeded to hurl the ball as hard as he could at us from a short distance. A big bloke with a good and powerful arm, he chucked them straight at our heads.

There was much gnashing of teeth and pointing of fingers over the emergence of World Series Cricket, and the announcement which rocked the Establishment to its very core came during the 1977 Australian tour of England. Doug believed the Australians' bad performance in England was in no way due to the WSC revolution.

A lot of critics blamed the worry of World Series Cricket for our poor performances in England in 1977, but to me that was a load of rubbish and a way of throwing off at the new outfit. After all, we knew about WSC during the Centenary Test and it didn't affect our performance there. That 1977 tour of England was a disaster. First and most importantly Dennis Lillee, after a long Australian season, decided that his back needed rest and he didn't make the trip. Thommo was coming back from his shoulder injury and to make matters for him a lot worse he suffered an elbow injury. We were in a rebuilding phase and we had several players who hadn't toured England before.

That put the onus on the more experienced blokes, like me, but again I failed in the Tests there, getting only 223 runs at 24.77. Added to our batting woes was the fielding and we dropped seventeen catches in the first four Tests. We won only five of the twenty-two matches and lost the Ashes three—nil. Thirteen of the seventeen Australian squad had signed with Kerry Packer's 'Circus', as the press liked to label it. There were four blokes in our squad not invited to join WSC: they were Craig Sergeant, Gary Cosier, Geoff Dymock and Kim Hughes, although early in the piece Jeff Thomson was released from his original contract. The thirteen guys who had signed up with WSC met Kerry Packer for the first time at London's Savoy Hotel. He wanted to know what problems the players might have with their employers and said he didn't expect there would be too many hassles. Several of the blokes were working in banks and Kerry said, 'Right, what bank do you work with?' A couple of the boys said they worked for the Commonwealth Bank and Kerry said that was little problem because he had a couple of healthy accounts with that bank. Rick McCosker said he was with the Rural Bank [of NSW]. Kerry wasn't quick here and told Rick that he might have a slight problem, but he could work things out there as well because his wife had an account at the Rural, and that too was a healthy account. That was one time Kerry didn't get it dead right, for the blokes at the Rural had trouble getting time off to play WSC.

Kerry told us the only thing that could stop WSC being a success was a mass walk-out. World Series Cricket hit the headlines for the first time in the second week of May 1977. At the time we were watching the rain at Hove. I was amazed that news didn't break a lot sooner, for there were by now so many people involved. There had been mention of WSC in South Africa weeks before when a well-informed gentleman spoke about it at a dinner. He explained the whole deal and was spot on, but no-one took him seriously. They couldn't believe what was going down. The press gave us a hard time. They even had a go at the way we dressed, unimpressed, it seems, about some of the team wearing casual blue jeans and T-shirts to the games.

Usually the Australians would play at Manchester for the First Test of the tour, but in 1977 Greg Chappell's Australians played England at Lord's for what was known as the Jubilee Test. The Jubilee Test was to commemorate 25 years of the reign of Queen Elizabeth II. Freddie scored 53 in the first dig and 10 in the second. The match was a draw, but it produced a total attendance of 101 050 and the record receipts—£220 384—for any cricket match in Britain.

With the new professionalism about to start, Freddie was among those who looked at the huge money being made in a very different light.

With the amount of money generated by the Jubilee Test, is it any wonder the players wanted a slice of that rich cake?

The England team also had a host of players who had signed with Packer: Tony Greig, Alan Knott, Dennis Amiss, Derek Underwood and Bob Woolmer. Greig was the first WSC man to suffer at the hands of the Establishment. He was immediately stripped of the England captaincy for the Ashes series. Mike Brearley took over for the series, although Greig was retained in all the games. The Second Test was played at Old Trafford, a ground that has always been kind to Freddie. He hit twin eighties there in 1968, and in 1977 he scored 88, before holing out to a poor delivery. Doug rues that poor shot.

Any chance I had of scoring a Test century in England went out the door when on 88 I hit a full toss from England off-spinner Geoff Miller straight to Greig at extra cover. One writer observed, 'Walters fell to a ball a schoolboy would have dispatched contemptuously.' He was right. We lost that Test by nine wickets and Greg Chappell read us the riot act. 'If you are not prepared to give 100 per cent in the field you won't play again on tour,' he said. Greg asked us for a total commitment. With six weeks to go, he asked that we strive to win all eight games left in our schedule. Sadly, we didn't have that success. Geoff Boycott returned, after three years in Test exile, for Trent Bridge and he reminded us of his staying power by scoring 107 in 420 minutes. Boycott was at his obstinate best in the England second innings, scoring 80 not out in 314 minutes. The headline in the Sydney Sun *read: 'Barnacle Boycott'. Never were truer words written.*

England won the Third Test by seven wickets.

In the Fourth Test at Headingly, Geoff Boycott became the first batsman to score his 100th first-class hundred in a Test match. Boycott went on to score 191 and the method of Boycott's batting, rather than his scoring strokes, made a big impact on Doug Walters. It was on 11 August 1977 that Freddie fully realised why he had failed so often in Tests in England.

After he had reached three figures and he must have been seeing the ball like a football, I watched in amazement as Boycott missed four balls in one over from Lillee by five or six inches. I couldn't believe that a class batsman, as Boycott surely was, could miss deliveries by such a long way. Then I realised that my technique in adjusting to the moving ball in England often led to my downfall. I vowed to play straight down the line like Boycott did that day at Headingly if ever I had the chance to tour England again with an Australian Test team.

Greg Chappell was intrigued when he learnt that Doug Walters would have used an entirely new approach to batting had he toured England in 1981.

Conditions in England have changed a lot since the 1960s and 1970s. The advent of ODI cricket and wicket preparation (covered wickets) has changed markedly. Since 1989 I haven't seen any Australian touring team experience the sort of seaming wickets I remembered from the 1960s and 1970s.

English bowling has changed as well. Every County had a [John] Snow, a [Derek] Shackelton, a [Geoff] Arnold, a [Brian] Statham, a [Ken] Palmer or a [Tom] Cartwright, men who could bowl a very tight line and length with good movement (each way) on helpful pitches.

Throw in Derek Underwood and one's technique and patience were thoroughly tested. Touring team's averages against England would have risen five or more points since the late 1980s, so Doug's timing was off as well. No other team could apply the same pressure to Doug, or anyone else, until the advent of the West Indies from 1977 to the late 1990s. Doug's attitude to batting was his greatest asset, but was not helpful to him when it came to batting against England under those conditions. When he was anxious he became very bottom-handed and that squared him up to the bowler and had him come across the line as he pushed his hands in front of the body, and, because he had such a good eye, he could catch up to the moving ball and nick it. I would be interested in how he intended to change his method if he had gone [to England] in 1981. Unless he loosened the bottom hand grip I doubt that he could have not followed the ball because once the hands get ahead of the body it is hard not to follow the ball.

Doug was one of the most instinctive players that I have ever seen. [Ricky] Ponting is another. At nineteen they were similar players but, perhaps, because Ponting is a full-time cricketer he has worked on his game and is now one of the best Australian players of all time.'[1]

As a youngster Doug played a lot of tennis at school. Possessing strong wrists and forearms, Doug had good court-craft, but when cricket took over he became an occasional tennis player. He was surprised to be invited to play in a tennis pro-am tournament at London's Queens Club, which hosts one of the lead-up tournaments to Wimbledon.

During the 1977 tour I was invited to play in a tennis pro-am tournament at London's Queens Club, which hosts one of the lead-up tournaments to Wimbledon. I happily accepted the invitation and was drawn to play with Mark Edmonson in the one-set, tie-break knockout competition. I could hit a tennis ball okay and Mark was keen to do well.

Surprisingly we saw some of the highly ranked pairs going by the board and we were very surprised (well, I was) to find ourselves in the final, against David Hookes and Drew McMillan.

That final was more nerve-wracking than facing fast bowlers in Test cricket and we soon found ourselves down 3–5 and love–40. I had visions of Hookesy giving me heaps about our impending defeat for the rest of the tour. Fortunately, Mark was serving (the pros were allowed only one service game in this tournament) and he turned the match around from our seemingly hopeless position. We came back to win the game, the set and the trophy. I can tell you that trophy takes pride of place above all others in my showcase at home.

Freddie took advantage of his victory to give Hookesy plenty of cheek and they joined a few of the other Australians for a couple of drinks to drown David's sorrows and celebrate Freddie's victory.

A notable absentee was my partner Mark Edmonson. He appeared some time later, just before the presentation of the trophy and the winner's cheque. There was a bit of heckling from the Australian contingent over distribution of the cheque. Mark was being reminded in no uncertain manner that he was obliged to hand over to me half the winnings. But Eddo ignored the heckling. He later took me aside and said that he hadn't received too many cheques of late and I was welcome to hang on to the trophy. Two years earlier Mark had won the Australian Open and I was over the moon about the trophy, so he seemed relieved that I wasn't all out for the money.

Freddie was more interested in getting his clutches on an ice-cold beer. Edmonson offered to buy him one, then he returned with a pint of warm English bitter. It was enough to test the patience of a saint. It wasn't the sort of dilemma he might face in combating a fast bowler, that split-second, whether to hook or duck the ball; this was far more serious.

Some Pommy lagers are okay, but there was no way I could come at this. No way, either, could I endanger my reputation by letting it get around that Doug Walters had knocked back a beer.

'Listen, Eddo,' I said, 'You're a lovely bloke and thanks to you I've had a great day, but if you don't get over to the bar pronto and trade this pint in for a cold lager, I'm going to stand up and announce that you have dudded me out of my share of the winner's cheque.'

Dougie got his cold beer.

During the 1977 tour Doug was given the opportunity to captain the team in the game against Glamorgan at St Helen's in Swansea. That match was drawn. The only other occasion that Doug led Australia was in the game against Minor Counties and he led his men to the first loss in history against them.

I captained Australia for the first time, against Glamorgan at St Helen's in Swansea. The game was drawn. I also led the side against Minor Counties in Australia's first-ever loss against them. However, I won't accept full responsibility for the defeat, for I had a bit of help from Kerry O'Keeffe. In the second innings I tried to pull one of their opening bowlers, got a top edge, and the ball crashed into my chin. I had to go to hospital and have seven stitches inserted in a cut and Kerry took over the captaincy. O'Keeffe set Minor Counties 207 to score in 165 minutes and they got them.

The Test series ended at The Oval, in a draw and, in what turned out to be Doug Walters' last Test match innings, he was bowled by gangling Bob Willis for 4. While Australian cricket was in turmoil, Doug believes England deserved to win the Ashes.

We were beaten by a better team. One of the more ridiculous attempts to find reasons why we lost so easily was the assertion by the press that we had seven wives on tour and their presence affected our cricket. In fact, most of the time when Caroline went on tour she had to stay at a different hotel because of orders from the team management. I never saw any sense in that for, if anything, it made things more difficult, and I often spent time organising transport for Caroline that would have been unnecessary had she been staying with me in the same hotel. One of the things that made Caroline happy about my switch to World Series Cricket was that World Series promised to look after the wives and they did. It was

*certainly a change for Caroline to be well looked after by officials, for if
the players were the poor relations by the Australian Cricket Board, our
wives had an even worse time of it.*

———

Throughout his career in State and Test cricket, Doug Walters has
been the most laid-back, phlegmatic and relaxed person you could
find anywhere.

His team-mates, the press and the public love the bloke for his
skill at the game, his earthiness and his loyalty. Everyone warmed
to his relaxed style, his carefree nature. The man in the street liked
his technique as a cricketer for here was a bloke who liked a drink,
like they did, who liked a smoke, like they did, and who played
the game every bit as much as they dreamed they might play the
game. Get to the game, have a quiet smoke, go out and hit a quick-
fire hundred, then sit in the relative calm of the dressing-room,
reach for a cold beer and light up a cigarette. Journalist Norm Tasker,
the bloke who rang the Marshdale telephone exchange with news
of Doug's selection in the NSW team, says:

> Doug was a supreme talent as a cricketer. A very natural talent.
> I once worked with him on a coaching series in *The Sun* aimed
> at kids, somewhere about 1969. I got the impression through
> that experience that he didn't really know what he did at the
> crease . . . he just did it. Just hit the bloody ball.

Maybe Norm hit upon Doug's batting secret. He simply hit
the ball. On true pitches where the ball came at a consistent height,
Doug reigned supreme. It was on the sluggish tracks of England,
where the ball darted off the seam that Doug struggled. Failing
in the Tests in England for a fourth successive time must have
weighed heavily on his mind as a new challenge loomed.

Yet his alert mind and laid-back attitude probably helped him through a tough period for Doug the batsman. When the 1977 Australian team returned from England most of the team were ostracised because they had dared to sign up for WSC. That was one psychological hurdle. There would be at least one more to come.

—m—

Australia had enough players signed up with WSC that they could field two sides—the number one team, under the captaincy of Ian Chappell would play the Supertests, and the number two team would play in the country areas. In the early match conditions, it was agreed that the fast bowlers would be given a bit of leeway in regards to overstepping the front line. They were supposed to allow about six inches, but the umpires let them go way past that mark. On the country pitches the wickets were pretty bad and the bounce was always variable. Freddie found himself out of the Supertests and on the country tour.

Ross Edwards and I were having lots of trouble with the short-pitched bowling and we were consistently edging to the gully area. This was something which had been happening to me for two or three seasons. In the off-season I received a phone call from Ross, who told me to be at Barry Knight's Cricket Centre at 3.30 p.m. that day.

Kerry Packer wanted us to spend some time at the nets and see if together we might iron out our batting woes. I was on time for I was told that Kerry would be there. Packer turned up a few minutes later. Kerry threw off his suit coat, rolled up his sleeves and proceeded to hurl the ball as hard as he could at us from a short distance. A big bloke with a good and powerful arm, he chucked them straight at our heads.

The former England all-rounder Barry Knight, who years earlier had emigrated to Sydney and started up his coaching centre, approached Packer and said that it might be advisable for him to use a tennis ball, lest he have the deaths of two of his men on his hands.

After that we used the soft ball, but you know, the ploy worked. I managed to sort out my back-lift, getting the bat to go back straighter. I used to take my bat back on an angle, aiming at third slip. I don't think I got to bringing the bat back as straight as Geoff Boycott or Greg Chappell but it became a lot straighter than it was. Kerry told us to hire a squash court and train together twice weekly. Rosco and I trained for two nights every week at that squash court centre and do you know Packer did not fail to ring the centre to check that we were there training. Not once did he miss. Obviously he wasn't too worried about the couple of bucks required to hire the court, but he did show a genuine interest in his players' welfare.

I came to greatly respect Packer for what he gave for the game and the players. He really cared about us; he cared about our welfare and our form. Kerry Packer played an active part in WSC. He went to all the main games and kept a close watch on proceedings. He invited all the WSC players and officials to his home around Christmas time in the second year of WSC. He mightn't have been making much money out of World Series, but that didn't stop him putting on a super party. No expense was spared and we had a great day.

But Doug's WSC days weren't the happiest in purely cricket terms. He played in the first Supertest against the West Indies at VFL Park, Waverley, in December 1977, scoring just 16 and 5, and was destined never to play another of these games. Doug became a regular on the country circuit, where we played the West Indies and the Rest of the World.

David Hookes was cruising to a startling century in the Second Supertest on the lightning-fast Sydney Showground wicket, when he hooked at an Andy Roberts bouncer, missed, and the ball delivered him a sickening blow to the jaw—the bone was shattered.

The Sydney wicket was fast, it was true, unlike most of the wickets in the country. But how could anyone gain form and confidence against fast bowlers on poor wickets, which were supposed to last two full days, but in reality they barely lasted one full session?

The variable bounce was the killer; one ball the batsman was fending away from his throat, the next trying to keep out a grubber. Doug may not have set WSC alight with a flurry of big scores, but he did retain his sense of humour and was a part of a revolution which brought professionalism and far better pay and conditions for our top cricketers.

Freddie enjoyed his second year of World Series Cricket. Kerry Packer also enjoyed it, for the introduction of night cricket helped transform the game. More than 40 000 people turned up at the SCG to watch the first big game of cricket under lights. That night's cricket did more than anything to bring closure to the revolution. The Establishment could see its power diminishing and so a compromise was likely.

A compromise had to happen for the sake of cricket. There was too much cricket being played in Australia at the time and I don't think there was enough room for both sides to succeed. I thought I'd be well and truly retired before the parties got together, but it was good to see both sides pulling together for the good of this great game.

I didn't get a lot of runs in WSC, but it's hard to notch a big score batting number six in a one-day game. My form was poor in the first WSC season [1977–78], but I was reasonably happy with my efforts in the second season. I made quite a few 30s and 40s in the one-day games and that's about all you can expect. The good thing we found about World Series Cricket was we were signed to play 55 days' cricket and you played those 55 days just about straight through, so it gave the players more time to spend with their wives and children.

Talking about big money, when we used to ride around in coaches going to WSC matches, it became a standard joke, whenever we saw a bloke in a checked coat, for someone to say, 'Hey, there's Kerry Packer with the big cheques.'

The batting helmet was 'born' during WSC. I remember Dennis Amiss going to the crease looking as though he'd be more at home on a motor bike than at a cricket ground.

In one up-country WSC match Gary Gilmour mimicked revving up a motorbike when Amiss came out to bat. The helmets were like the motorcycle policeman's helmet, complete with a visor that you could lift up like a car boot. As Doug points out, the big cricket revolution wasn't just about pay and conditions, cricket under lights and coloured clothing: there were moves afoot for the batting helmet to become part of every player's kit.

Since that first Amiss' model, the helmet has been modified and stream-lined and these days the helmets they wear do not affect your neck the way the old, heavier ones certainly did. Helmets were ridiculed when they first came in and the World Series boys were called 'squibs', but it wasn't long before the Establishment players were wearing them. And why not? It's no fun having a bloke tear in and try to rip your head off from 20 metres and I, for one, will take any protection that's on offer.

Unlike many others who joined WSC, Doug never experienced any ill-will from any source over his leaving the traditional game.

I never experienced any resentment from anybody over my joining World Series Cricket. When we came back to the fold, we were treated like the Prodigal Son. We'd been away, but now we were back and there would be plenty of goodies for everyone. If I had my time over I'd sign with World Series again.

The main disappointment I suffered was not being allowed to play club cricket. That's grass roots cricket, and I missed it. I thought that action [by the Australian Cricket Board and the State associations] in stopping players who had signed with WSC in playing grade cricket was petty.

I didn't think I'd play for New South Wales again, let alone Australia, when the 1979–80 season began. I thought they'd feel I was too old and stick with one of the younger blokes who played when WSC was on.

Even the bloke who used to put that sign up on the Hill at the SCG had given up on me and even presented me with the sign. Now what can you do with a 12-metre-long strip of canvas which reads, DOUG WALTERS STAND?

A few years later the SCG Trust named the stand on the old Sydney Hill, The Doug Walters Stand. The stand has been demolished and a new stand has been under construction for some time. SCG Trust chairman Mr Rodney Cavalier said the new stand will not carry Doug Walters' name. 'The new stand will be named after a great cricketer who played in the pre-television era. Such names as Dave and Syd Gregory, Charlie MacCartney and Victor Trumper come to mind,' he said. 'While the Doug Walters Stand has gone, that does not mean that Dougie will not be otherwise recognised somewhere in the new stand.'[3]

Freddie had a consistent year with the bat: 27 and 0* versus Western Australia at the SCG; 83 and 10* versus Victoria at the SCG; 43 and 80 versus South Australia at Adelaide; 83 and 14 versus Queensland at the SCG; 24 and 34* versus Victoria at the MCG; 5 versus Tasmania at Launceston; 16 versus Queensland at the Gabba; 62 versus England XI in Canberra; 72* and 35 versus South Australia at the SCG.   * denotes not out

My new-found consistency pleased me no end. And I was rapt in being picked again for Australia in the one-day matches. I played in two and was twelfth man for another three.

It was great to be back with the boys and playing for Australia again.

The Sheffield Shield match against South Australia at the SCG was a volatile game if ever there was one, and it featured a long-running battle between Ian Chappell and Len Pascoe. Chappell hit 158 in the SA first innings and he continued to bait Lennie throughout. At one stage Chappelli wandered over to a point and banged in a stump, indicating that Freddie was bowling too wide and he couldn't reach them. Immediately after that little bit of by-play, Chappelli drove at a wide out-swinger from Freddie and he snicked it waist-high, straight to Rick McCosker at first slip. Freddie leapt high into the air with excitement only to see McCosker turf what was a simple, waist-high catch.

Freddie scored a first-innings 72 not out and in the second I had him caught at slip by Chappell for 35.

Getting Doug Walters was worth at least three wickets in one for me. He was a brilliant player of off-break bowling, the best I've ever seen. Batting a second time, South Australia was blasted out for 69, Pascoe getting 7/18. South Australia had to win the Sheffield Shield, but alas, New South Wales won by a mile.

Straight after the game, Chappelli took a bottle of beer into the victor's room, saying, 'Well done everyone,' and especially well-bowled to Len Pascoe.

But Lennie was in no mood to accept Chappelli's words. He sprang from his bench seat and grabbed Chappelli by the throat, pinning him to the wall. He charged Chappell with not affording him the respect he deserved. Chappelli replied: 'Len, have you ever thought that I might have been trying to annoy you because you're the best bowler in the side?' Chappelli's words helped pacify Lennie, but his ruse had failed, for Pascoe responded to the SA captain's taunts during the game and he bowled SA out for a pathetic 69. At least Chappelli talking to Lennie post-match prevented mayhem of another kind.

New Zealand and India were scheduled to tour in the 1980–81 season and it wasn't beyond the realms of possibility that Doug Walters could get back into the Australian team.

I thought this season would be my swan song. The NSW Cricket Association must have thought so too for it did me the great honour of granting me a benefit year: I formed a committee that handled the organisation of events. A lot fell to Caroline to organise as I was away for much of the time playing cricket. We played in Tooheys cricket matches around the country areas of New South Wales. These were tough games. We had to visit about seven hotels and clubs and have a drink with the locals for a couple of days before the game. This was all part of the Tooheys promotion. It was tough work!

I must admit that at the start of the new season I thought, 'Wouldn't it be great if I could get a couple of scores and make the Australian team?' I was hardly needed to bat early on for the NSW early order got so many runs. Then came the match against South Australia in Sydney. I was seeing the ball pretty well. When I was 41 I played at a ball from medium-pacer Geoff Attenborough, and the South Australians made a concerted appeal. The umpire was unimpressed and called over. I am afraid he made a mistake.

Doug made a mistake in edging the ball and the umpire could not have missed the deflection, for the wicketkeeper had to move a good couple of paces to his left to accept the ball. We could only assume the umpire did not hear the snick, that familiar willow on leather sound which came loud and clear to us behind the wicket.

Doug survived and went on to play a classic Walters innings, a knock full of adventurous shots, cuts, drives, even the sweep shot.

I went on to make 186. Without that score New South Wales would probably have been beaten and I wouldn't have made the Australian team again. So I was not the slightest bit sorry for standing my ground and I would do it all again under the same circumstances.

That 186 was an outstanding innings, one of the best I had seen from Freddie in any form of cricket. He cut and drove, even swept, with power and precision. He was ruthless in this knock and highly calculating. Perhaps in his subconscious he reckoned this was very much his last chance of making an impact and getting another go wearing the baggy green cap.

Freddie was picked for the first Test against New Zealand in Brisbane. His greatest fan, John Bracewell, debuted for the Kiwis in that match and got to bowl, albeit briefly, to his hero, who eventually fell, bowled by Lance Cairns for 17. In the second Test Freddie hit 55 and then scored 1 and 40 against Queensland at the SCG, before playing the Third Test versus New Zealand at the MCG. There he scored 107, but not before much drama and controversy. Australia was 9/261 when the hope of the side, last man Jim Higgs, who you'll recall failed to score a single run on the 1975 Australian tour of England, sauntered out on the MCG to join Freddie.

I was on 61 when Higgsy joined me. He took centre and I knew there were two balls to go, so I thought he was wasting his time. The first ball from Lance Cairns shaved his off stump, and then came the second ball. It was short and lifting, and Higgsy just put his hands above his head and gloved it straight to the keeper. We started to go off and from the bowler's end, Umpire Robin Bailhache yelled, 'No-ball!' and I said, 'Robin, what was that for?' and he said 'Doug, that is the experimental law we are having this year and fast bowlers can't bowl short-pitched balls to blokes who can't bat.' I said, 'We all know Higgsy can't bat, but are you calling him [Cairns] a fast bowler?' So they allowed Higgs to bat on. I got out for a hundred [107] and Higgsy went crook; reckoned I could have stuck around until he got his ton. 'I did the right thing by you, Freddie. Now it's your turn,' he laughed.

Higgs scored 6 not out. He faced 61 balls and batted for 94 minutes. He hit one four. Freddie scored 107 off 206 balls in 276 minutes with six fours. It was his last of fifteen Test centuries.

Freddie played three more Tests that summer—against India, scoring 67 at the SCG, 20 and 33 in Adelaide and 78 and 18 not out at the MCG. His final first-class knock for New South Wales was against Tasmania at the SCG. He scored 55. It was 7 March 1981: the last of his 258 first-class matches. The side was selected for England in 1981 and Doug Walters' name was missing from the list. His Test career was effectively over and he decided to retire.

Former WA, SA and Test batsman John Inverarity admired Doug Walters for his determination to be himself as a batsman.

Doug invariably played the same way, sticking to his natural game and remaining untroubled and not distracted by the state of the game. He kept a clear head and just played. Many players have unwittingly impeded their development by both changing their method and by attempting to adapt too much to the situations of the moment. Doug just played and his wonderful record is testimony to not only his abundance of natural talent and athletic prowess, but also to the fact that he did not allow himself to be diverted from his most familiar and trusted pathway. The management of most modern first-class teams would have been greatly challenged by some aspects of Doug's match preparation and lifestyle. I suspect they would have considered him to be intolerably unprofessional in some ways. All credit to Doug for being such a shining beacon in the cause for anti-earnest, boring, excessive professionalism. His way would be a ray of sunshine today. I am reminded of the refreshing remarks made by Scolari, the coach of Portugal in the 2006 Football World Cup: 'My priority is to ensure that players feel more amateur than professional. Thirty to 40 years ago the effort was the other way. Now there is so much professionalism we have to revert to urging the players to like the game, love it, do it with joy.'

Doug Walters played with unbridled joy shining through and he gave great joy to hundreds of thousands of fans.[4]

And it was a long and enjoyable journey for Freddie.

Kevin Douglas Walters: career in statistics

Batting

Category Matches inns no runs hs ave
Tests 74 125 14 5357 250 48.26
ODIs 28 24 6 513 59 28.50
First-class 258 426 57 16180 253 43.84
List A 49 40 11 940 71 32.41

Bowling

Category Matches balls runs wkts bbi bbm ave econ
Tests 74 3295 1425 49 5/66 7/89 29.08 2.59
ODIs 28 314 273 4 2/24 2/24 68.25 5.21

First-class 258 14576 6782 190 7/63 8/103 35.69 2.79
List A 49 1107 825 29 4/28 4/28 28.44 4.47

In Tests Doug Walters took 43 catches and in all first class matches he took 149 catches.

chapter fifteen
happy
ENDING

Those who knew Freddie well were a little unsure as to how their remarkable friend would settle down to a life not playing cricket at the highest level: indeed, a life not playing cricket at all.

Freddie was disappointed in not making the 1981 Australian tour of England, if only because he was denied the chance to prove his theory on 'the way to bat in England'. It was at Headingly, Leeds where Freddie saw the 'batting light'. He stood at slip and found himself laughing at Geoff Boycott's lamentable efforts to lay bat on ball to a succession of Len Pascoe deliveries.

I couldn't believe that Boycott could play and miss by such a long way some four balls in a row. I laughed. But I stopped laughing pretty quickly when I realised that Boycott's playing and missing had shown me the way to bat on the seaming wickets in England.

Freddie always reacted rapidly to a ball which changed direction. His hand–eye coordination was better than most and in reacting in this manner on slow wickets Freddie actually caught up with the ball. So often he found he would get a thick edge and the ball would fly at catchable height somewhere in the region of gully.

On Australian pitches when the ball moved it went quickly, Freddie played and missed... and survived. Boycott, who in 1977 went on to score 191 in that Leeds Test, played straight down the line. It was the English way. If the ball moved in or away it missed the bat. An in-swinger hit the batsman on the front pad and the out-swinger, or leg-cutter missed the outside edge. Freddie resolved to use that batting strategy if he made the 1981 team to England.

I used this new technique in my last Australian summer and it worked okay. But while I resolved to bat that way in England, I wasn't picked for the tour, so I never got the chance to test my theory.

Freddie eased nicely into retirement from cricket. He continues to tend his Carlingford home vegetable patch where a weed is despatched with all the finality of a long-hop being disappearing over the mid-wicket boundary by a savage Doug Walters pull shot. He continues to follow the races avidly and, as in his cricket career, Freddie has more wins than losses. He works his crosswords, always on the lookout for a new card trick and has been the star of more after-dinner speaking engagements than the mountain of runs he scored in Test cricket.

Often Freddie is invited back to the same speaking venue and urged to tell the same stories, in the same sequence, to further entertain with his myriad card tricks and then drink with the mob until the wee hours. Recently Greg Matthews rang and asked Freddie if he could stand-in for him and do a charity gig in Melbourne. Freddie accepted. The deal was he would fly to Melbourne and be collected at Melbourne airport and conveyed to the charity venue.

The charity had something to do with TV personality Tony Barber. I got to Melbourne airport, but no-one turned up to meet me. I stayed three hours, then I caught a return flight home. A day or so later, I enquired about the charity 'do' and before I had time to explain, I was told, 'Mate, you were terrific. Freddie, they loved you. Fantastic stuff.' To this day I wonder about that experience.

Freddie says he keeps his asking price at a reasonable level so he continues to get regular work, to the tune of some hundred gigs a year. He used to team with ex-champion jockey Malcolm Johnson, the man who rode into turf history by riding Kingston Town to 25 career wins.

We'd bounce off each other. I'd talk about my era, but not always. Malcolm is a great character and we seem to 'gel'. I have worked alongside some of Australia's best comedians, including Calvin the Grey, Brian Doyle and Johnny Garfield.

When he is not away speaking at a show or hosting a tour for cricket tragics, Freddie, wearing shorts, tracksuit top and thongs, will be sitting in the downstairs patio, under the yawning perspex, within third slip's reach of the pristine swimming pool and vegetable patch, at his Carlingford home, some 40 minutes from Sydney centre. He'll sip coffee and light up a smoke. The racing form studied, the crossword done and the sun sneaking up the yard arm . . . it's time to knock the head off one.

Neighbours drop by to have a chat and share a beer, for Freddie is the most welcoming of human beings.

Since he gave the game away, Doug had a long run of commercials with Max Walker and three successful joke books, one by himself and two others, one with Rodney Marsh and the other with Mark Waugh. He has also helped promote beer, such as Toohey's 2.2 ale. And he has a Chinese connection. China became an annual excursion for Freddie, with a touring company of ex-Test and State cricketers, organised by former Waverley Cricket Club president, Phil O'Sullivan.

On that first China trip in 1984, there was planned a warm-up match for the team against Kowloon Cricket Club in Hong Kong. Carolyn and Doug brought their second-born son, Lynton, with them, reasoning that a trip to China would broaden the youngster's education (Lynton was then eight years old). A Hong Kong harbour cruise was organised and the tour party was invited to dinner on the island of Lama.

The hospitality on board that junk was fabulous and I tucked into the Chinese fare and the odd XXXX beer. After a while I realised that I hadn't seen Lynton for awhile. The harbour seemed a bit rough and I feared Lynton might be up the front of the vessel, with some of the more courageous cricketers. If you've ever been on a junk, you will know that the railing doesn't go all the way round and I picked the worst possible time to go for a walk. Just as I reached the un-railed section of the boat, we hit a big wave. There was no rail to hang on to and overboard I went. I plunged ever so ungracefully over the side into the middle of Victoria Harbour. Thankfully, Lady Luck was with me this night, for a very alert captain was the only person on the junk to see me fall overboard.

Captain 'Rescue' swiftly brought the junk astern and had the lifebuoy over the side and next to the floundering Walters so fast that he didn't have to think, just hang on and have the ship's crew haul him back on deck.

Carolyn was not at all amused. For a minute she must have had visions of returning to Sydney a widow.

The Walters' 'Overboard in Hong Kong' tale has been re-told and embellished to the extent that it has become part of the legend of Doug.

There were about 60 people on board that night and yet I have met a lot of people who swear they were on that junk. Not only did they see me fall overboard, they also swear that I broke the surface of Victoria Harbour, holding a glass of beer in one hand and a soggy cigarette in the other.

—⁂—

On 4 January 2006, 150 people turned up to help Freddie celebrate his 60th birthday. Who else but Doug Walters could have such a party in the front bar of his local watering hole—the Great Northern Hotel, Chatswood?

Next day I discovered I needed about 100 sips to get through my first beer of the day. At the party I tried to have at least one drink with everyone there, but I failed. Mind you, I only failed having a drink with every single person there by three . . .

Let's see . . . Normie and Tabsy, Evil and Beatle, Chappelli and Crazy and Benauds and . . . the list goes on.

Freddie has slipped into cricket retirement like feet into the most comfortable slippers. He won't change and no-one would ever want him to change. Freddie, however, isn't afraid to speak out when the occasion warrants . . .

305

chapter sixteen
don't 'BAG' the CAP

They are not professionals ... they were all invited to play and, if they don't like the conditions, there are 500 000 other cricketers in Australia who would love to take their places.[1]

– Alan Barnes

Every schoolboy cricketer in Australia yearns to play Test cricket. He yearns to pull on the coveted baggy-green cap and walk that Test stage which has hosted myriad stars from Trumper to Bradman to Warne. The baggy-green cap is as much Australian as the kangaroo, the Sydney Harbour Bridge and the slouch hat. It is a part of the national identity. Yet in more than 130 years of Test cricket, less than 400 players have worn the baggy-green. For the majority of players, the path to the Test stage is a long and weary struggle. Clarrie Grimmett toiled for years for recognition, spending seven years in veritable isolation in Sydney during and after the Great War, then in Melbourne, before he found his haven in Adelaide, eventually making his Test debut at the age of 32.

Grimmett was Australia's 121st Test player. Don Bradman has the number 124; one of Doug's heroes, Keith Miller is number 169; Peter Burge, who advised Doug to continue attacking as a batsman, is number 200 and Doug is Australia's 237th Test cricketer.

Batsmen such as Norm O'Neill and Ian Chappell had to perform consistently over a number of seasons to finally make the Test squad. And so it was with Doug. He played for New South Wales at the age of seventeen, was an immediate success, but didn't play his first Test until December 1965, a few days before his twentieth birthday.

Along with a list of champions, there was no easy path for Doug to play Test cricket, and it is little wonder that he gets a bit miffed when he sees the Australian selectors virtually giving away a baggy-green.

The Australian selectors have blundered seriously in recent times.

Two off-spinners—Nathan Hauritz (Test player number 390) and Daniel Cullen (number 397)—have each been presented with a baggy-green cap and have played in a Test match without performance on the board.

> *Your mate—SA off-spinner Dan Cullen—has been on the scene for ten minutes, turns up in Bangladesh and is put straight into a Test match with Shane Warne and Stuart MacGill. I regard Cullen's inclusion in that Test match as an insult to the other two spinners.*

Cullen made his debut in the Second Test against Bangladesh at Chittagong in April 2006, a game made famous by nightwatchman Jason Gillespie getting 201 not out.

Because both Warne and MacGill were in the eleven and obviously would play a big part in the make-up of the attack on a slow pitch, Cullen bowled sparingly. He sent down seven overs in each innings for a total of 1/54 for the match. Warne bowled 54.2 overs for a return of 8/160 and MacGill bowled 44.4 overs to notch 7/173.

I presume Cullen's selection was to do with Stuart Clarke, who had a successful tour of South Africa, opting out of the Bangladesh tour because his missus is having a kid, which was ridiculous. There have been a helluva lot of cricketers in the past who didn't get home for Christmas and weren't at home for their birthday, let alone being home for the birth of their children. I think doctors are better equipped today to handle the situation [child birth] than was the case 50 years ago, but I cannot accept the giving away of Australian caps, even in a one-day situation. You pick your best team and you pick your best team every time.

I don't agree with the rotation system, but whether it is a Test match or a one-day international, you've got to earn an Australian cap.

In the lead-up season (2005–06) to his Test debut, Cullen took just 27 wickets for 1293 runs in State cricket, for an average of 47.89. After the Chittagong Test, Cullen played five matches for Somerset in English County Cricket, bowling a total of 119 overs and taking 7/381—an average of 54.43. He then played two matches for Australia A against Pakistan A and India A for a return of 2/168—an average of 84.

Last summer (2006–07), Cullen's figures for South Australia in first-class cricket read: 13 wickets for 530 runs at an average of 40.78. He played six matches, having been dropped from a few Pura Cup matches in a generally disastrous year for the Redbacks. Despite another average season, Cullen was named among the 25 cricketers given a lucrative national contract. In the early stages of

2007–08, Cullen was still struggling for first-class wickets. However, if Cullen can turn his game around and get back to the sort of form which ensures his performance starts to match his potential, Doug Walters will be among the first to praise him.

Two years earlier the Australian selectors also picked badly by selecting two rookie spinners to support Shane Warne on the crucial tour of India.

Queensland off-spinner Nathan Hauritz, who had taken 16 Pura Cup wickets at 64 runs apiece, was, amazingly, picked for that Test tour, along with Victorian all-rounder, Cameron White. Hauritz was, at the time, bowling poorly and White never really threatened to do much outside of a few tight overs in one-day games. Hauritz's inclusion came back to haunt the Test selectors, for on the eve of the last Test match Shane Warne broke a finger which ruled him out of the game. Stuart MacGill had, stupidly, not even been selected for the tour, and because White was not an option to play in the Test match, Hauritz was handed a Test cap. He took five wickets for the game, but the Indian batsmen targeted him in their second innings on a pitch which was a minefield.

While Hauritz got 2/87 in the Indian second innings, occasional spinner Michael Clarke took 6/9. Struggling to get a regular game for Queensland, Hauritz moved to New South Wales. Last summer he played five Pura Cup matches, bowling a total of 87.4 overs taking 4/254—an average of 63.5 runs per wicket. Still in their early twenties, both Hauritz and Cullen have the chance to turn their cricket around and match performance with potential.

—⁓—

Our Test selectors handing out baggy-green Test caps 'willy nilly' is one of Doug's major concerns about the modern game.

But he is also concerned about many of our Test players not playing club or State cricket whenever that chance presented itself.

Glenn McGrath rarely played club or State cricket, whereas Jason Gillespie, whose international career may be resurrected on the strength of his new national contract, always jumps at the chance to play.

We all got our start in the game in grade cricket, and if the players are fit and available to play they should play. The players talk about the need for rest. Well, bowling ten overs in four spells in a one-day game, even for the fastest bowler, let alone a medium-pacer or a spinner, is not a real big ask. I wouldn't back Australia to beat anyone in a one-day match, but I would back them every time in a Test match.

I don't think Shane Warne should have been allowed to opt out of one-day cricket. The reason given was that by doing so it would lengthen the time he had left to play Test matches. I think if you are available to play for Australia you must make yourself available to play every match—Test or one-day game—in which you have been picked. I also don't agree with players picking one tour and not another. Some of the Englishmen have done this recently. Fine if you don't want to go on a certain tour, whether it is the subcontinent or wherever, but do not expect to get picked in the next Test team when the players return. Glenn McGrath missing South Africa and Bangladesh because of his wife, Jane's, serious illness is quite another matter, and I certainly agreed with him staying at home to help care for her.

—◊◊—

Doug is very happy with the manner in which Australia, especially, goes about its Test cricket.

I love the way our team plays the Test matches, well, up until recently and maybe that could be a reflection on Ricky Ponting's captaincy, I'm not sure. I haven't got a high regard for Ricky Ponting as a captain anyway, at this stage.

I think he's certainly the number one batsman in the world. If he wasn't as good a batsman . . . he's hiding his own blunders as captain by the scores he's putting on the board. I think he's made plenty of very basic mistakes in captaincy. He's often batted on too long. I think Allan Border began that trend of batting the opposition out of a match. AB against England would like the game to go on to the last session of the fifth day, and he got away with it most of the time. Mark Taylor took over and proved 'we could win Test matches in two and a half days by playing a bit of aggressive cricket'. Ponting seems to be in the AB mould, where he thinks Test cricket has got to always go over five days . . . We are not playing the same aggressive cricket which has been so successful over the past three or four years.

The latest five–nil drubbing by Australia in the Ashes series 2006–07, would tend to argue strongly against that view, but England were palpably weak. Technically, they were totally outclassed, and mentally, they simply could not cope. Michael Vaughan was out, so too Marcus Trescothick, and fast bowler Simon Jones. Ponting could afford to bat on and on at any time, because consistently they bowled the Poms out in less than a day.

Doug played Test cricket under six different Australian captains: Brian Booth, Bob Simpson, Bill Lawry, Barry Jarman, and Ian and Greg Chappell. He regards Ian Chappell as far and away the best captain he ever played under.

I was in Bathurst one night at a function. Bathurst is Brian Booth's home town. I had two prizes to give away at the end of the evening. I said I'll get rid of those pretty easily. The first two hands up by anyone knowing who was my first Test captain gets the prizes. And a lot of hands went up and a lot of names were called out among the 500-strong gathering, but not the name we were looking for, and I had to say that this bloke was named the 'Bathurst Bradman' who boarded with Mrs Brown at Bexley, and still no-one in the crowded room could name the player.

This bloke also played hockey for Australia in the 1956 Melbourne Olympics. Finally, one bloke put his hand up. He got both prizes. Then there was Bob Simpson. He missed the first Test because of a broken thumb and that's why Brian Booth captained the side in Brisbane. Simpson returned for the Second, Third and Fourth Tests, then he got chicken pox and Brian Booth captained my Fifth Test match. Then I went into National Service, and when I came out, Simmo had finished and Bill Lawry was the captain. Even the two Tests I played against India while I was still in Nashos, Lawry was captain. Next came Barry Jarman, who led the team side at Headingly, Leeds, after Lawry had broken a finger. Then there was Ian Chappell and Greg Chappell.

You ask me who was the best—well, there's no comparison between any of those guys. Ian Chappell was so superior it wasn't funny. Ian just understood cricket very well and he understood cricketers even better.

If Ian Chappell was the best captain he played under, who were the bowlers who most troubled Doug Walters?

I'd have to say John Snow [England fast bowler] was the first fast bowler I had difficulties with as far as quick bowlers go. Snow was the most accurate fast bowler I faced. He didn't waste a delivery, and when he bowled his bouncer he was at you and you had to play every ball. Snow didn't bowl his bouncer that went more than a couple of inches over your head.

Snow in the 1970–71 series against England operated on wickets that were generally variable in bounce, and I regard him as probably the first of the moderns to get the ball up at you off a good length and make you play the ball in front of your face. I'm sure the West Indies copied John Snow's method... Snow was one of those blokes who got at you a lot quicker than it appeared if you were watching from the dressing-room or the sidelines. South Africa's Mike Proctor also worried me. I always found it difficult to play the unorthodox bowlers.

Proctor charged into the wicket and bowled off the wrong foot. He bowled predominately late in-swingers, but he could bowl a good leg-cutter and a bouncer which came in, and seemed to follow you as you tried to sway back out of the line of the ball. He wasn't tall, but broad-shouldered and robust, like a Ray Lindwall or Fred Trueman. He was strong as an ox and operated at a speed round the pace of the West Indian great Malcolm Marshall.

We were all taught as kids to watch the ball as it came out of the bowler's hand, but these unorthodox bowlers made it difficult to pick up the flight of the ball. When you don't see the ball—because he's hiding it behind his back or bowling off the wrong foot—it is tough to pick up. When I talk about the best bowler I ever saw, Dennis Lillee, and the quickest bowler, Jeff Thomson, people say, 'How do you know if you never faced them?' I faced them two Sheffield Shield matches every year and every other day in the nets.

I think I've faced more balls from Dennis Lillee and Jeff Thomson than I faced from all the other bowlers in the world put together, so I think I have a fair idea of who was the best and who was the quickest. They would come back with, 'Yes, but those guys wouldn't have bowled quick at you in the nets.'

I say, 'You wanna bet?'

As far as spinners were concerned, Derek Underwood was the best, Bishen Bedi was number two.

During his eras Doug didn't seriously rate any of the leg-spinners. The best in international cricket was Pakistan's Intikhab Alam, and in Sheffield Shield cricket there was an assortment of leggies. The best 'leggie' of the era was undoubtedly Victoria's Jim Higgs, then came Queensland's ebullient Malcolm Franke; following them were South Australia's Terry Jenner, who was clever and subtle with changes of pace and use of the bowling crease, NSW leggies

Bob Holland and John Watkins, and the long-striding Chinaman bowler David 'Cracker' Hourn. Finally came the leg-spinner Bob Paulsen, who modelled his action on Richie Benaud, and while he didn't quite get to that standard, he was a good servant for Queensland, then Western Australia. In the twilight of Doug's career, Queensland Trevor Hohns bowled steady leg-breaks, but he was never the type of spinner to run through a side, rather he was a solid middle to late order batsman who bowled a bit. South Australia's Peter Sleep, who also began in the late 1970s, was more a batsman who bowled and never developed into a genuine front-line bowler for his State or country.

I don't think I came across a leg-spinner who was all that accurate and you knew you'd have a gift two or three balls an over if you could just sit on him and see him by. The odd good leg-spinner they bowled was off-put by a half-tracker or a full toss at least once or twice an over. So I can't think of a leg-spinner in my time that I really rate.

—m—

Doug believes today's Australian players should not be bleating about playing too much cricket.

The fact is, first-class players in the 1960s and 1970s played as many days cricket as Ponting's team. We didn't play as many Tests as they do today, but with grade, Shield and Test matches all thrown in, we played at least as many games as they play today.

There's a lot of people in Australia who would like to work as many days as the Australian players and get paid like the guys are today.

Our tour of Ceylon, India and South Africa in 1969 wasn't brilliantly organised. Ricky Ponting is complaining about the reverse. Going from South Africa to Bangladesh he complained of playing too much cricket.

It's not as if you are up against the world's best. Going from South Africa to Bangladesh . . . playing Bangladesh is a walk in the park.

I don't agree with Ponting's argument. Too much cricket? That's what you want to do as a cricketer, play cricket.

Doug might also smile wryly when noting that a number of Test men, including Gilchrist and Ponting, have signed on for more cricket under the new Indian breakaway competition.

These players today are getting very good money. Being away on tour goes with the territory. After the brief Bangladesh tour the players began a four-months' break. How many Australian workers on big money get the equivalent of long-service leave every year? It annoys me when the players come out and say that Cricket Australia and the ICC have it wrong. On occasions the schedule may be too tight, but they are certainly not playing too much cricket.

You'd hardly class playing Bangladesh as being in a serious Test match. For the Australian players to say that they are in danger of being burnt out five months down the track—I can't cop their argument there.

Doug also believes that the national coaching system is not working to its full potential. He says that when Rod Marsh ran the academy in Adelaide he had the 'cream of the crop' up-and-comers all in the one place.

They were our future Test players. The State associations need to pull their head in and have their best men at the main Australian academy.

When Rod Marsh left the Australian Cricket Academy in 2001 to take up the role with the England and Wales Cricket Board (ECB), former rugby star Bennett King was appointed to take Marsh's place. The Australian Cricket Board (now Cricket Australia) appointed a consultancy team to review the activities of the academy which Marsh ran.

The consultants interviewed a lot of people (apparently) but they did not talk to Marsh, who masterminded the success of the academy for eleven years. Neither did they speak to Wayne Phillips, who ran the overseas coaching program, nor Dennis Lillee, master fast-bowling coach. The academy subsequently moved to its base in Brisbane at the Allan Border Oval. It has been renamed the Australian Cricket Centre of Excellence.

I really don't know whether they have the right personnel to coach at the academy.

But I do think the academy is a good stepping stone for potential Test players. However, I think it should be for players under the age of nineteen. And I believe that the Under-19 competition itself is holding youngsters back. The Under-19s should be scrapped.

The problem we face in Australian cricket right now is that we aren't bringing through enough young players. If a player looks the goods at the Under-17s stage, the trend is to wait until he gets into the Under-19s before they consider him for further honours.

Trouble with that is a lot of these blokes are not getting a decent chance in the State side until they are well into their twenties. Meantime, the incumbent players are fiercely hanging on to their positions. We get the situation of a player aged 35 or more getting injured or being dropped and he is replaced by a player aged 32 or 33.

In a few years' time we will be having a lot of players retiring round the same age. If we don't bring on the young blokes we are going to be in trouble in terms of depth and balance.

These are words from a player who began his career with New South Wales at the age of seventeen.

He was playing alongside his heroes, Richie Benaud, Norm O'Neill, Bob Simpson, Brian Booth, Peter Philpott, Frank Misson and Johnny Martin. Only Doug Ford among the NSW regulars had not played Test cricket. Doug Walters reckons that experience at such a tender age gave him a walk-up start to his career.

—m—

The Big Cricket War of 1977, which saw World Series Cricket financed by media magnate Kerry Packer challenging the very existence of cricket as we had all come to know it, had an outcome for which today's Test men can thank their lucky stars. They can thank the Ian Chappells, the Dennis Lillees and the Doug Walterses of this world for they, along with others, including the younger brigade like David Hookes, put their futures on the line. They secured a better deal, and a financial upward trend for our best cricketers evolved.

Imagine Ricky Ponting's men and their lot if WSC had not happened along. They would still be playing cricket for a pittance, and Shane Warne may have had to stick to a baked beans diet throughout his career. Packer won most of the battles and the war, for he got his way with TV rights and it was, and has been, television which has brought such wealth to the game at the highest level.

While the 1974–75 Ashes series Down Under produced winning cricket with Jeff Thomson and Dennis Lillee delivering their blistering firepower, Ian Chappell's men were paid peanuts. Chappell did succeed in getting the players a pay increase, from $200 to $400 a Test, but it was still a long way short of the mark for elite athletes who had become, because of time away from work, a veritable corporate luxury to their firms. Unlike Dennis Lillee and Ian Chappell especially, Doug Walters never publicly agitated for a better deal from the Board, but he was among the silent majority within the playing group.

He was a part of the players' strike in South Africa when we voted against a fifth Test against the Springboks because of the Board's refusal to pay us an extra $500. That stand by Bill Lawry's men in 1970 and Ian Chappell's constant request for better pay and conditions from the Australian Cricket Board prompted Board secretary Alan Barnes to say, 'They are not professionals ... they were all invited to play and, if they don't like the conditions, there are 500 000 other cricketers in Australia who would love to take their places.'[2]

Today, with the infusion of millions of TV and other sponsorship dollars, the Board, now Cricket Australia, pays the top players big money. The State teams also have the money to handsomely reward even the most modestly gifted of State players.

However, are the clubs in country cricket doing better than before World Series Cricket happened along? Are the city grade clubs doing better? Where does all the money go?

Country cricket is no better off and I'm not sure that grade cricket is any better off. Before WSC that money allocation from the Board was split down to the last dollar and sent out to every big and little affiliated club. Dungog Cricket Association got about twenty bucks. That amount wouldn't have bought them two cricket balls, even in those days. Now they are not getting a penny, so I guess twenty bucks was better than nothing.

They are supposedly spending that money by coaches going out to the various country regions and guiding the youngsters and generally promoting cricket, but I haven't seen any evidence of that. I've seen a lot of evidence of putting another floor in the NSW Cricket Association building and employing six more guys. I don't know what these blokes do. We need to see more coaching and promotion in the country areas ...

If they—NSW Cricket—don't promote the game in the country, they're not right in the head. Quite a large percentage—still more than 60 per cent—of NSW blokes that have gone on to play for Australia came from the bush. And I am talking about the entire time cricket has been played in Australia.

Think of some of them: Don Bradman, Bill O'Reilly, Doug Walters, Alan Davidson, Johnny Martin, Gary Gilmour, John Gleeson, Geoff Lawson, Michael Slater, Glenn McGrath and Mark Taylor; the list goes on.

However, Doug disagrees with the private school system which disallows their talented young cricketers from playing grade cricket in lieu of school games.

In New South Wales only three private school students—Jim Burke, Peter Taylor and Phil Emery—played Test cricket. I put that down to the private schools' ban on their cricketers not being allowed to play in the grade cricket competition at weekends. I know there is a heap of talent among these lads, but none seems to kick on after private schooling. They probably go on to university, get a job and do other things than play cricket at the weekends. If these players were given a chance to play for a grade club during their school days, I am sure that a percentage would stay with the game and that more would go on to play from their State and for Australia. For now, the club ban is robbing cricket of a valuable talent resource. And it continues at a time when cricket is competing with other sports to get the best talent from the same pool.

—∞—

Doug has strong views in another direction—suspect bowling actions.

Chuckers should be identified at an early age. They should be weeded out by the time they are in their early teens. I don't believe in the technology which is being used to measure 15 degrees flex or whatever.
A bloke either chucks or he doesn't.

Years ago we didn't bother much about a slow bowler who threw. We only cared about the quicks with suspect actions.

I've never been able to spin an off-break when I tried to bowl one. Yet, in the backyard I used to experiment, and when I threw an off-break I could turn it three feet.

Does Murali throw? To me Murali appears to throw the ball. He might have a deformed arm and rubber wrist, whatever. I don't think that matters. What matters is if the bowler looks to be throwing. Disability or not, a bloke who looks like he throws should be banned from bowling in any cricket match.

I used to do a lot of coaching in Sri Lanka. Whether technically Murali does or does not throw isn't really the issue. What does count is that there are hundreds of kids over there trying to emulate Murali, and for those without a deformed arm and a rubber wrist, they really do throw the ball. And that is where common sense with these kids must prevail.

It is too late to do anything about Murali because of how long he has been in the game and how much success he has had at the highest level. Were he to be banned from bowling at this stage of his career, I think there would be a fair bit of litigation.

What world cricket must do is weed out the chuckers long before we let them onto the first-class arena.

On a lighter note and with typical Walters' humour, Freddie will take you through a lengthy discourse on how he thinks Murali actually bends and flexes his elbow through 165 degrees of contortion, way above the so-called ICC benchmark of 15 degrees of 'allowed flex'.

—⚏—

Doug marvels at the ability of the greats of today, Ricky Ponting, Adam Gilchrist, Brian Lara and Sachin Tendulkar. He was delighted to watch the skill of Shane Warne, and how he bowled in tandem with Glenn McGrath, to place pressure on the opposition over so many Test matches.

And he believes the game is in good health worldwide, however, Freddie stresses that the International Cricket Conference has an immediate and important role to play.

Australia dominates the world scene. But it is important that the lesser teams, like Bangladesh and Zimbabwe, play in the top competition, while at the same time getting their structure up to speed. The ICC has the expertise and knowledge to help with the infrastructure and coaching needs for these countries.

I understand that Bangladesh plays a lot of one-day matches and very little two- or three-day games. The structure needs to be fixed to enable Bangladesh to have a level playing field with the rest of the Test-playing nations. For world cricket to prosper there has to be a tougher, tighter competition.

—⚌—

Along with his special brand of humour, Freddie is also a man of great compassion.

A year or so ago, when Doug learnt about Gary 'Gus' Gilmour's dire predicament, having to undergo a life-saving liver transplant, he rang Gus.

'Hey, Gus. How many livers do we get?'

'Freddie, I think we only get one.'

'Okay, Gus. If that's the case, you can have half of my liver.'

'No, thanks, Freddie . . . I'll take my chances.'

Gus had his transplant and I thought I'd let him settle down for a few days after the operation before I rang him. I rang a couple of days after the great footballer, George Best, died.

'Hey, Gus . . . you'd be a nice sort of fella?'

'How's that, Freddie?'
'Well, you knock back mine . . . and take on George Best's liver!'

—ₘ—

Why did Freddie drink so much? Did he ever worry about the influence his drinking might have on other members of the Australian team?

Freddie has always been his own man and whatever the others did was up to them. He couldn't always find a drinking mate late into the evening. When he hit that hundred in a session against Northern Districts in New Zealand back in 1974, Doug achieved the feat without hitting a single boundary.

I did a lot of running that day . . . and I worked up a healthy thirst.

It is largely a myth that Doug Walters was a poor trainer. In fact, he trained full bore at every session I saw. He would dash about like a terrier, always bowled a lengthy stint at the crease, and had a long fielding session. Freddie batted in the nets as he batted in the middle. He was always totally committed to the task at hand.

Technique was never an issue for Doug in Australia. He came at you with a bit of a crooked bat, but that was his way and he had an eye like a stinking fish. Any ball which moved appreciably on our hard, fast tracks he missed. In England he would have 'caught' up with it and nicked it. But for all his casualness and legendary liking for a drink or smoke and his laid-back attitude, Doug thought a lot about his batting.

I could close my eyes and 'visualise' where the field was set. I knew exactly where all the fieldsmen were. When I batted in the nets I trained myself to visualise the field setting. There were some great players like Norm O'Neill and Mark Waugh who, early in their careers, tended to pick out the field, but they eventually got it right. At practice I always wanted to train with a purpose. I knew exactly where I had to hit the ball to get maximum benefit from the shot. It was all in my mind's eye.

How often do we get an unplayable ball? Rarely.

Usually a batsman gets out through a lack of concentration. And once you get to a hundred, you are obviously on top of everything, and the next hundred should be a lot easier, but it is amazing how many players get out just after they reach a hundred. I don't think you can put it down to fatigue. Fitness, or a lack of it, is not the problem. No matter who was bowling I visualised the field setting. I would always 'see' the gap between cover and mid-off. If you're not batting or bowling with a purpose, you're wasting your time in the nets. A lot of batsmen hit the ball straight back to the bowler because they are too lazy to pick it up out of the back of the net.

A lot of players do not practice properly in the nets. If a batsman doesn't get into the habit of visualising the field placement, he will not consistently take advantage of the bad ball. If you get into bad habits you'll find that when you get a gift of a full toss you'll hit it straight to a fieldsman at mid-off or mid-on. Then you know you have wasted four runs, and often a batsman will get himself out because he gets frustrated. And the frustration usually comes from missing opportunities because you have failed to prepare.

—Ⱳ—

Everyone knows stories about Doug Walters and his love of cards.

You know, stories like me saying, 'Hold the hand, I'll be back in a minute,' and going out to bat. I did that a few times and naturally, now and again, I was back quickly, but it's a fact of life that people only remember those times when I was back quickly. I've heard blokes tell that story and make it sound as though I purposely made a duck, because I had a good hand.

I don't know if Rick McCosker believes that story or not, but he barred cards in the dressing-room when he was NSW captain in the 1980–81 season.

So K.D. Walters is now the crossword king. He bought a book of crosswords and religiously did them during that last summer, but must have been relieved to play a lot of Test cricket that season and so it was back to the cards.

—ɯ—

Former Test fast bowler Len Pascoe, who often hires Doug for speaking engagements, fondly recalls those halcyon days at the Sydney Cricket Ground:

Freddie would sit at the end of the long table at the SCG, one eye on the game another on his cards, with a cigarette in the ash tray, while he did the crossword puzzle. A wicket would fall and he would say, 'Don't touch the cards, I'll be back in a minute,' and there were times he was back before his cigarette went out. No histrionics, no sledging the umps, he just sat back down and continued his hand. However, when he did occupy the crease we witnessed a genius at work; no spinner was safe, as was the case in Sydney, New South Wales versus South Australia, where he devastated their Test spinners for a brilliant 186.

When he got out he calmly walked in, sat down and asked if anyone had moved his cards.[3]

Recently, I interviewed Doug in Colombo. The city was tense. Two days before we met, a suicide bomber struck at an army camp just behind the Taj Samundra Hotel, on the Galle Face Road, where I was staying. Doug was booked in at the plush Cinnamon Grand

Hotel, only 300 yards down the road. That night, as I began the short walk, the road was blocked with police and army commandos, each brandishing an automatic weapon. I caught a cab and the driver left me at a bridge, just at the rear of Doug's hotel. There I was confronted by a Sri Lankan Army commando, complete with battle fatigues and his finger on the trigger of an AK-47 assault rifle.

'Passport?'

'I don't need a passport to see Doug Walters. What I do need is a slab of beer and a carton of cigarettes.'

—∿—

One of England's great fast bowlers, Bob Willis, the man Freddie hit for six to bring up that century in a session at Perth in December, 1974, recalled the day England regained the Ashes under Ray Illingworth by bowling out Australia, led for the first time by Ian Chappell, for 160 in the second innings of the Seventh Test to win by 62 runs. Doug had been dismissed for 1.

> We got off the field dead tired, but happy to win. It meant the Ashes, a tough battle, and we knew the Aussies would be bitterly disappointed. As we got into the rooms there sat Doug waiting for us with an ice-cold beer. What a brilliant bloke.[4]

Ian Chappell always maintained that he would have hated to go on a Test tour without Doug Walters in his team. As Chappelli has always said, they broke the mould the day Doug was born. My wife Christine and I have known Doug and Caroline over a long time. And we're aware that, whatever the occasion, Doug always seems to have an ace up his sleeve. While editing this manuscript, Christine looked up and said:

'You know, Doug really is *one of a kind*.'

Endnotes

Chapter 1

1 Doug Walters to author, Sydney, March 2006.
2 Told to author by Ray Johnston, August 2006.
3 ibid.
4 Ray Johnston, telephone conversation with author, September 2006.
5 Bill O'Reilly, *Sydney Morning Herald*, 14 December 1965.
6 Lyrics courtesy Ian Quinn, August 2006.

Chapter 2

1 Tom Keneally in email to author, 6 October 2006.
2 Richie Benaud in email to author, 31 October 2006.
3 Norman Tasker in email to author, 1 September 2006.
4 Ian Wooldridge, Introduction, *Two for the Road*, by Doug Walters and Rod Marsh, Swan Publishing, 1992, pp. 92–3.
5 Alan McGilvray, talking to author, Sydney, 1981.
6 Ian Wooldridge, *London Evening Standard*, 13 December 1965.
7 Quotes sourced from *Woman's Day* article by Susan Dunlop, 'Cricket Runs in the Family', 21 February 1966, pp. 56–7.

8 Selected quotes by Jim Fuller as reported in the *Dungog Chronicle*, 19 January 1966.
9 Letter to Doug Walters from Ian Johnson, dated 4 March 1966.

Chapter 3

1 *The National Service Scheme 1964–1972*, Australian War Memorial, by Sue Langford, p. 11.
2 ibid., pp. 11–12.
3 In April 2007, the remains of two soldiers were found in Vietnam. They are believed to be two of the six missing in action from the year 1965 (official Australian Army figures differ, depending upon the official or department you contact).
4 Roger McDonald, *Barry Humphries' Flashbacks*, 1999, Harper-Collins, p. 89.
5 Ian Wooldridge, who wrote the foreword to Doug Walters and Rod Marsh's book, *Two for the Road*, 1992, Swan Publishing, Nedlands, WA, p. 94.
6 ibid., p. 96.

Chapter 4

1 Caroline Walters to author, Sydney, October 2006.
2 Letter to K.D. Walters from Keith Miller, dated 7 March 1968.
3 Letter from Australian Army—permission to proceed overseas, 19 April 1968.
4 Paul Sheahan, email to author, dated 25 August 2006.
5 'Brilliance of Walters in Bold Relief', by Jack Fingleton, *The Times*, 11 June 1968.
6 Letter to Doug Walters c/- Australian Cricket Team c/- Australia House, London from Mayor A.W. Hammett dated 14 June 1968.
7 Caroline Walters, email to author, 2 November 2006.
8 ibid.
9 ibid.
10 Don Bradman, letter—in part to author, dated 26 June 1985.

Chapter 5

1 Phil Tresidder, *Sydney Sun*, 11 February 1969.
2 Richie Benaud, *Daily Mirror*, 12 February 1969.
3 Ian Chappell to author, Sydney, 2004.
4 Sir Donald Bradman letter to Doug Walters, dated 19 February 1969.
5 Letter from Stephen Wigney to Doug Walters, undated, but received early in the summer of 1968–69. Stephen Wigney's letter is pasted in one of Doug's

scrapbooks, next to a cheque for two shillings and three-pence, given to him by a Hobart fan. The cheque is dated 21 January 1966 and was never cashed.

Chapter 6

1 'Grave Concern Felt for Cricketers' Welfare', *Sydney Sun*, by Phil Tresidder, 24 December 1969.

Chapter 7

1 AM, ABC Radio with Tony Easterly, 22 April 2004.
2 Trevor Howard to author, 20 January 1970.
3 Phil Tresidder, *Sydney Sun*, January 1970.
4 Among Doug Walters' newspaper clippings, author unknown.
5 Eric Litchfield, *Rand Daily Mail*, 22 March 1970.
6 Phil Tresidder, *Sydney Sun*, containing grabs from Afrikaanse newspaper *Die Burger* (editorial), Cape Town; *The Times*, *The Daily Telegraph*, and *London Sun*, 22 March 1970.
7 Australian team manager Fred Bennett at Jan Smuts Airport, Johannesburg, March 1970.

Chapter 8

1 Bobby Simpson, 'Pads Up', *Sydney Sun*, 14 March 1970.
2 Sir Donald Bradman, letter to author dated 14 August 1992.
3 Ross Duncan to author, Brisbane, 2006.
4 'Historic 100 By Walters Before Lunch', *Daily Mirror*, 6 January 1972.
5 Ian Chappell, in conversation with author, September 2006.
6 Dennis Lillee, in conversation with author, 11 September 2006.

Chapter 9

1 'Australians Have Flexibility But May Lack Variety', E.W. Swanton, *Daily Telegraph*, Friday 28 April 1972.
2 ibid.
3 'Eye on the Ashes: England Must Nail Doug Early—Or Feel the lash', Ray Illingworth, London *Mirror*, May 1972.
4 Cricket writer Mike Coward, email to author, dated 2 September 2006.
5 'Dad's Army Goes Barmy', Ted Dexter, *London Daily Express*, 10 June 1972.

6 Ian Chappell, in conversation with author, October 2006.
7 ibid.

Chapter 10

1 'Walters Answers His Critics With A Chanceless 159', Phil Wilkins, *Sydney Morning Herald*, 6 December 1972.
2 Ian Chappell in *Passing Tests*, Lynton Press, Coromandel Valley, South Australia, 1973, p. 43.
3 Ian Chappell, in telephone conversation with author, September 2006.
4 ibid.
5 Phil Wilkins, *The Sun-Herald*, 25 March 1973.
6 Ian Chappell, in telephone conversation with author, September 2006.
7 Rodney Marsh, in conversation with author, Adelaide Oval, 15 September 2006.

Chapter 11

1 Sir Donald Bradman, in conversation with author, Adelaide, 1991.
2 Ross Edwards, in email to author, July 2006.
3 Bob Willis, in conversation with author, May 2007.
4 ibid.
5 Ross Edwards, in email to author, July 2006.
6 ibid.
7 Sir Donald Bradman, letter to author, dated 8 June 1984.
8 Brendon Bracewell, in email to author, August 2006.
9 John Bracewell, in email to author, September 2006.
10 Christine Wallace, *The Private Don*, Allen & Unwin, Sydney, 2004, p. 69.
11 E.W. 'Jim' Swanton, *Swanton in Australia*, Collins, London, p. 151.

Chapter 12

1 Ian Chappell, Headingly, Leeds, August 1975.
2 Ian Chappell in conversation with author, August 2006.
3 Upon his return from the 1975 England tour, Doug was awarded the MBE at Government House, Sydney, by NSW Governor Sir Roden Cutler.
4 *Wisden Cricketers' Almanack*, Sporting Handbooks Ltd, London, 1976 edn, p. 330.
5 Richard Knott, *Cricket Wit and Wisdom*, Running Press, Philadelphia–London, 1996, p. 109.
6 John Arlott, BBC Sports Radio, 1975 Lord's Test coverage, 5 August 1975.

7   Among Doug Walters' private collection of newspaper cuttings and repeated in Jonathon Rice's *One Hundred Lord's Tests*, Metheun, London, 2001.
8   Ian Chappell, in conversation with author, Sydney, 2004.

Chapter 13

1   Sir Donald Bradman, in conversation with author, Melbourne, March 1977.
2   Doctor Donald Beard, in conversation with author, Adelaide, 1977.

Chapter 14

1   Greg Chappell, in email to author, September 2006.
2   Norman Tasker, in email to author, September 2006.
3   Rodney Cavalier to author, 2008.
4   John Inverarity, in email to author, 14 August 2006.

Chapter 16

1   Australian Cricket Board secretary Alan Barnes, *The Australian*, 4 January 1975.
2   ibid.
3   NSW and Test team-mate Len Pascoe in email to author, September 2006.
4   Bob Willis, in telephone conversation with author, May 2007.